Fredrik Lång, born in 1947, is a researcher and writer. His literary production consists of nearly thirty works in the form of novels of ideas, essays, aphorisms, and philosophical works. Lång is known as the author of the idea-historical work *Bild och tanke*, which deals with the parallel development of art and thinking from antiquity up to Marcel Duchamp, romance novels and novels of ideas about, e.g., Leonardo da Vinci and Pythagoras.

Fredrik Lång has received many awards, including the State Literature Prize in 1985 for *Sommaren med Sue,* the Finland Prize in 2002, and the biggest Finnish literary prize, the Tollander Prize, in 2021. His latest books include the essay collection, *Geosofi—Bilder på en utställning* (2020), and the novel *Farväl Nappari* (2023).

Fredrik Lång

IDEA AND IMAGE

On the Genesis of Categorical Perception

Translated by Andreas Hemming Oliver
Brotherton Joe Scott-Oliver

AUSTIN MACAULEY PUBLISHERS®

LONDON * CAMBRIDGE * NEW YORK * SHARJAH

A CIP catalogue record for this title is available from the British Library.

ISBN 9781035844821 (Paperback)
ISBN 9781035844838 (ePub e-book)

www.austinmacauley.com

First Published 2024
Austin Macauley Publishers Ltd®
1 Canada Square
Canary Wharf
London
E14 5AA

Table of Contents

*Whosoever scorns painting is unjust to
truth; and he is also unjust to all the
wisdom
that has been bestowed upon poets.*

Philostratus (sophist, 3rd
century)

Preface

When *Idea and Image* appeared in Swedish in 1999, the prevailing current of ideas in philosophy and art theory that wanted to be in step with the times was called postmodernism. In 1979, Lyotard had published *La condition postmoderne*, in which he declared, among other things, the death of the so-called grand narrative; the kind of teleological historiography created by Hegel and Marx that was still represented during Lyotard's lifetime by, for example, Sartre or by feminist historiography. These metanarratives were stories of liberation, they were the stories of human evolution from the past to the present that pointed towards a bright future of ever-increasing freedom.

These narratives, rooted in the optimism of the Enlightenment and the belief in progress, were now considered dead. They were relegated to history. All that remained were local narratives and limited rationality.

To try to arouse interest in that intellectual climate for a book which, on the contrary, declares that it is in fact still possible to write a so-called grand narrative, to sketch the outlines of an arc from antiquity to the present day which, on the same premises, presents the development of knowledge and art during this period, but which, instead of leading to a message of freedom, instead announces a coming abandonment, a rejection, and a retreat from freedom as an ideal, proved impossible. Finding a publisher, in Finland or in Sweden, proved not to be possible despite several attempts.

Thus, the book finally, many years after it was finished, was published by my own small press, Draken, in 1999.

Since then, of course, a lot has happened, and more will happen. Incidentally, according to informed sources, postmodernism is said to have died at 1.30 in the afternoon of 23 June 2011, while the philosophers Markus Gabriel and Maurizio Ferraris were having lunch together in Naples.

The first version of the manuscript was finished in the spring of 1995 and has since only been haphazardly updated. The long delay in publication is, unfortunately, nothing more than a symptom of the lack of interest in the publishing world for manuscripts of this kind. For the Finnish edition[1], some passages that I consider superfluous have been deleted, but no substantial changes were made. This is also true for those points of which I have slightly different view today.

The insightful critique of Docent, now Professor Vesa Oittinen gave me the courage to delete long digressions and superfluous passages from the first preliminary manuscript. With M.A. Lars Christiansen, I had detailed and useful discussions about Petrarch. However, I am most indebted to Professor Sven Sandström in Lund, who, despite other compelling assignments, took the time to read and comment on the manuscript line by line and page by page. Without his careful reading, mistakes that later would have embarrassed me would probably have been allowed to pass.

For the Finnish translation, PhD Jarkko S. Tuusvuori made several updates to the footnotes and the literature used.

The illustrations are by Isa Fellman, and the complicated layout of the manuscript for the Swedish edition was done by Trygve Söderling. To them, too, I owe a great debt of gratitude.

1. Introduction

Art is, as I see it, the mirror humans have set up in front of them to confirm the truth in the understanding they have of their existence. Art expresses what it is, and what it has been, to be human. In this verification, man does not only see that the perception he has of himself is true (this is what I am, this is what my surroundings are like, this is what my humanity looks like), but he also verifies the truthfulness of his own form of life.

And this is what art actually is about: creating symbolic forms that visually manifest the truth and beauty of the current form of life, and thus the only permanent subtext in the ever-changing view on what is "true" or "beautiful".

Conversely, art can also function as a carnival mirror, exposing the asymmetries and the deficiencies of the human way of life, while simultaneously making an attempt to realign these flaws. This is another thing that art has in common with thinking and theory. Art can both support and undermine the values that make up the criteria for the quality of life valid at a specific moment in time. The latter by portraying ideals that at the time are incompatible with generally accepted, life-sustaining, ideologically or productively correct ideals.

In short, by painting a picture that it concretely and literally is impossible to live in. This art depicts, as will be made clear further on, at first an inhuman world and later on an unnatural world.

The former "constructive" form of art dominates, as history and the civilising process usually exhibits "constructive" epochs; times when understanding is increased, power is consolidated, production is enhanced, while rationality and the insights into the conditions of life become deeper. However, there are two eras when this essentially is not the case, and during which, the virtues named above receive negative connotations. In other words, times when the foundations of life's values are fundamentally challenged and the level of rationality (at least apparently) is diminishing.

The first of these eras is late antiquity, where we can see how the ruling (mostly Athenian) values are undermined and disassembled. The second is so close to us that gaining any knowledge about it remains a challenging prospect. It is our own chaotic, multifaceted and contradictory time, of which we can only reach an incomplete, vague and uncertain knowledge (that perhaps only barely can be called knowledge), through a form of analogous reasoning with history as the known and the present as the unknown variable.

This, however, is the destination of the long detour through the history of images, art and human understanding up to the vibrating *now* that does not allow itself to be captured in any readymade pattern. Of course, the journey itself is also the end goal, the expansive gallery of images and concepts that mankind has left behind in his estate built through the millennia.

For me, art history is much more than the history of works of art. The foundational idea behind this book is that for every era, the most essential or pertinent art in image form expresses the deepest possible understanding of its own time. Art is, as is cognition, an interpretation of a contemporary existence, executed in the framework of the current metaphysical categories provided by thinking.

What this somewhat cryptical formulation actually means will hopefully become evident after further reading; it is included here as a means of explaining why so much space has to be given to the examination of the knowledge-creating social environment in which art came into being and of which it always has been an integral part. Every picture tells more than a thousand words and every consequential work of art includes a proposition about, and is a confirmation of, the values of its time. That this is the case can be seen in the, often rabid, disagreements on the changes in visual imagery.

Countless people have sacrificed comfort, happiness, societal esteem or peace of mind in the name of beauty, compelled by a force preventing them from acting otherwise. If pictures were only "ornaments" or "decoration", this would be unthinkable. That is why the art created by an era should be scrutinised as meticulously as the values shaping the concurrent form of life as well as those underlying the creation of knowledge at that particular time.

Seeing and Knowing

I will start by making a couple of difficult but important demarcations. Symbolised knowing and depicting operate under the same conditions, both work with the insights, understandings, and procedures of selection that are in consonance with the self-interpretations of the prevalent *form of power*, *production*, and *life.* In this sense, all art and all knowledge is ideological: there is no detached, independent knowing or depicting. Even the attempt of becoming a total outsider or gaining absolute independence expresses a, albeit negative, relationship to existing power or general values.

Why is this the case? Aristotle states in the first sentence of his *Metaphysics,* that "all men naturally desire knowledge". Furthering this argument, one could say that all men by nature strive for a betterment of their life, or at least strive, to maintain their current quality of life.

As knowledge is in league with power (and to a greater degree with the Greeks[2] than with Francis Bacon) and because power in its varying shapes is the authority that guarantees a good life for those that control it, but is also involved in the determination of what is true and beautiful, one can group both the endeavours of gaining useful knowledge, manifesting beauty as well the sustainment of a good life into one single, at this point somewhat diffuse, concept of "power".

Both truth and beauty orient and reorient themselves in the same manner as iron filings in a magnetic field in accordance with the shifting polarities of power, and the sensitivity and readiness to arrange themselves in agreement with the demands of power is nothing else than an instance of the practical opportunism that "by nature" characterises so much of human virtue. This is due to the simple reason that truth-seeking is filled with and convinced of the rectitudeness of itself, because its goal, "the good life", or "the better life", is in an absolute sense, good. There is no further argument that extends beyond this one.

When has an artist or a thinker wanted to demolish one world in order to create a worse one?

The symbolic forms of every era express, as ideas or images, more or less clearly the metaphysical foundations that thinking needs to actualise the optimal forms of life of its time. Art and knowledge do not only depict "the real", but also reveal the underlying framework that the intellect needs to maintain the coherence and unity of its interpretations of this "reality". The Egyptian hieratic scale, using size to denote importance; the disjunct way of the Greeks to portray nature; medieval icons, the central perspective of naturalism—all are interpretations of existence that are and have to be in harmony with the general functionings of society.

And all four, for their time typical reductions of the visual representations of the multitude of existence, were all regarded as similarly "natural"; they were perceived as the natural image of "true nature".

Seeing is never a purely optical process in which an impression on the retina produces a "picture" in an unmediated fashion, instead an instance of understanding is always included. If seeing catches a glimpse of something "unintelligible", then it does not rest until it has arranged, interpreted and understood it, and this understanding is done in accordance with the available models of interpretation.

The *reproductive* seeing or image creation is thus *doubly* subordinated to the valid modes of understanding: firstly during the seeing itself, and secondly in the process of the mental rendering of the image, subject to the prevailing practices and conventions regarding the depiction.

THE DOUBLE MOUTH
When vision fails to interpret what is seen, the gaze becomes confused and begins to switch between different options.

One such strong convention is that we (see? and) depict in accordance with a *conceptual* continuity rather than a spatial continuity. If we, for example, are painting a tree on a field, we tend to make a distinction between tree and background, even though there is no qualitative difference in the visual impression between them. Instead of using the continuity of the surface of the image, filling it point by point, starting for example in the top-left corner, we start by drawing the tree and then the background or vice versa.

For the Greeks, whose thinking was dominated by abstract concepts and who lacked logically consistent interpretations of, for example, "space" or "nature", this phenomenon resulted in a special form of art that I will call "hieroglyphical". It might also be noted that both impressionism and especially pointillism succinctly problematised the relationship between the surface of an image and "reality"—but one has to bear in mind that the knowing concerning this reality then also was a totally different one.

Power and Metaphysics

In this way, metaphysics becomes an important part in the understanding of art, because it is the common denominator that both the theoretical as well as the visual depiction refers to. Metaphysics is, while still remaining in the company of Aristotle, 'knowledge of certain principles and causes[3].' When trying to trace the outlines of the metaphysics of a certain epoch, one can get quite far by examining how knowing during this epoch defines the word "truth", and furthermore by investigating in what manner something is viewed as a cause for something else (as overall reason, final cause or explanatory foundation, first principle, etc.).

A sufficiently deep and nuanced historical treatise on the concept of cause would actually be enough to create a good idea of the metamorphoses that metaphysics has gone through. The symbolic worlds of theories and images both follow and are dependent on the metamorphoses of metaphysics, while also being involved in said changes. At times, knowing can foresee a coming change in the foundations of thinking, but just as often, it is art, with its seemingly freer position, which is first in expressing the budding change.

In the intricate interplay between the human intellect and the guiles of history, "truth" and "beauty" always seem to make their way to the pinnacle of universal and valid foundations for assessment.

Because metaphysics is and always has been in the service of power—power understood as the necessary consolidation needed by the forms of life to perpetuate themselves, and here understood without any conspiratory paranoia: power is as necessary as our interpretations; as unavoidable as our simple wish to live together and live well—metaphysics is in some manner always sociomorphic[i]. Metaphysics is the subtlest argument for the validity of the social and productive claims of power, because metaphysics always presents power as sanctioned by a higher authority, either a "divine" or a "natural" one, and is thus both definitive and unavoidable.

For example, in our time, we find it completely natural to extract the trappings of a good life from nature. At the same time, the conception we have of nature is that its foundational principles, its metaphysical substance, is given by categories such as mechanical work, effect and energy. Thus metaphysics establishes a necessary symmetry between the way of understanding and the way of life. Also naturalism in visual arts imagined the principles of depiction in accordance with an instrumentally perceived reality.

This can be seen most clearly with Leonardo da Vinci. He was probably the first to create an ontological foundational principle based on one hand, the deep insights he had into the utility of machines and tools, and on the other, the knowledge he had of their manner of effect. 'Instrumental or mechanical science is most noble and useful beyond all others since by means of it all animate bodies that have motion perform all their operations,' Leonardo writes.[4] Thus he perceived that *all* animate bodies, both crafted, mechanical as well as natural, could be interpreted in mechanical or instrumental terms.

Moreover, as will be made clear later on, Leonardo spoke about "nature's work" and that a correct picture of nature emerges when it is depicted as being at work; when the effects that are noted are supposed to be induced by mechanical causes. In this manner, we reach a symmetry between three levels; the social, the ontological and the epistemological. This is how a complete understanding of natural things is established.

This is, however, nothing unique for our time, instead *all* relevant understanding is of this kind, in other words equally sociosymmetrical or sociomorphic. The social is interpreted into the object in the manner that the object enters the social. The type of metaphysics that man has maintained during various eras is a sociomorphic net thrown over existence and with which he very

---

[i] The word "sociomorphic" is used here in the original German sense "von der Gesellschaft, den sozialen Verhältnissen geformt" and in this sense appears in the German philosopher Ernst Topitsch's book Erkenntnis und Illusion. I use the term in a more general manner than Topitsch in that I consider any scientific or religious interpretation of nature to be sociomorphic.

effectively has highlighted certain aspects of it, while others have methodically been made invisible.

No one has yet proven that force, work, etc. would be unconditionally "natural" concepts, in the same manner that ideas would exist in the manner that Plato meant, or that nature, as was the case when relations of power were more concrete, would be inhabited by active gods.

Nature is a socially, thus humanly necessary amendment, as Nietzsche said. This is how it is, and has always been, and I cannot imagine that it could be different in the future.

I will speak a lot on metaphysics in connection with interpretation because the underlying metaphysics always determine the rules of interpretation. Every interpretation, both theoretical and visual is conditioned, and these conditions are given by the actual conditions of living—the hopes and expectations that in interplay with a total experience of the humanly and socially possible *right then,* determine the prospects of life. The socially effective and successful seems to always grant a model of how existence in its totality is supposed to function.

In this manner, existence as a whole is always a *cosmos*—where the ancient Greek word κόσμος in its original meaning stands for the "correct order of society" and in its metaphysical meaning "the orderly structure of the universe". As in heaven, so on earth and *vice versa.*

A fundamental postulate, pervasive in the modern perception of knowledge since the times of Nicolaus Cusanus and Giambattista Vico, is that man can only understand what he himself has made. In Nietzsche, we find it as a critique of knowledge-based pragmatism in the following statement:

'We have measured the value of the world according to categories that refer to a purely fictitious world. Conclusion: All values which we have tried, hitherto, to lend the world some worth, from our point of view, and with which we have therefore deprived it of all worth. [And] all these values, are, psychologically, the results of certain views of utility, established for the purpose of maintaining and increasing the dominion of certain communities: but falsely projected into the nature of things. It is always man's exaggerated ingeniousness to regard himself as the sense and measure of all things.'[5]

With such a view on the developments of art and knowing, many simplifications and schematisations regarding their historical course have to be made in order to reveal the broader view. The first schematic on the use of power is as follows:

History mainly exhibits two forms of power relations:

a. societies with concrete "physical" power (monarchies)
    1. The patchwork of kingdoms in archaic Greece; concrete models of interpretation, polytheistic interpretations.
    2. The remains of the Roman Empire; concrete monotheistic interpretations.
b. societies with abstract, codified power (democracies)
    1. Athenian democracy; abstract models of interpretation: "words", "ideas".
    2. Modern democracies with abstract models of interpretation: "work", "energy".

Thus I perceive the gods as concrete, sociomorphic projections to general existence of prevalent concrete power relations, while the "ideas" of Plato or the "power" (*Kraft*) of Kant, are examples of abstract relations of power conducting abstract interpretations of existence in accordance with the principles that maintain the socially successful in these democracies.[ii]

Technical Instrumentalism

Perhaps somewhat surprisingly, I will denote the type of reason that created both the high cultures of the Greek epoch as well as our own (in category b above) with the term *technical instrumentalism*. For our own time this denotation is well established, but when applied to ancient Greece it is somewhat puzzling at first glance.[iii] Nevertheless, I maintain that technical instrumentalism is an adequate denotation of the successful *ideology* that the Greeks surrounded their exclusive form of life, and the reason why, will be given in the following:

[ii] Hegel uses, quite secondly, a similar division in his *Aesthetics* (Chapter III.B.ii. 1 .a). Speaking of the difference between the concrete and the abstract exercise of power, Hegel says that the codified, abstract law only punishes but never takes revenge. The same is true of the entities of the cosmologies of the democratic societies: they never take revenge, but follow strict, inexorable laws.

[iii] For example in the light of the opposition between the ancient and the modern that is expressed in e.g. Heidegger. I have to ask the reader to accept the interpretation as a working hypothesis for the time being, as it is of crucial importance in order to be able to gain on my approach to understanding history in general. The value of the interpretation can be determined when this writing has come to an end.

With technical or technological instrumentalism, I mean the interlinked network of thought, that within the framework of theoretical and practical knowledge consciously and consistently develops techniques and methods, that through the use of clearly defined tools or *instruments* achieve the, also consciously formulated, requirements for "a good life". With technology, I then understand the methods and devices used for production of artefacts for any purpose. Technology is "a labour-saving device". And this is exactly how technical instrumentalism worked even in antiquity and especially in Athens.

On a conceptual level, it is not difficult to discover the technical-instrumental nature of Greek ideology. For both Plato and Aristotle, the art of ruling or statecraft was the highest form of art (*politikê tékhnē* or *epistêmê*). Its object was the care of the state *(polis)* and it was primarily tasked with securing a good life for those who deserved it, and secondly, as an unavoidable consequence of the first task, to maintain a despotic rule over those who did not deserve anything else, i.e., the slaves.

As slaves during classical times by definition and in relation to the societal aim were tools (*instrumentum; instrumentum vocale* in Varro's translation of Aristotle into Latin)[6]. One interpretation of technical instrumentalism on the Greek form of societal, and self, understanding could be 'the art of maintaining the conditions for a good life through despotism over the slaves and egalitarian power among the free.' In other words, technical instrumentalism in its Greek form is the political art of ruling over each and every one as they deserve in the name of the common good—like-over-like and despotically over those who are viewed as tools.

The exposition of Aristotle in his *Politics* is clear enough. 'And inasmuch as in all the sciences and arts the End is a good, and the greatest good and good in the highest degree in the most authoritative of all, which is the political faculty.'[7] To reach its end of "the good life", statecraft also needs knowledge about the means, even if the means are not included in the end.

Aristotle continues, 'But when of two related things one is a means and the other an end, in their case there is nothing in common except for the one to act and the other to receive the action. I mean for instance the relation between any instrument or artificer and the work that they produce: between a house and a builder there is nothing that is produced in common, but the builder's craft exists for the sake of the house. Hence although states need property, the property is no part of the state. And there are many living things that fall under the head of property [i.e., slaves and livestock].'

Thus, they not a part of the state and are only its instruments: 'And the state is one form of partnership of similar people, and its object is the best life that is possible.'[8] The relationship between the instruments and their users is transferred *practically* through the power apparatus of the state, the citizen militia.

'The proper object of practising military training is not in order that men may enslave those who do not deserve slavery, but in order that first they may themselves avoid becoming enslaved to others; then so that they may seek suzerainty for the benefit of the subject people, but not for the sake of world-wide despotism; and thirdly to hold despotic power over those who deserve to be slaves.'[9]

The *theoretical* relationship between the exercise of power and its object was shaped in the lively discussion on the configuration of the state conducted by philosophers, politicians and city planners, which as a whole creates the *ideology* formed around the functions of classical technical instrumentalism. There are almost no conceptions during the golden age of Greek philosophy that are not connected to the idea of society in some shape or form, as man indeed is, as Aristotle puts it, a social animal.

Even the areas where the Greek philosophers excelled, ethics, epistemology and politics, are wholly permeated by the ideology that encircled their views on state power and societal governance. It could not have been any other way.

Man, a social animal; the slave, a talking tool. The necessary symbiosis between the state and its instruments with the aim of achieving the good life could be rephrased as technical instrumentalism; the highly developed and sophisticated political art to use slaves for the common good.

If the slave would have had the possibility to use the tools at his disposal in his own manner, he would have started to think about their use, how to make them better, how to use them more efficiently and with less effort—for his own utility. Now this possibility was out of the question. Instead, the *slave owner* could think about ways in which to use the *slave* in better and more efficient ways, as Xenophon does in his *Ways and Means.*[10] This was the Greek way of *rationalising*; to use the *instruments* at their disposal more efficiently in order to reach a good life.

These forms of technical instrumentalism, both the ancient and the modern, are as well requirements for the theoretical self-reflections that both forms of life do conduct. It seems as if it indeed is the instrumental character, with—as Hegel might have thought—an instrument inserted between the reflection and its object, that is necessary for abstractions to be created, as the etymology of the word indicates *(abstrahere* = pull away).

In the non-instrumental contexts of life, the world and the understanding of it are so embedded within each other, that the categories of understanding cannot detach themselves from their original extantness in the world. The perception of a sovereign *I* (also in a collective form as an active *subject*) cannot crystallise either under these conditions—and of the same reason. For *me* to reach the conclusion, that it is *I* or *we* who determine the conditions of my or our life, i.e., for me to reach the insight that *my* will is worth something, the visible traces of the active use of instruments—*my* instruments—is needed.

To wait for the Nile to flood or for the rain to fall does not give the same insight. Technical instrumentalism as a production strategy is the knowing and the knowledge that arises when the useful effects of the insertion of an *instrument* between the categories of subject and object have become obvious. At the same time, as knowing actively develops methods for the use of these instruments, it also ensures that the use of these instruments is absolutely "natural".

It also seems as if the forms of life, because of this crystallisation of the subject, at the same time (and due to the distance that the living or non-living instrument inserted between the subject and the object brings about) pulls away an object, whose basis for interpretation, even though the object is a *result* of a subject's instrumental intervention, is postulated as being *unconditionally real* or natural.

Both the ancient and the modern democracies can thus be seen as scientific-technical forms of life. Forms of life, in which the indispensable tools or instruments for the realisation of the good life shape the nature of science. The tool is an actually existing practical form of reasoning, dividing subject from object, active from passive or *logos* from *physis*. Or as Hegel puts it: 'The tool is the existing rational middle, the existing universality, of the practical process; it appears on the side of the active against the passive; it is itself passive on the side of the labourer, and active against what is worked on.'[11]

This formal concurrence between classical and modern does actually enable us to recognise ourselves in much of the ancient world. Nevertheless, the differences are of course enormous, and just as important—actually it is two completely different ways of relating to the world. The type of ethics that functions as a moral compass in our culture, is totally incompatible with the views of the leading Greeks on what constitutes a good and productive life. Where we would call on ourselves to *work!* the Greeks would instead say *rule!*[iv]

Subjectivity and Objectivity

What is expressed in art is mainly a visualisation of the *personality* or subjectivity of man, and just like knowledge, personality can only exist through its actual, social and collective realisation. One can only speak of subjectivity in relation to a certain kind of sociality; the self is only valid and active through its socially directed actions. The efficiency of these actions determine the intensity of the self-perception of oneself, while the efficiency is dependent on how actively the subject can realise its ambitions with the help of the tools—in the form of social institutions, political forms of organisation, military power and technical tools—available at the time.

That is why there is nothing strange in the fact that the knowledge that surrounds the functions of these tools is subsumed into and becomes an important part of the subject's view of itself. Naturally, the subject integrates the creation of its own position in its self-understanding.

To understand man and his view of himself, one has to understand the foundation of his power—or powerlessness. It is, nevertheless, not always easy to keep the meaning of the concept of *subject* clear and pure. It is especially difficult when one turns to late antiquity, when the concept in its historical form appears, but with a diametrically opposite understanding than the current use in philosophy and grammar.

Subjectus would, in accordance with its political connotations in Imperial Rome where it meant "subservient", "influenced by", "under the control of", etc., more closely be translated with the word "object" in *our* understanding of the word. As we shall see, the personalities in both concrete forms of power in the schema above (a.1 and a.2) are characterised by being *subjectus*, subservient and

---

iv When Martha Nussbaum implies that the political economy of Aristotle could be named "social democracy" she actually presumes that the classical ideology of production is a form of "technical instrumentalism", as it would of course be a mockery of *historical* social democracy to assume that people would be used as tools. See *Aristotelian Social Democracy* in *Liberalism and the Good*, ed, B. Douglas et al. 1990, p. 203 – 252 subordinated in both a psychological and epistemological manner as well as in their capability of free action.

That is why I have tried to use the Latin term to denote this other, inverted form of subjectivity. The question of why and how a reversal of this meaning has happened, and what visual self-image the metamorphoses of the subject has led to, will occupy a large part of this treatise.

Image – Idea

A similar difficulty, but one that could also illuminate certain points, concerns the word *idea* and its history. The roots of the concept are in the Greek word for *image,* related to *idein,* "to see". Thus there is a spontaneously felt correctness in the proposition I am planning to expound, namely that symbolical knowing has arisen in symbiosis with the forms of "depicting seeing". Still today, we speak of intellectual conceptions as "images", and one can express understanding and visual perception with the same words: *I see.*

Following Foucault, one could say that the depicting images of seeing and the systematised shapes of understanding follow the same deep, fundamental laws. Or in the words of Cassirer: '*Concept* and *Form* are synonyms; they unite without distinction in the meaning of *eidos*.'[12]

Thanks to the conceptual "transparency" and the spontaneity that characterises the earliest philosophical thinking, concerning concepts like cosmos and idea, and a whole swarm of related words, like *aletheia* with the double meaning relating to both knowledge and visuality of "the true" and "the visible", it is possible to summarise the proposition that I aim to pull out in its historical entirety in the following manner:

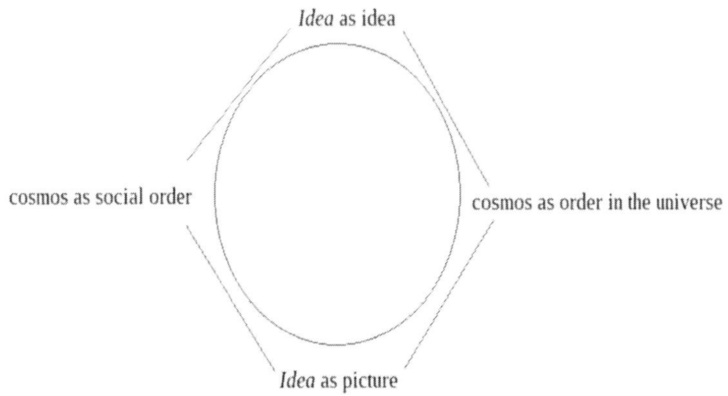

which one should read in the manner that the idea or the image in both its intellectual as well as its visual form reflects on and interprets existence, while at the same time being an instrument for expounding or facilitating a universal order that the societal order can recognise itself in or make use of.

One could say that reason refurbishes its surroundings until it can recognise them and say: I have been here before.

Religion and Knowing

Another relation which immediately should be determined is that between faith and knowledge; between myth and philosophy or theology and science. Both provide symbolic forms for interpreting the world in a broad sense, and in such a manner that the interpretation coherently and without contradiction is aligned with the actual life experiences of the time in question.

The biggest difference—and it is no difference of principle, but one that originates in differences of everyday experiences—is characterised by the fact that religion and its explanatory instance *the myth*[v] perceives truth as "given" and the psychological impulses as "fancies", e.g., "temptation" in Christianity or "anger" in the epics of Homer, while science views truth as "assumed", "inferred" or as something one strives to achieve; in the manner of Socrates or Descartes.

Religion and myth thus have a passive relation to the truth and to the basis for actions and have a *subiectum* as a subject, whereas science actively strives for truth and subject-philosophically is characterised by active knowledge agents with their own motives for action. However, this is an aspect that is derived from the societal dimension and the relations of power: myth and religion exist as dominant modes of thinking in vegetative and static natural economies with monarchic forms of rule, whereas science only has existed during intense, intervening, self-aware and democratic modes of production such as the Greek form of slave production and within the modern industrial mode of production.

In short, that which we call science is the self-understanding of technical instrumentalism. But both myth and science are "true": myth is true in certain circumstances, with events in reality validating its truthfulness in accordance

---

[v] Both religion as well as science consist of *"hardware"* and language-based *"software"*. Procedures and institutions belong to the former; myth and theory to the latter.

with the criteria for "truth" that are given in the same context, something that is also true for the sciences.

Or as Wittgenstein expresses it: 'At the basis of the whole modern view of the world lies the illusion that the so-called laws of nature are the explanations of natural phenomena. So people stop short at natural laws as something unassailable, as did the ancients at God and Fate. And they are both right and wrong. But the ancients were clearer, in so far as they recognised one clear terminus, whereas the modern system makes it appear as though *everything* were explained.'[13]

It is important to dissolve the relative differences between religion and secularised knowing as a foundation for the interpretation of existence, also because they tend to maintain an inappropriate barrier between religious and secular image production. Both are true interpretations of man at the time; for example, all the spiritual or magical "power" that was imbued in the sacral images is an articulation for the specific "weakness", submission and passivity that man only could give a mental expression of in this manner under the given circumstances.

And because art and knowing in *all* its forms expresses the experiences that man has of his possibilities (in life or the afterlife) to live a good life, in that context there is no difference between religious and secular art; between religious myth creation and scientific reflection.

History

There are other ways of marking the differences in the modus of being that through the capacity of thought result in either myth or philosophy. A useful distinction has been made by Max Weber. He speaks of societies either based on *status* or on *contractus*.[14] The legal and economic principles of status-based societies are mostly concurrent with those that apply to subsistence economy, which means concrete, physical power and status-bearing, physical units of value, such as cattle, horsemen, or tracts of land and dogmatic cosmologies with anthropomorphic explanatory structures.

Group a. in the schematic above is thus status-based. The *contractus-*societies are instead built on reciprocal and mutually agreed upon values, such as democracy, codified law, abstract units of value (money) and on a discursive, self-correcting thinking with abstract and sociomorphic explanatory models.

Institutions and forms of thinking of the *contractus-type* are indicative of urban, commercial societies (group b.).

The type of historical analysis I am conducting is of a chronologically parallel nature. I will compare two temporally different, but structurally similar developments with each other; two periods during which the societal form gradually, in a similar but not identical manner, transforms from a status society to a contractus society—and back to a revised status society. This view of history is best visualised as a mighty spiral, slowly and majestically turning or developing around the unattainable origo of history.

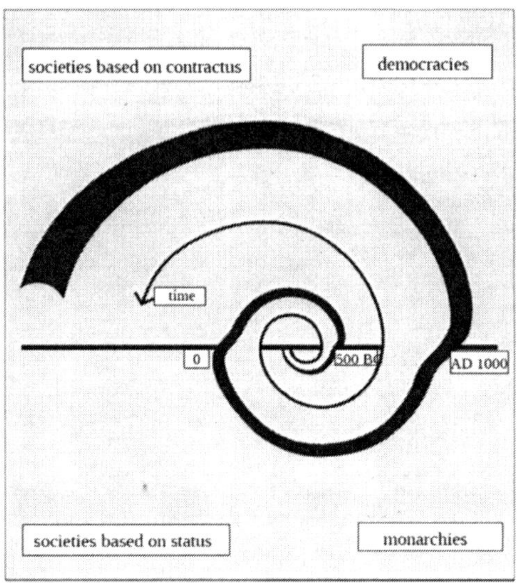

In the historical parallel narrative, I will mainly follow the outer trail of the figure, beginning in the transition from late antiquity to the Middle Ages and ending with the projects aligned towards the future of our own time. This is because my primary interest has been to gather material for the understanding of the present—and also because the historical traces of human activity are so much clearer at these times.

The self-expressions of antiquity, through words and images, will only appear parenthetically, as the differently coloured and differently textured backdrop against which the later democratisation and demythologisation that we call the modern hopefully will stand out so much clearer. Because I am convinced that there is a deep-set structural uniformity between the classical and the modern form of life, and that it can be characterised by the concept of "technical instrumentalism", even though the "technical instrumentalism" of the

Greeks, just as their democracy or their self-awareness was of a totally different nature than ours.

This concurrence enables the fruitful study of two phenomena in two different contexts, to recognise similar stages in a chain of events, the same elements in a multitude of causes, which in a best-case scenario allows us to distinguish the actual factors that produced the phenomenon, from the transitory or the immaterial ones.

We begin where we will end; in the lost and resigned retreat of a self-aware epoch from pretentious claims to power and presumptuous values of subjectivity.

2. The All-Seeing Eye

The Deconstruction of Political Rationality

As is entailed in the concept of flourishing, a reduction of the Athenian self-perception and perception of freedom had already begun during its philosophical golden age—because if Athenian philosophy would have continued to deepen, that which we now see as its pinnacle would only be viewed as a bud yet to flower—as thinking after Plato and Aristotle did not intensify and was not conducted in the same general, pretentious spirit, but was instead replaced by subject-philosophically reductive schools of thought such as stoicism, scepticism, epicureanism and cynicism.

The subject-philosophically reductive part (which will be dealt with in the last chapter) consists of the fact that thinking no longer makes claims on having a political function, a ruling role, as is the case with Aristotle, and even more so with Plato, but that it instead refuses to engage in politics and the practical use of power. Instead, it finds its aims and its meaning in the private and the solitary. The political use of power is no longer the entity that can uphold reason or belief in the future.

While Plato and Aristotle maintain that the most distinguished role of the free man is to engage in public life and in politics, Epicurus sees *not* engaging in politics as a virtue. The Attican demand for being in the public eye is replaced in the Epicurean circles by the exhortation that it is best to "live in obscurity".

Instead of political activity, Stoics emphasise passivity, and instead of *ruling* philosophy focuses on *serving*. This is seen most clearly in the folksy form of Stoicism, Christianity, which in itself is a doctrine well-versed in the art of submission. But the Christian virtues were well prepared in the Stoic principles of knowledge: resignation, suffering and austerity. Stoics also showed respect for real work (*filoponia*)—in contrast to Plato and Aristotle, who denigrated the experience of work and instead favoured criteria of value that related to the political use of power.

The aim of high philosophy, to exercise state power over others as they deserved, was reduced by the Epicureans and the Stoics to a call for self-control. The demand for statal self-sufficiency or *autarchy* was transformed into a more modest demand for personal steadfastness or self-sufficiency (*ataraxy*).

This is a decisive step in the transformation of the classical: a specific, local and collectively anchored view on rationality disappears, the concrete and for the instrumental character of thinking decisive connection between *logos* and *polis* is severed; what remains is a, to some extent, stateless but individualised subjectivity, and one that is more generally defined than the Athenian body political, as even women and slaves could express it.

However, the two interpretations of subjectivity and self-understanding lie closer to each other than what is apparent at a first glance: both concern the Greek theme of "power", and as long as the analogy between state and individual was valid and man was perceived as a *micropolis*, the step from power in the *polis* to power in the individual was small.

The change that took place can be seen as given by the premises that prevailed: if man is a *zoon politikon*, a political being, not only must the defining characteristics such as freedom and slavery in the city body be laid down in his understanding of himself and his existence, but then also must the change which in its effect obliterated the city-state and abolished the absolute difference between Greek and barbarian be absorbed into man's self-image and in the definition of his species' ability to act and rule. Which in fact also happened.[vi]

[vi] It is interesting to note, and no coincidence, that the two historical periods of democracy and conscious, instrumental production, in their consolidation phase exhibit a collectively defined individuality that conforms itself with power, as in the Aristotelian *political animal* or as in Francis Bacons identification of scientifical knowledge with power – because it is both necessary to be unified to realise the potentials of existence as it is easy to be so when it seems possible. While periods of decline, when the productive possibilities are exhausted or begin to show tendencies of counterproductivity, are afflicted by *spiritual* or *subject erosion*. The Cynical, Epicurean, Stoic or Christian ways of perceiving humanity are very much eroded in relation to the concept of *power* – but are still just as unavoidable, necessary and in the long run beneficial. Technical instrumentalism in both its ancient and its modern form includes the promise that existence can be *created* in a rational manner, and a promise of something positive can garner interest and induce cooperation, whereas a *broken promise* only creates confusion and disorientation.

One of the most beautiful promises of classical philosophy, the promise of the good life, could not be realised on the same terms in a more general manner as city-states ballooned over all existing boundaries and the category "human" was generalised, both in the framework of the Alexandrian empire, but especially in Imperial Rome. The foundation for the Hellenic cultural flourishing was "democratic slavery", something that could not expand successfully.

It was as already Cleon knew: democracy can only flourish inside the city walls. Aristotle prompted his pupil, Alexander (a half-barbarian with the epithet "the Great"), in vain to 'establish friendly relations with those who are of like character to our own and have the same interests, and with whom we are obliged to co-operate in matters of great importance; for such friendship is most likely to be permanent. We must make those men our allies, who are most righteous and are possessed of considerable power and live near at hand; those who are the contrary must be our enemies.'[15]

In that case, the Athenian values could have been maintained. But Alexander did not do it. Instead, he treated everyone the same way. He 'recognised and rewarded excellence in others, regardless of whether they were Macedonian, Greek, or barbarian, and he wanted to go beyond the violent parochialism of traditional Macedonian attitudes towards others by extending his policy of "mixing", from clothing to court protocols to military units to entire populations.'[16] Macedonian Greater Greece thus became a melting pot where the, in a local community like Athens, functional and for the good life necessary division between free men and barbarians was erased.

Aristotle's argument that slavery is natural and thus just was possible to maintain only as long as Athens was a sovereign self-sufficient state. But when Alexander, much to the dismay of Aristotle, began treating Greeks and non-Greeks alike, the other argument, that slavery is due to chance, became just as "natural". It was close that Plato would have been sold as a slave, when he on the return from Syracuse was caught by the Spartans and was shipped to Aigina. Plato as a slave: would it have depended on chance, on the military power of some state or the fact that he actually deserved it? When the strong writes history, the weak deserves his fate; the victor does not believe in chance, only in his own superiority.

As the ethnic (in its original meaning "people") and the ethic not only share the same root but also tend to follow one another, it became impossible in the multicultural Hellenistic empire or in Imperial Rome to maintain the, for Plato's and Aristotle's thinking, crucial distinction between humans and presumptive tools; barbarians. Stoic thinking abandoned the confined *polis*-based rationality and became cosmopolitan, but in the dissolution of the given collective subjectivity and rationality another form of autarchy than a state-led crystallised in the core of thinking. The autarchy of the individual virtues emerged as an ideal. As a counterweight to a cosmopolitan universality, the Stoics formulated a claim for *personal* autonomy.

Already the Sophist Antiphon claimed that all men, Greek and barbarian, 'in all aspects have the same nature.' In his modest version of Plato's academy, Epicurus allowed both women and slaves to join the gatherings. And in the Roman Empire, accommodating weakness, the central administration had to expand the concept of "Roman" as the borders of the Empire expanded. This was due to the fact that the conquered peoples exhibited the bad habits of either refusing to bow down to the central authority or demanding civic rights in the Roman state.

Just as in Athens, democracy did not survive this enormous expansion. The city of Rome became a cosmopolitan metropolis packed to the brim with immigrants with their exotic customs and esoteric religions, all the while demanding to be viewed as Romans, even though the only thing that they shared was being *subject* to the same Emperor. A new form of community emerged, independent of ethnic or linguistic unity: citizenship became synonymous with *subordination*.

The citizenry of Rome, belying their diverse origins, were *subject* to the same ruler; the same lord. Here the word "subordination" should not be misunderstood: in the same manner that Christians experienced a paradoxical pride in being servants of God, as it meant that they were God's chosen, the citizens of the Roman state proudly declared: *civis romanus sum*, I am a Roman citizen.[17]

The difference between free men and slaves still existed, but it was not as absolute as in Athens. The right of purchasing one's freedom after a number of years was widespread and contributed to integrating the slaves and thus also *slave mentality* into society. The changes in political culture were reflected in the ethics of Stoicism, which theoretically revoked the qualitative difference that Plato had made between master and slave by acknowledging that all men had *dignity*; a human dignity.[18]

Perhaps it is possible to turn around Hegel's penetrating observation that before the servility of the slave the master loses his humanity and conversely claim that before the humbleness of the master, the slave regains his humanity. At least that is how it happened.

As the new power relations compelled servility in Stoic philosophy, they were transferred via a sociomorphic generalisation to cosmic conditions. With the introduction of an old oriental principle that Christianity would steward later on, man was made a spiritual slave to an almighty lord. Ethical values underwent a similar change: where e.g., Aristotle had emphasised political activity and ruling as the contents of a consummate life, the Stoics saw passivity, suffering and subservience as its meaning.

A similar pattern can be seen with the principles of knowledge: the forms of knowledge that were in liaison with political power became homeless, whereas the ability to empathise with passivity and suffering became knowledge. One should note that the Stoics, even though the principles for their worldview hardly can be motivated in another way than as a justified reaction to an ideology of rulers and slaveowners in dissolution, did not do much to improve the conditions of the slaves. Stoics, such as Seneca, were at the most upset about slavery, but nothing more.

Stoic philosophy actually expresses the dilemma of the ancient way of life very well: it was generally not possible to live with slavery or to accept the results of its abolition. To live a good life without slaves would have required, as Aristotle humorously points out, that 'every tool could perform its own work when ordered, or by seeing what to do in advance. [---] If thus shuttles wove and quills played harps of themselves, master-craftsmen would have no need of assistants and masters no need of slaves.'[19]

That was the dilemma of late antiquity, and it was a real dilemma as it lacked a rational solution according to contemporary thinking. Hegel calls a consciousness in such a situation "unhappy". Because everyone could not be rulers; i.e., as the shuttles were not yet moving of their own accord and work had to be done, the practical way out was to make a virtue out of a necessity and thus the implicit catchphrase became: as we all are or want to be the same, but as not all can be masters, let us all be slaves.

With the restoration of despotic power in Rome, a process whose political innovations extend from Augustus, via Gallienus to Constantine, the democratic elements[vii] in both knowing and image production slowly disappear. The new form of power inexorably excretes new symbolic forms in the way that knowing and art again are brought into consonance with it.

Stoicism became *the* intellectual position in Rome, and later on, without any substantive changes, fused into a religion and a form of mandated state-thinking as Christianity. Stoicism (and Christianity) thus became the ideological umbrella under which the Greek subject-object division between master and slave could be overcome.

We could, following Hegel, say that the theoretical dissension between free men and slaves was reconciled under the protective blanket of Stoicism and Christianity, but in a peculiar manner insofar as *everyone* (including emperors) initially became servants; servants of the Lord, while only much later on (which at the same time marks the end of the historical purpose of Christianity) becoming masters and subjects. In practice, large swathes of barbarians and redeemed slaves were integrated into the realm of the human as subjects to the emperor and citizens in the state of Rome.

The concept of *humanitas*, which in Athens could not have been possible to formulate so as to encompass a majority of the population, instead being the applicable to only a very limited elite, became in Rome the refuge where human and inhuman, free men and slaves could, at least in principle, meet at the same level. For example, the emperor, Marcus Aurelius, and the redeemed slave, Epictetus, could both operate successfully within the same Stoic "party". The great human "reconciliation" and fraternisation was conducted under the watchful and masterful eye of the Lord and Superior.

[vii] Edward Gibbon: *The Decline and Fall of the Roman Empire* 1952, p. 154. The expanded meaning of the word *dominus* tells us something about how the relationship between ruler and subject changed and how due to its connotations in the realm of everyday language and everyday experience became this relationship became more concrete and direct. For Republicans, *dominiatus* meant "tyranny". Emperor Antonius Pius (86–161), on the other hand, did not hesitate to say of himself that *ego men tou kosmou kyrios* – I am the ruler of the world. With Diocletian this course of development later culminated when he adopted as his title the name of Iuppiter, or Jupiter. See e.g., A. H. M. Jones, *The Decline of the Ancient World,* 2014, p. 122.

It is also interesting to see how the epistemology that most clearly mirrored the way that the dominating societal class used power was transformed. 'Ultimately the theory of Ideas, originally a philosophy of human reason, was transformed almost into a logic of divine thought.'[20] In the writings of St Augustine, man *surrenders* his own claims to reason—a manoeuvre going in the opposite direction compared with the spiritual development from Heraclitus to Anaxagoras, during which reason gradually was *internalised*, given a name and an undertaking.

In reference to a famous theme in visual arts, we can say that Philosophy (represented by three wise men in the philosophical and three kings in the political context) fell on their knees before the Miracle—that belief in the Unbelievable acquired greater weight than the certainty of the Obvious.

Thinking as a whole is, in other words, subsumed in the same paradox that the slave has been forced to live with this whole time; the slaveowner tells him that he is not human and he believes it in the end. That he, in absence of actual possibilities to express his own will, finds himself actually agreeing to the fact that he lacks both reason and will—as they are found somewhere else. As an aside, one can mention that it was Emperor Diocletian (243–313) who began demanding genuflection (*adoratio*) out of his subjects.

The philosopher Plotinus wrote eulogies to Emperor Gallienus (218–268) *The Great Maker* and *Poet (poietes)*. So far—five hundred years and two tattered empires—were Plotinus and neoplatonism away from the platonic supposition that it was the *philosopher* who should rule.

As a characterisation of an epoch, Nietzsche's assertion that Christianity is an expression of a slave morality is only valid for these early times. But only for them. Nietzsche does not recognise the division in the Christian philosophy of power, that it temporarily accepts slave morality and submits itself to a Lord, but at the same time, as it is the slave that works on all things and has an essential knowledge about them, slowly makes himself a secondary master; a master over nature.

This double role as an agent for both master and slave morality seems to be pre-formulated already in the Christ figure: the Lord is not only Lord and Ruler and the master of thralls, but also their *Saviour*.

The knowledge or the art of ruling the state (and in its original form administering the household and ruling over slaves; something which Plato made no difference between in principle, and which Aristotle also criticised him for) was at core of Athenian thought—while knowledge in the art of *being ruled by another* was non-existent. Self-restraint was admittedly one of the manly virtues, but to be submitted to the will of another was unthinkable.

However, in the situation that the new political realities forged for thinking, it was imperative to learn submission and obedience—and also passivity, and a certain theoretical muteness. In the same manner, that the patient is supposed to be attentive of his illnesses in front of the physician and not of the physician's knowledge and competence, the slave-consciousness observes only its guilt and its limitations, not the unrestricted freedom of action of his master. The self-consciousness of power, its wisdom, which had been the self-evident core of philosophical discourse, was placed at the far edges of the beyond, as the holy but inaccessible junction of concealed connections.

A total reversal of the perspective of power and powerlessness took place.

Knowledge and power, "meeting as one" not only with Francis Bacon, but already with both Plato and Aristotle, are not separated at this stage from one another, but have become unattainable and are now located at an endless distance. If curiosity, as according to Aristotle,[21] had been the liberating wind that swept away the stale breath of drunken mysticism and opened the door for sober philosophy, then the doors were shut again when St Augustine[22] condemned curiosity and inquisitiveness.

The desire for knowledge, that had been an expression of freedom of action and the possibility of self-realisation, and that above all was linked with the instrumental insight that it is man that with the help of his political tools himself creates the good life, was turned, when actual freedom was circumscribed, when the desire for knowledge lacked a real substrate via which it in accordance with the traditional criteria for rationality (political power) even could attempt such a self-realisation—was now turned over to its opposite and became a *prohibition* against curiosity; a denial of the self-conscious subject.

Philosophy in the sense of Aristotle or Socrates disenfranchised itself. It is impossible to see the individual as a carrier of her own independent capacities of reason in a theocratic or pseudo-theocratic power structure. The *logos* or the *ratio*, i.e., the form of reason that since Heraclitus and Anaxagoras had been an internalised function of the soul, and a private, discursive, dialogic property, and the associated *idea of the scientific* was transformed into its opposite, the *idea of God* (Hans Blumenberg).

The emperor and his figure of legitimacy, God, was the actual societal subject, the actual authority under whose aegis societal transformation could be effected. One should note, that even though the level of rationality in thinking, from a narrow Athenian—and from our modern—perspective, was lowered as the scientific idea was abandoned, there is no reason to act with condescension towards this epistemological turn.

It was inevitable in the same way that monarchy, by the grace of God, was inevitable and was *de facto* an expansion of rationality—but at the same time a hollowing out of the self-conscious Athenian subjectivity anchored in democracy and the *polis*. This is due to the fact that one always has to relate the concept of "rationality" to the subject, i.e., the question of *whose* conception about truth and justice is realised. The *intensive* rationality of the Greeks, by definition limited to an exclusive group, gave way to an *extensive* development as the concept of subject was generalised.

In Christianity, everyone (who was Christian) took part of (the divine) reason, and even if it wasn't as ostentatious and brilliant as that of the Athenian schools, then, if one could quantify reason and calculate a product of the number of subjects and the amount of reason, the expanded form of reason would surely be larger. And, nevertheless, it was the Stoic and Christian form of life that prepared the (with the present as a measuring stick) reasonable displacement of the real correlate of reason from a dependence of ruling and idleness to an alliance with work, experimentation and material production.

Such is the significance of the Middle Ages, epistemologically, but as will be revealed, also iconologically and substantially.

The Picture of Despotism

During imperial times, not only were the forms of governing and understanding of a pyramidal society reinstated, but also the monolithic perception of images as a visual language of power. It would have offended the democratic Greeks if they would have found an image of their ruler on their coins—as the symbolic unification between value and valuation was so important, and the coin was the most widespread measure of value.

– But after the death of Alexander, those who wanted to refer to his greatness as a support for their own claims to power struck his likeness on their coins. In the Roman Empire, image and legitimacy snuck closer to each other; signs and understanding were submitted in a more obvious way to the functions of power.

To embellish his importance, Marcus Junius Brutus struck the picture of his legendary predecessor, Lucius Junius Brutus, on his coins—where previously only gods or the almost divine Alexander had resided.

Caesar completed his intent and let himself be glorified as the guarantor for the continuation of the Empire and the value of its coins. In 44 BC, he usurped total power, proclaimed himself *dictator perpetuo* and let the first coins be minted with portraits of an emperor.

This tradition was continued by his successors, so that when Augustus in 12 BC let himself be appointed Pontifex Maximus and high priest, possessor of the highest clerical office, demigod and *cosmocrator*, only the nomenclature was reorganised according to the actual symbolism of the currency (according to which the portrait, the effigy, had been reserved for the gods). Iconologically, the ascension of the emperor to godhood was well prepared.

The– Caesar, the Emperor—became a numismatic being through the power of his office. The inauguration of the pyramid and the obelisk as a symbol of power was followed up by numerous imperial statues and the ubiquitous imperial coinage. The victory of the despotic principles had gotten a worthy and literally valuable conclusion.

A larger variant of the constant presence of imperial power were the busts and statues of the emperors that were erected to represent the central administration in all parts of the vast empire.[23] One could imagine the imperial busts as the political banners and loudspeakers or as the propaganda of their time, if it wasn't so that propaganda strictly speaking aims to persuade an opponent and spread an ideology and historically belongs to the vocabulary of the Counter-Reformation.

The symbolic imperial presence did not have this function, but instead had the purpose of constantly reminding the citizens of their *submission*, of their inevitable role as *subjectus* in relation to the emperor. Propaganda, in the shape of bombastic reason, is a part of a dual conflict of power: Catholicism vs.

Protestantism; socialism vs. capitalism, etc. This was not the case in Rome. Rome was unequalled and all-mighty.

The powerful pressure and the from a ruling role originating, palpable arrogance with which Constantine met his subjects in the former state capital of Rome and forced them to obedience can be seen clearly in the colossal sculpture, originally placed in the Basilica of Constantine in the Forum, and is now shown in the yard of the Conservatory Palace.

'The first Christian Emperor was honoured with such an idol. However, this has to be seen as a sign of the times, as a testimony of Constantine's peculiar view on Christianity as well as a crushing defeat of faith in a moment of victory for the church. [---] It is the holy majesty of the image of the oriental ruler we finally meet in a true Roman form. The enormous eyes and their spiritualisation come from the east; in the portrait of Constantine there are elements of old oriental art.'

'[---] The "holy" in the image of Constantine was highly topical in the 4th century and deeply allied with the spiritual powers that carried the Christian faith to victory; Christianity was not an oriental religion by happenstance.'[24]

Constantine I / Constantine I or some of his sons

The brutalisation of power was accompanied by a brutalisation of taste and an increasing vulgarity in art. The constant wars created an avenue for the most ruthless, and in the uncouth ceremony of the military camp, the uneducated emperors had no reason to conceal their violent temper or their often simple background. Out of sight of the capital, the rulers also easily forgot the origins of their lawful power and its character. The position of emperor had been created by unifying a number of offices that still revealed their republican origins and thus had to be concealed by even more pretentious and bombastic titles.

To all the previous titles the rulers added one that required even more submission, *dominus*; lord. The epithet *dominus* originally did not mean the power of a ruler over his subjects, or as the title *imperator,* that of a military leader over his soldiers, but explicitly the despotic power of a master over his own slaves.[i] The iconography completed the epistemological and political reinstatement of despotism and absolute knowledge—especially after Diocletian demanded a regal likeness (*similitudo*) in the imperial busts and portraits.

The simplifications, the excerpts and the banalisations in iconography and form enhanced the effect of the few pictorial forms of the imperial myth. Artistic design or genealogical features; exquisite archaic forms hardly played any role outside Rome. But, in the words of Zanker, also in the capital of Rome, 'the future was hardly to move in the direction of increased refinement and elaboration. The simplified visual language gradually taking root in Italy outside Rome held its own and sometimes even had an influence back in Rome.'[25]

When power finally became completely spiritualised as Christianity became the state religion, a whole cluster of epithets moved from the voluntarily abdicated emperor to the newly instated Jesus Christ. The emperor had been called *Lumen Imperii*—The Light of the Empire. The Christ figure was given, as can be seen e.g., in the Monreale cathedral outside Palermo, the inscription EGO SUM LUX MUNDI. Also in the terminology, the spiritual ruler had become Lord over a people—a people that spiritually and ideologically had become servants.

Christ the Almighty

The transition from concrete imperial power to a spiritual power within Christianity happens without changes in the iconography.[viii] The Christian ruler, *Christ Pantocrator,* in the Daphni mosaic from the early 12th century, the Almighty who is the father and the son in the same figure, is depicted with the same piercing gaze as Constantine. The iconographic origins of the Byzantine Christ figure in an amalgamation of concrete imperial power and legitimising holiness appear clearly in the second bust of Constantine, situated in the same place as the colossal statue.

As a grim echo of the visualisation of the Roman empire's true principles of power, the epithet of ruling push forward in the features of the son of Man. The

---

[viii] The same applies to both ideology and the view on knowledge. If one wants to find a break in the epistemological development it lies between Aristotle and his successors, the Stoics, Cynics and the Epicureans – but also in this break it is possible, as we shall see to, interpret a deep-lying continuity. To see something unconditionally new in Christianity is an unfortunate mistake that originates in the narrow reliocentricity of our continent.

same penetrative jailer eyes, the same brutal determination to *rule*, the same arrogantly curved, majestically contemptuous mouth.

Christ Pantocrator (11th century) from the Church of Daphni

One can see the staring eyes as an oriental influence, but it is not essential, because the crucial thing here is that exactly this rigid form of the presence of power was incorporated into western iconography and in addition overtook a dynamic. living and often dramatic imagery. The attributes of power are the same in the Christ figure as in the images of the divine emperor, the placement in the church is the same as that which previously was reserved for Jupiter and the masterful eyes instil the same feeling of inferiority in the beholder (who actually is more of a beholdee than a beholder) as the imperial gaze was meant to convey. In the constant emphasis that man is a servant and a slave to the lord, the first phase of the transformation in the ancient societal dichotomy is manifest, that all men actually, on an abstract level, in relation to eternity and the omnipotent power, are the same. The concrete masterful gaze of the slave owner— *dominus*—with the right to punish, is replaced in a symbolic manner by the (nevertheless concretely existing) emperor's gaze, that in turn is replaced by the abstract and eternally absent gaze of the Lord.

With Christianity as a state religion, the god and his primary earthly deputies become increasingly absent and abstract. Absence—absolute absence—does not mean enfeeblement, but the opposite. His power grows more and more, at the expense of all the people who are subordinate. The double or triple figure of the

Lord is omnipresent—especially when He has ensured himself of a worldly apparatus of power. Not only is man as a social or political being defined by his submission; his whole spiritual and psychological dimension takes the same shape.

The Lord as an all-encompassing dominant not only gains a social, but also an ontological gravitas. The epistemology that now is valid could be borrowed from Isaiah 7.9: 'If you will not believe, you surely shall not last.' *Existence in itself* is permeated by the will of the Lord. Now, as always, the legitimacy of the government is secured by the symmetry between *microcosm* and *macrocosm*: Byzantine autocracy works, according to a 10th century commentator, in accordance with the order and harmony that 'represent[s] in miniature the order and rhythm with which the Creator has infused the universe.'[26]

It would be wrong to say that the citizens of the Greek democracies (i.e., the free men) would have had a free will as we understand it.[ix] The utility of the state and the utility of the family preceded all individual concerns and the notion of the "freedom" of the will was subsumed to the collective well-being. Thus, it would be misleading to claim that that which had never existed now had disappeared.

But private argumentative reasonings had occurred, and real dia-logos had taken place, but above all, an individually based form of reason existed and a conception about freedom (*eleutheria*) versus fate that one could not have translated to any other language at the time. As these categories intellectually had been a part of the characteristics of democratic despotism, man or humanity perceived as *being equal* had to get rid of them. Or rather keep them where they had always been, with the despot, but make him categorically different and absolutely absent.

The qualities of the slave owner now resided with the totally absent but always present God; He possessed the Word, the Will, the Reason and the Freedom. We can see this as the *negative*. The *positive* is that without the instrumentally productive interlude of the Hellenes these categories would never even have been formulated. They would, generally speaking, not even have *existed*, not even as something unreachable. The paradox of freedom would

---

[ix] Just as wrong as it would be to say that they lived in a "democracy" of our kind – the politics of *apartheid* in South Africa would have been startlingly "democratic" in comparison. Freedom in the Greek sense related to the state in the same way that Plato's dialectics relate to the idea, i.e. in the dynamical, troubling way that the relative or *relativising* relates to the absolute. The analogy works both ways.

never have been formulated, reason would not have reached independence and the singular will would never have become part of the human experience.

History would still have taken place in a milieu decided by fate, where the Homeric heroes (or later on the Vikings who also lacked the classical experience) shaped their destinies.

We can also reverse the picture of the state of things, and instead focus on the view on existence of the societal majority, previously viewed as objects devoid of reason, i.e., the slaves. Then we see that *nothing changes* as the transformation from the lordly philosophy of the Greeks to Christianity *actually takes place*. With the Lord as lord, the Word, the Reason and the Will still reside with the Ruler—the lord, whose superiority is contingent on the fact that he possesses these qualities.

He, in his heavenly figure, can be identified as Lord precisely due to them. Even the only will that the slave was allowed to carry, the wish to be free, remains with the same expression and the same location in the hierarchy of wills: in the strategy of Paul, the Apostle, to fashion Christianity into a sort of "Stoicism for the people", the word *salvation* that was used in an eschatological manner, was in some texts the same as the word for the "manumission of slaves" used in everyday language.[27]

Original Sin

During their often very dramatic history, the Jews had to endure many trials and tribulations, which they in an admirable way managed to get through without perishing as a people. Perhaps this is why Jewish thinking has been engrained with the perception that the entire Jewish people carried a *collective debt*—one could not think that misfortunes would happen a *people* if they would not have been guilty of something, and an effect must have a cause (or a debt, according to the cosmological strategies of the time).

In the case of the Jews, a whole people perceived themselves as guilty or indebted, something that—as one had managed to survive all the misfortunes— was mitigated by a belief that they also were chosen.

The Christian religion, that started among the Jews, did not have a people at first, and almost no history or traditions associated with it. That is why it had to become a missionary religion, that *spread* its gospel. To convince people that it was necessary to believe in Christ, Paul transformed the Jewish thought of a national sin or debt with a collective salvation into something *individual*; to something that primarily concerned a singular person.

Now, the ethical detached itself from the ethnic. Both sin and salvation became concerns for the individual. The stoic, individualistic position that one should have command over oneself still reflects an ideology of mastery. In Christianity, caring for oneself was transformed into a practice mirroring that of the slave: now the primary aim was *salvation*, in other words purchasing one's freedom.

The Greek intellectual concept of the soul, *logos*, did not reach the same degree of individuality and independence as the Stoic or the Christian ones. But it was neither possible nor necessary: in the same manner as the meaning of the word *logos* semantically was anchored in the language usage of common Greek, (signifying meaning,) the Greek conception of personality was always part of a state-mediated (male) collectivity. That is why statelessness was perceived as a punishment worse than death.

The *daimonion* of Socrates as a personal possession thus becomes an exception that actually challenged the power of the state, but even Socrates chose the justice of the state above an individual one and death instead of exile and statelessness.[x]

A servant of Christ, a slave in an abstract meaning, as, could be perceived in his essence, i.e., pertaining to the *soul*, as an *individuality*. Thus, being part of a state or class no longer defines the essence of a person, and instead has been replaced by personal virtue. 'There is neither Jew nor Greek, there is neither slave nor free, there is no male and female, for you are all one in Christ Jesus,' Paul writes to the Galatians.[28]

Thus a new and untested substance is added into the great cauldron in which the civilisatory process slowly steeps. Both the Epicureans and the Stoics had, admittedly, cut the ties between ethics and the state and in that manner individualised morality as previously mentioned, but here the Platonic idea about the supremacy of the soul forges a deeper alliance with the notion that it is the individual who realises his own destiny. This is a very peculiar union, as the components originate from two opposite camps.

Plato's perception on the ruling role of the soul is formed as an analogy which uses the power of the free men in the state as its template, while working

---

[x] The fate of Socrates is in some way as contradictory as the conflict between dialectics and idea in the thinking of Plato, and with exactly the same ingredients.

on one's *own* fate is a slave virtue that to some extent had been adopted in some Sophist, Epicurean and Stoic circles. This alliance is so strange that it could only have been forged in the face of eternity.

Another thing that is clear is that the personality and humanity of the concrete slave, whose psychological and epistemological conditions were adopted by the new form of spiritual slavery, could not be defined within the context of stately cohesion, as was commonly done by the Greeks. Because to be a slave meant *not* belonging to a pertinent and self-defining collective. The slave was—and had to be—like Ibsen's Mountain King: *sig selv nok!*—enough for oneself.

The only thing the slave could hope for was that he or she, after years of hard work, could purchase her freedom. Work and servitude were the virtues of the slave, the source of his knowledge—and the seed for his hope of salvation.

Just as little the servants of Christ could unequivocally tie themselves to the collective destiny of the Jews. The human value that became dominant as Christianity became the state religion had to find its own formula. And it became: God is the Lord, we all are slaves to the Lord, we all have a sinful or bad soul, the soul is immortal and a sign of humanity, and we all are equal as we all are responsible for the salvation of our own, individual, soul.

In the Old Testament, the words that are used for "salvation" usually have the root *jascha*. '"Yasha" primitively means "to be or make wide". Evil and danger are always regarded as narrowing conditions or effects. From the 'narrow' place, the sufferer cries out. When help has come he is in a 'wide' place. [---] Hence "Yasha" and its derivatives express "victory".'[29] Thus "salvation" is closely linked with the "peace" that the happy unfolding of life under the blessed auspices of Jehovah could bring.

Salvation in the form of "victory in war", "liberation from ones enemies", etc.; referred to the felicitous conditions that determined the fate of the *people*. Christians, however, were not a "people", they lacked ethnic cohesion, and thus the sin (in the form of an original sin), and consequently also salvation had to be both generalised and individualised. As Paul wrote to the Romans: '*Everyone who calls on the name of the Lord shall be saved.*'[30]

The salvation that the earliest form of Christianity promised was firmly linked with the release from bondage and slavery in a conceptual sense—thus one understands that the promise of deliverance from the evils and the injustices of the world fostered great hope among the people that had no power of their destiny and were not even seen as human. Because in front of the Heavenly Lord, everyone was equal, free and unfree; master and slave.

In a comment to Paul's First Epistle to the Corinthians, the 5th century Syrian bishop, Theodoret of Cyrus, writes: 'We are not our own lords; we have been bought with a price; and while living, therefore, we are the Lord's, and when dead we are the Lord's; that is, neither art thou his master, nor is he thine; for One we all have for our Lord. For to this end Christ both died, and rose, and revived, that He might he Lord, both of the dead and the living. He is the Master of all, who for our sakes gave Himself up to death, who destroyed the power of death, and has promised salvation to us all. To Him, then, are we subject, as from Him having received life.'[31]

Something that still even Seneca had viewed as incompatible, namely work and knowledge, were now joined in the serving of God, the essence for all insight.

The common characteristic that made a human indistinguishable from another and gave everyone a task to fulfil throughout life was the fact—unknown among the Jews—that *everyone was a sinner*. In relation to the mentality of the slave owner, the concepts remain remarkably intact, but are reversed. The dichotomy body—soul still remains, and is still existentially separated in the same manner that separates life from death, but now on an axis of time—all men must *die*—and not on an "axis of struggle" as in the life and death struggle of the master and the slave where only the one that dares risk his life is free.

But above all, the values of life are shaped from the viewpoint of the corporeal, namely that of the slave, that previously was illogical, powerless, sinful and evil. The domain of the pure soul on the other hand, where all good things reside and that possess all the virtues and the joys of the master, is accessible only when the abstract slave has reached the frontier in front of which the actual slave lost his freedom i.e., before the doors of death.

The common inheritance of all men thus had negative connotations in Christian teachings, as something evil, as an inevitable inclination to sin that only the faith of salvation in the hereafter could save oneself from (this lies in stark contrast to Stoicism, where the universal was a common human *dignity*). Even so, the conception of a general corporality, a general original sin, was an important civilisatory step as it at the same time, as the counterpart to sin, generated the perception that individuality in the form of personal responsibility exists, and that a general global solidarity exists between all people.

This is also expressed negatively, as compassion—it is often the case in history, that something positive initially appears as something negative, and that it only later on can be overcome and overturned.

The Gaze

The Ruler that rules in absentia becomes an All-seeing Lord in image rendition, represented by the Eye or the Gaze. It is not the beholder that beholds the image of God, instead God beholds man. The image is not thus an "image", but a sacrosanct creation for the initiated that ritually has been given aspects of the strength and superiority of the Lord. Both the imperial gaze as well as the overseeing gaze of Christ the Almighty renders a notion of *being watched* in the person watching, a notion of subordination, of being a *subjectum*.[xi]

The feelings of inadequacy and *shame* are a form of consent of the correctness of the existing hierarchy. *I* am, in the eyes of the Lord, a sinner, and thus His potential punishment is just. This consent can perhaps also explain why successful slave uprisings did not take place during antiquity. When power has a pyramidal shape, powerlessness must reproduce a similar shape. Thus, even the confused slave uprisings had to reproduce similar mini-pyramidal shapes.

Why? Because they also needed a leader of divine origin, as that is how power, reason and truth could be identified. Power secretes power of the same form. The short-lived despotically ruled slave states in Sicily did not eradicate slavery, but perverted it by making the previous lords and foremen into slaves. Into the slaves of the slaves.

If we cling to the perception, that the type of mentality gradually developing within Stoicism and Christianity meant that the slavish aspects of existence formed a valid morality and a mode of understanding existence, then the continuity between the Athenian logic of domination is maintained, but also the later development of the human self-image and self-understanding can best be understood from this perspective. It is unnecessary, as Nietzsche does, to present derogatory assessments on the essence of slave morality.

[xi] The reversal of the viewer's perspective, to which I will return later, emerges in an interesting way from the shift in meaning of the words *subjectum* and *objectum*. "*Subjectum* originally designates precisely what we call an object today; and *objectum*, to the contrary, means in the Middle Ages what we grasp as represented and opposed to us in mere thought, what is intended subjectively in today's sense." Heidegger: *Being and Truth*, 2010 p. 35 Transl. G Fried and R Polt.

Admittedly man was subject to an, in power and capabilities, absolutely overwhelming Lord, but on the other hand, he—or the majority of the citizens—now had the categories of knowledge on his side. As a subject, he had adequate knowledge about himself—a step forward in comparison with Greek high philosophy. Man does indeed possess his knowledge in a passive manner, but this gives the correct picture of his submission. It is the slave himself that defines his slavery, which also is the strength of the slave.

Later on, when the slave becomes aware of his own power and the fruits of his labour, then he is no longer a slave but a *worker*, then *he* rewrites, as we shall see, precisely as all others who have come to power and become aware of their strength; then he rewrites the conditions of existence in accordance with *his* criteria, being altogether different from those of the master and originating from a totally opposite praxis.

It is impossible to reconstruct the experiences and the thoughts of the slaves as almost no sources exist, according to one who has researched slavery in the ancient world.[32] On the other hand, one could say that *everything* is preserved, in a later, spiritualised form, and that it is the manifest certainty that the Lord is the lord and that the only thing worth living for is the hope of salvation and freedom.

The relationship between Lord, the God, and His servants, this generalised and abstract slave existence for the part of humanity that had looked up to Rome, I call, in accordance with its iconological expressions and psychological experiences, an *ofthalmos*-relationship, The Greek word *ofthalmos* or *óps* in the singular was the eye of a master or a ruler, or the eye of heaven. God or His representative appear in both words and images as a constantly present and all-seeing eye.[xii]

And when power lies within the eyes of a jailer that at any given moment can open the hatch and see you in your inferiority, the feeling of constantly being seen is expressed as *shame.* Under the stern gaze of the Lord, you are always guilty.

As Sartre puts it: 'Consider for example shame. Here we are dealing with a mode of consciousness, [---] a non-positional self-consciousness, conscious (of) itself as shame; as such, it is an example of what the Germans call *Erlebnis*, and it is accessible to reflection. In addition its structure is intentional; it is a shameful apprehension of something and this something is me. I am ashamed of what I

[xii] "For His eyes are upon the ways of a man, And He sees all his steps." *Job 34:21*

am. Shame, therefore, realises an intimate relation of myself to myself. Through shame, I have discovered an aspect of my being.'

'Yet although certain complex forms derived from shame can appear on the reflective plane, shame is not originally a phenomenon of reflection. In fact, no matter what results one can obtain in solitude by the religious practice of shame, it is in its primary structure shame before somebody. I have just made an awkward or vulgar gesture. This gesture clings to me; I neither judge it nor blame it. I simply live it. I realise it in the mode of for-itself.'

'But now suddenly, I raise my head. Somebody was there and has seen me. Suddenly, I realise the vulgarity of my gesture, and I am ashamed. It is certain that my shame is not reflective, for the presence of another in my consciousness, even as a catalyst, is incompatible with the reflective attitude; in the field of my reflection I can never meet with anything but the consciousness which is mine. But the Other is the indispensable mediator between myself and me. I am ashamed of myself as I appear to the Other. By the mere appearance of the Other, I am put in the position of passing judgment on myself as on an object, for it is as an object that I appear to the Other.'[33]

The Jewish, collectively felt feeling of *guilt*, becomes, in an individualised understanding of personality, a personal admission of *shame*. But to only refer to a Jewish origin is not enough to explain why this form of self-denigration now could grow into a general feeling, within another, radically different culture. History never functions on borrowed premises. How was it that the *joie de vivre*, the worship of corporeal beauty and the hedonistic indulgence in all sensual pleasures—not to mention the *shamelessness* so central in both Greek and Roman life, are infiltrated and outflanked by their complete opposites: life-denial and guilt-consciousness.

For this metamorphosis to be meaningful, the impulses have to be found in society itself; within its most vital parts, and again it is: the relationship between the (actual) master and the (actual) thrall. 'I am a slave to the degree that my being is dependent at the centre of a freedom which is not mine and which is the very condition of my being,' Sartre writes.[34] For medieval man, all interpretations of existence—intellectual and visual—verified that this was the case. He was a slave to his own being; he accepted the judgement of the Lord.

The feeling of shame *is* this judgement; shame is, as Sartre also says, the shame of oneself. The servant makes the judgement of the master his own: that it is shameful to be forced to work and to be master of none. Man as servant is deprived of his possibility to set himself above the judgement of the Lord, and in his interpretation of the world, he accepts this.

To be a slave means accepting a faith almost equal to death: as mute, as meaningless and as powerless, but with one important difference: it was stained with the lingering shame of not having chosen a more honourable fate: death. And as long as power was confident and complete, the slave could not keep the judgement of power at bay: the Lord's contempt for work and slavery were absorbed by the slave and turned into self-contempt—also by the spiritual slave. In the dualistic world of Plato, man was also divided into a free and a "banausic" part: the soul represented freedom or ruling while the corporeal represented manual labour and commerce. Then, when the Stoics dissolved the Platonic state-personality, it had significant consequences for the perception of personality. The concept of slave was generalised (or was placed tangentially to the conditions in society) so that the free (man) who was a slave to his own bodily lusts and passions generally could be seen as a slave in a spiritual sense—and conversely a slave that exhibited great self-restraint could be recognised as (spiritually) free and thus worthy of respect.

To depict barbarians with large, exposed genitalia was an old theme in Greek vase painting. Barbarity was equalled with unrestrained and bodily lust; i.e., as the incapability of the barbarians to *rule* over themselves. (*Within* the Greek civilisatory process, one can clearly see in images how men are "tamed"; how sexual aspects are toned down in favour of virtues of moderation such as *sofrosyne* and *ataraxia*. See also the chapter on individualism below.)

When slave morality became general morality, it could not avert the judgement that master morality already had passed: that the slave—an embodiment of corporality—lacked *logos*; that the slave thus was lustful and unrestrained and that it was very, very bad. A creature that cannot control itself does not deserve a better fate than to be someone's slave. Thus, slave morality does not (yet) manage to remove the curse of master morality (a fate shared with *nature*, as we shall see later on), instead creating a strange moral code, consisting of self-contempt, shame and a denial of the experiences of the body.

And, as a counterbalance to this misery, a longing for the guidance of the Lord. Almost only one positive value exists in the temporal world, to serve well. But that is something that the master also can welcome.

Foucault and Sartre on the Gaze

The relationship between power and submission in the form of being constantly under (spiritual) surveillance by an All-seeing-Eye, was later on even adapted for practical applications. In his analysis of power as it is constructed in relation to *Discipline and punish*, Michel Foucault offers a chapter on the Panopticon, the model of a prison invented by the English utilitarian philosopher, Jeremy Bentham, and built like the spokes in a wheel with hub in the middle from where all the prisoners could be surveilled in one glance.

"The Panopticon", Foucault writes, 'is a marvellous machine which, whatever use one may wish to put it to, produces homogeneous effects of power. A real subjection is born mechanically from a fictitious relation. So it is not necessary to use force to constrain the convict to good behaviour, the madman to calm, the worker to work, the schoolboy to application, the patient to the observation of the regulations. Bentham was surprised that panoptic institutions could be so light: there were no more bars, no more chains, no more heavy locks; all that was needed was that the separations should be clear and the openings well arranged.'

'[---] The efficiency of power, its constraining force have, in a sense, passed over to the other side—to the side of its surface of application. He who is subjected to a field of visibility, and who knows it, assumes responsibility for the constraints of power; he makes them play spontaneously upon himself; he inscribes in himself the power relation in which he simultaneously plays both roles; he becomes the principle of his own subjection.'[35] In fact, no probation officer is even needed, it is enough there *could be* an eye looking at you from the centre of the power.

Bentham himself mentions this to be the "Essential Points of the Plan". 'The essence of it consists, then, in the centrality of the inspector's situation, combined with the well-known and most effectual contrivances for seeing without being seen.'[36]

In an interview with Jean-Pierre Barou and Michelle Perrot Foucault emphasises this: 'There is no need for arms, physical violence, material constraints. Just a gaze. An inspecting gaze, a gaze which each individual under its weight will end by interiorising to the point that he is his own overseer, each individual thus exercising this surveillance over, and against, himself. A superb formula: power exercised continuously and for what turns out to be a minimal cost.'[37]

The term *ofthalmos* as an expression of the masterful gaze in an unequal lord-servant reality has a reversal in Sartre's phenomenological analysis of the gaze in equal, democratic societies. Sartre's analysis has its epistemological roots in Hegel's analysis of the original encounter between two individuals; that which makes one the lord and the other the slave. But as it is not possible to enslave people in a democratic society, the relations between individuals have to be expressed in a more subtle way.

We can call these kind of relationships that Sartre analyses *dia-optical*—encounters eye to eye. As the phenomenological analysis of Sartre according to me is of great interest also in a historical (and especially in an art historical) context, it seems necessary to recapitulate it.

The stylised encounter between people that Sartre expounds in *Being and Nothingness* (and that Hegel had done earlier in *The Phenomenology of Spirit*) concerns the process of how equality (or inequality) is determined. Or about how the subject constantly has to assert his subjectivity against other subjects to be able to maintain his self-image.

In the decisive first phase of the encounter, before an identification and a mutual recognition between the two who are under each other's gaze takes place, one is the object of the other, and vice versa. In Sartre's theory on social relations, the section on how this imbalance is eliminated and both beholders can see the other as subjects is a central piece. We shall remain for a while in the situation where this imbalance still exists, when the other still is an object for the subject. If this transitory situation prevails, it expresses that the object feels shame of himself. Shame is the psychological expression that the *beheld* admits the correctness of the judgement of the *beholder*, and the verdict is that the beheld is *shameful*. As long as the beheld cannot nullify the gaze of the beholder and make him *seen* as well, he accepts the verdict, *shameful,* of himself.

To See the Other

I am in a public park. Not far away, there is a lawn and along the edge of that lawn there are benches. A man passes by those benches. I see this man; I apprehend him as an object and at the same time as a man. What does this signify? What do I mean when I assert that this object is a man? If I were to think of him as being only a puppet, I should apply to him the categories which I ordinarily use to group temporal spatial "things".

That is, I should apprehend him as being "beside" the benches, two yards and twenty inches from the lawn, as exercising a certain pressure on the ground, etc. His relation with other objects would be of the purely additive type; this means that I could have him disappear without the relations of the other objects around him being perceptibly changed.

In short, no new relation would appear through him between those things in my universe: grouped and synthesised from my point of view into instrumental complexes, they would from his disintegrate into multiplicities of indifferent relations.

Perceiving him as a man, on the other hand, is not to apprehend an additive relation between the chair and him; it is to register an organisation without distance of the things in my universe around that privileged object. [---]

Thus suddenly, an object has appeared which has stolen the world from me. Everything is in place; everything still exists for me; but everything is traversed by an invisible flight and fixed in the direction of a new object. The appearance of the Other in the world corresponds therefore to a fixed sliding of the whole universe, to a decentralisation of the world which undermines the centralisation which I am simultaneously effecting.

But the Other is still an object for me. He belongs to my distances; the man is there, twenty paces from me, he is turning his back on me.

Being and Nothingness, p. 254-

To Be Seen

If the Other-as-object is defined in connection with the world as the object which sees what I see, then my fundamental connection with the Other-as-subject must be able to be referred back to my permanent possibility of being seen by the Other. It is in and through the revelation of my being-as-object for the Other that I must be able to apprehend the presence of his being-as-subject.

For just as the Other is a probable object for me-as-subject, so I can discover myself in the process of becoming by a probable object for only a certain subject. [---]

I have observed that I cannot be an object for an object. A radical conversion of the Other is necessary if he is to escape objectivity. Therefore, I cannot consider the look which the Other directs on me as one of the possible manifestations of his objective being; the Other cannot look at me as he looks at the grass. Furthermore, my objectivity cannot itself derive for me from the Objectivity of the world since I am precisely the one by whom there is a world; that is, the one who on principle cannot be an object for himself.

Thus this relation which I call "being-seen-by-another", far from being merely one of the relations signified by the word man, represents an irreducible fact which cannot be deduced either from the essence of the Other-as-object, or from my being-as-subject. On the contrary, if the concept of the Other-as-object is to have any meaning, this can be only as the result of the conversion and the degradation of that original relation.

In a word, my apprehension of the Other in the world as probably being a man refers to my permanent possibility of being-seen-by-him; that is, to the permanent possibility that a subject who sees me may be substituted for the object seen by me. "Being-seen-by-the-Other" is the truth of "seeing-the-Other". [---]

The look which the eyes manifest, no matter what kind of eyes they are is a pure reference to myself. What I apprehend immediately when I hear the branches crackling behind me is not that there is someone there; it is that I am vulnerable, that I have a body which can be hurt, that I occupy a place and that I can not in any case escape from the space in which I am without defence—in short, that I am seen. Thus the look is first an intermediary which refers from me to myself. What is the nature of this intermediary? What does being seen mean for me?

Let us imagine that moved by jealousy, curiosity, or vice, I have just glued my ear to the door and looked through a keyhole. [---] But all of a sudden I hear footsteps in the hall. Someone is looking at me! What does this mean? It means that I am suddenly affected in my being and that essential modifications appear in my structure—modifications which I can apprehend and fix conceptually by means of the reflective cogito.

First of all, I now exist as myself for my unreflective consciousness. It is this irruption of the self which has been most often described: I see myself because somebody sees me—as it is usually expressed. This way of putting it is not wholly exact. [---] It is shame or pride which reveals to me the Other's look and myself at the end of that look. It is the shame or pride which makes me live, not know the situation of being looked at.

Now, shame, [---] is shame of self; it is the recognition of the fact that I am indeed that object which the Other is looking at and judging. I can be ashamed only as my freedom escapes me in order to become a given object. [---] The Others' look makes me be beyond my being in this world and puts me in the midst of the world which is at once this world and beyond this world. What sort of relations can I enter into with this being which I am and which shame reveals to me?

In the first place there is a relation of being. I am this being. I do not for an instant think of denying it; my shame is a confession.

Being and Nothingness p. 256-

This is shame as the mode of being for the self, after being seen. We shall not delve into the reciprocal relation to the other, where the other is like myself, that Sartre expands on in the following chapter, but this form of reciprocal dia-optics should be kept in mind when we reach Giotto and the intense exchanges of glances that take place *within* the picture plane in his paintings.

One should note that in the hypostasing of the gaze in the Byzantine image tradition, a visual confirmation is made of the condition that man is utterly inferior; that the psychological expression of inferiority is shame; that man is *absolutely shameful*, even afflicted by original sin and that he lacks every possibility to annul his vulnerability, to be free, to become a *subject*. And man, in turn, cannot see God, cannot *meet* his gaze, but is constantly exposed to His thorough scrutiny and his dreadful but at the same time just judgement that cannot be questioned.

This is what this category of images states. Man could not, and was not allowed to, gaze inquisitively upon his Maker as he himself was gazed upon. And creation was also encircled by prohibitions to gaze upon it. In the tenth book of his *Confessions*, Augustine writes about *voluptas oculorum*—the lust of the eyes—and he maintains that the lust to see was the most pernicious of the sensual pleasures and also the likeliest culprit in endangering one's spiritual health.

As the sense of sight is set to instant gratification, it is simultaneously the sense of curiosity and thus pernicious. Theoretical muteness and visual blindness are constructed of the same socially valid elements.

Through the maintenance of the image of an all-seeing God, man continually fortifies the conception of his own inferiority. The concession is transmitted through the acknowledgement that the judging Lord is absolutely noble and good. The image of the Lord's beaming omnipotence also signals that man is absolutely inferior. We can never completely understand what it meant to live under these conditions—as little as we can fully understand the Greek lifestyle—but we can examine the mechanisms of its self-understanding. One of these mechanisms is images. Another one can be seen in the categories of knowledge. We can also reverse the angle of approach and look at how *impotent* man, man that accepted that absolute power and absolute reason existed outside himself, conducted himself. In the introductory chapter to his fascinating study on *The Autumn of the Middle Ages*, Johan Huizinga vividly portrays the type of mentality that the *lack* of self-reflective individuality and autonomous will leads to. The people that lived then, acted—lacking responsibility, power and authority—akin to children, without constraint, impressionably, impetuously and unreasonably.

But one has to remember that they all were the "God's children", and that no perceptible difference or difference in principle (such as a personal faculty of reasoning, something that was internalised once again at the dawn of the modern era, and became the foundation of knowledge for Descartes) existed between children and adults is corroborated by for example the fact that adults engaged in activities that we now call "children's games". Or perhaps this can be seen even more vividly in the manner that contemporary children were depicted, as tiny adults.

The picture of the Middle Ages would not be complete, Huizinga writes, without 'that of the vehement passion possessing princes and peoples alike.[38]' The deluge of unfettered lust, passionate piousness or bloodthirsty anger that gives the Middle Ages its frightening outlines is juxtaposed with the real power of ancient man, with the concomitant ethical call to rule over himself, fetter his passions and behave temperately and reasonably. Or juxtaposed against the moderating mechanisms that enter self-restraint into the mental registry of modern man.

The Post-Despotic Society

The watchful gaze of God and man's constant preoccupation with his sin and shame is a constant theme in scholastic moral philosophy. When Boetius of Dacia in 524 writes about God as all-seeing, that He 'with one glance of His intelligence He sees all that has been, that is, and that is to come. He alone can see all things, so truly He may be called the Sun'—it is clear that he writes about a Neoplatonic rather than a Christian God. God in the Old Testament is also a seeing as the Christian God. But not for all eternity.

Of the images in which humanity manifests its origins, its dreams, its hopes and wishes and the extent of its knowledge and abilities, there are two series that express exceptionally well how "freedom" as a budding idea and actual concept has been visualised. The two series are very different, as they were made in completely different circumstances. One is an excerpt from a series of statues, showing an increasing awareness of freedom fashioned as sculptural independence, while the other shows how actual power is deconstructed.

At the same time, they exhibit a similarity in meaning as both, in their way, depict *idols*: human ideals. The first series is from archaic Greek times, the second is medieval.

During a short period of time of around one hundred years, the Greeks created both the institutional framework as well as the spiritual and visual forms for their freedom. This is undoubtedly one of the most significant periods ever in the formative process of both the intellect and the type of depiction that we are familiar with today.

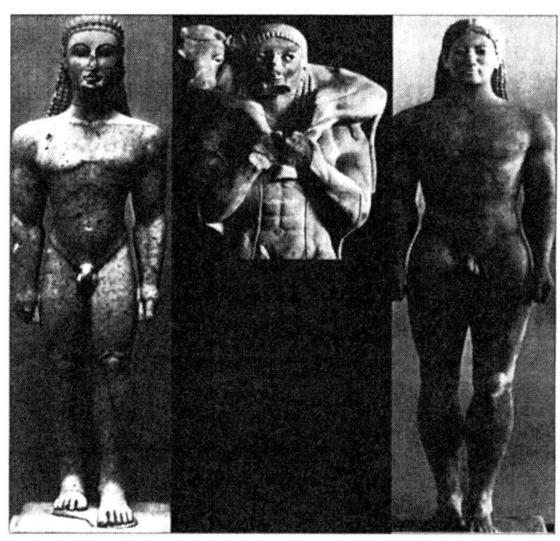

Four Idols: *Kouros* c. 600 BC, *The Calf Bearer* c. 570 BC, *Kroisos* c. 525 BC, *The Kritios Boy* c. 480 BC

In the first image, in the archaic dawn, we see how man hesitantly, as if awakened from a deep slumber, treads onto classical ground. During the archaic period, he still stands in an Egyptian pose, rigid, solemn and somewhat soulless. His movements are stiff and uncertain, he lacks a clear vision of his resources and his capacity to move, but already in the next image he has, at the same pace that he has released himself from the cyclical grip of destiny characterising the natural state, taken the step out into freedom, unconstrained, innocently smiling, *animated* by his own will and own intentions that light up his facial expressions.

It is not my intention to neutralise the mystery of the archaic smile, but as I see it, the smile expresses unpretentious and proud surprise, *this I is me*; this I in the picture is like me. The soul, *logos*, is in me. I am like the idol; independent and spiritual. The smile is this recognition.[xiii] The smile is an expression for the

---

[xiii] To continue the Sartre-Hegel discussion on the first encounter to its epistemological present, I want to add something on Levinas. It seems to me, that the difference between Hegel's and Levinas' way of perceiving the encounter isn't as much about the difference in its phenomenology – but that it actually is about two totally different types of encounters. If we start from the type of original existence where tribal society defines its borders concretely with a palissade (or city walls) then the Hegelian encounter is characterised by the fact that it takes place over this barrier – the self is standing across a tribal Other – while the encounter described by Levinas, the open, smiling, face-to-face encounter happens within the palissade, and is an encounter that confirms that which already has been established with the palissade as its concrete manifestation, i.e. tribal

reciprocity lacking in the *ofthalmos*-relationship, but that now, for the first time, materially manifests the pride and relief that all men are equal and that I am like the other and like the ideal—sculpted in stone.

During the same century that Sappho creates the poetic self and Heraclitus invents the soul, man chisels an image of himself in the sculpted, soulful features. And this is not a general Greek creation (thus one cannot find the causal links in the "race" or the "language", etc.) but explicitly an Ionic, with its roots in the commerce, the equality and the entrepreneurship that also were the prerequisites for democracy and philosophy.

Just as sculpture liberated itself from its material confines and escaped its prison of marble (Michelangelo), through the use of their political instruments, the Ionic Greeks liberated themselves from their uninfluenceable earth-bound destiny. And it happened consciously, with a clear conception of both their *goals* and their *means.*[xiv]

The final form, the so-called *Kritian Boy* from around 480 BC, depicts a man that (almost) literally *stands on his own two feet*. He has stepped away from the natural state and its way of life, detached himself from the formless grip of the stone slab to meet the world with the justified and magnificent pride that grows from the insight that it isn't nature's draconian laws but his own man-made laws that are the foundations of civilisation. A material manifestation of a self-aware man.

The flip-side of Greek freedom was the brutal power with which it maintained its institutions and values. Every ideal of freedom breathes some form of power, whose odour is the only thing lingering when freedom has lost its means of power and has thus consumed its *logos*. That is what happened with Greek freedom.

The freedom that was recreated during the Renaissance, is different from the Greek. During late antiquity and the Middle Ages, freedom already *existed*, or it

---

sameness. The archaic smile is the confirmation this encounter triggers. In the case of Hegel, on the other hand, the original encounter takes place along a line of battle, over the palissade and it results in a society of slave owners, where one is the owner and the other is the slave. The divine eye watches over this conflict, as it maintains the perception of the Master on a slave-creature. The frozen gaze of God is an expression for a frozen form of violence, for all the violence that has been written down in the constitution of the society of slaveowners; a society that in the end was penetrated and overpowered by this violence. It is the gradual playing out of this conflict that the Divine eye beholds.

[xiv] Such as in the reconstruction of Miletus led by Hippodamus in 479 BC, after which the city became and orderly and "rational" grid city.

had existed in a real and active form, but now, in a post-despotic society, it only existed as a concept, as a memory and an infinitely distant abstraction; as the freedom of the Lord. The *living* interpretations and signs had congealed into *power* and could only be reproduced within the forms of ruling, with the attributes of power.

The new freedom, that so to speak emerged "in the pores" of the medieval social body, meant not only, as in archaic Greece, a release from the grip of nature. It also had to liberate itself from the grip of the *polis,* from the societal forms of power of antiquity, i.e., from the categories and conceptions that were used by antiquity in completing its aspirations for power.

It does not happen, or does not happen *primarily* as during archaic Greek times that man figuratively gives himself more room to manoeuvre, more freedom. The image of man's growing freedom is portrayed in reverse during late medieval times, so that the Lord's position of power is less and less striking and that He becomes more humanlike. Which is the same thing as saying that man/the servant receives more power and freedom, insofar as he becomes more like Him, who previously has had sole possession of the power and the freedom.

Four images of Christ: *Pantocrator, Christ on a throne with Mary and John, Pietá, The Suffering Christ*

In the first picture, *Christ Pantocrator*, the ruler is alone, solitary and all-mighty. In the second, the *Deësis*, He is flanked by two creatures of earthly origin, Mary and John, the Apostle, that function as *mediators* between the earthly and the heavenly life, and whose intercessions will ameliorate His absolute judgement—a role that Mary later on had to bear on her own. These two archetypal pictures of Byzantine origins are medieval. The two latter ones, the *Pietà* and the *Man of Sorrows* are from the late Middle Ages, Gothic, and of Western origins.

The clearest sign of the change in the attitude towards life can be seen in the images where compassion is sacralised and generalised to also encompass the God. If not before, then at least at that point the sphere of the divine is subsumed into the human. Compassion, that in its first incarnation, was to join people of different gender, race, and societal position into an all-embracing (Roman) humanity, is borrowed to mediate between the abstract Lord and the abstract servant. When the servant can, or rather has to, feel compassion with his master, then the master has become human in the eyes of the servant.

The thing that is interesting with the *Pièta*-motif is that it lacks precedent in the Scriptures. As a sculpted embodiment of a feeling, not only expressing deference during the difficult hour of grief, but also expressing human sympathy and unity with the divine family, the *Pièta* (and the *Mater Dolorosa*-figure) are genuine contemporary creations, imprinted in the self-esteem of the time by its foremost interpreters.

On Meeting the Gaze of God

A millennium after its origins, the image of Christ Almighty had been dethroned and substituted with more timid representatives for the Creator. The spiritual tyranny, as it had manifested itself in the harshly judgemental gaze and in other attributes of power, gradually receded and left room for a relationship based on a higher level of reciprocity. But as always, a phenomenon reaches insight of itself only when its role has been played out. The review comes when the play is over.

Roger van der Weyden: Self-portrait (tapestry replica)

One of the most interesting texts on the gaze of God is written by Nicolaus Cusanus (1401–1464); the great philosopher on the boundary between scholasticism and natural science. In the small book *De visione Dei* (*On the Vision of God*), written for the monks at the Tegernsee monastery, Nicolaus initially writes about a self-portrait by Rogier van der Weyden he had seen in the Town Hall of Brussels.[xv]

The picture has the peculiar feature, that wherever one stands in the room, one appears to be *gazed upon* by the eyes of the self-portrait. If one moves from one side of the room to the other, it appears as if the gaze would follow. And that is what the gaze of God is like, Nicolaus writes, omnipresent, gazing upon all. And God is called "God" (*Theo*) because He sees all, as Nicolaus (incorrectly) believed that the word *Theo* has its roots in *theorein,* "to see", "to behold".[xvi]

But Nicolaus Cusanus, who in his thinking is standing on the doorstep to the modern age, and that had already experienced the dioptic images of a Giotto or a Roger van der Weyden, is able to—and this is something new—*resist* the all-seeing gaze of the Lord and assert himself on his own terms. The God of Nicolaus is "both a seeing and a seen God", according to Walter Schulz.[39] In the gaze that Nicolaus directs at God, the difference between God and man or the stellar and the elementary world that has been in place since Aristotle and Augustine, is undone.

Theoretically, God becomes a known being, while man, also in images, becomes a *seeing* man. Augustine's condemnation of the "lust of the eyes" is gradually invalidated. And in the moment that the gaze falls upon the Creator, the eyes are also opened towards Creation, and neither no longer looks as previously imagined. A reciprocal relationship between God and man is established, and as is the foundation for all reciprocity, no longer is man only dependent on God, but God also becomes dependent on man.

It is the eye contact and the love relationship that enables this reciprocity: *"Domine, videre tuum est amare;* O Lord, Your seeing is loving", Nicolaus writes. 'You, O Lord, do not at all allow me to conceive, by any stretch of the imagination, that You, Lord, love anything other than me more than me, for it is me alone whom Your gaze does not desert. And since where Your eye is present Your love is also present, I experience that You love me, because Your eyes are most attentively upon me, Your lowly servant. O Lord, Your seeing is loving;

[xv] The painting has been lost, but there should be a copy in the form of a tapestry in Bern; see Cassirer 1927, p. 32.

[xvi] "Now, O brother contemplative, draw near to the icon of God and situate yourself first in the east, then in the south, and finally in the west. The icon's gaze looks at you in equal measure in every region and does not desert you no matter where you go." Nicolaus Cusanus: *De visione Dei*, chapter i. Transl. Jasper Hopkins.

and just as Your gaze regards me so attentively that it never turns away from me, so neither does Your love.'

'And since Your love is always with me and is nothing other, Lord, than You Yourself, who love me, You Yourself are always with me, O Lord. You do not desert me, Lord; You safeguard me on all sides because You most carefully watch over me. Your Being, O Lord, does not forsake my being, for I exist insofar as You are with me. And since Your seeing is Your being, I exist because You look upon me. And if You were to withdraw Your countenance from me, I would not at all continue to exist.'

'But I know that Your gaze is that maximal goodness which cannot fail to impart itself to whatever is capable of receiving it. Therefore, You can never forsake me, as long as I am capable of receiving You.'

'Hence, I must see to it that, as best I can, I be made more and more capable of receiving You. But I know that the capability which conduces to union is only likeness; but incapability results from unlikeness. Therefore, if by every possible means I make myself like unto Your goodness, then according to my degree of likeness thereto I will be capable of receiving truth.'[40]

It is due to this reciprocity that love as a gauge of the characteristics of interpersonal relationships is an interesting indicator of possible mental states in both Greek and medieval behaviour. The Greeks were not familiar with the type of sentimentality that we express with the words "compassion" or "loving one's neighbour".

The pinnacle for the Greek state was *autarchy*—and in accordance with the logic of opportunism statuating that 'individual virtue must be structured as a virtue of the state' (Foucault), the male ideal of freedom (*sofrosyne*) shied away from all forms of dependence or attachment, especially from a potential *reciprocity* between a man and a lower being such as a woman—or, Woe! a dependence on this unworthy being. Thus, love could not be the foundation for the relationship between a man and a woman. The foundations for these relationships were steeped in older traditions from pre-individualistic times with the demands (and continuation) of clan, family and house at the forefront.[xvii]

But, in Christianity (and actually already among the Epicureans), things are different. Love and *compassion* denotes something crucial in the general conduct

---

[xvii] This can also be one explanation of the widespread homoeroticism in Greece: it was the only way to unify mutual affection and physical love. On the other hand, a delicate problem of inequality emerged – highlighted by Foucault – as the roles of the *sexual* act itself could be divided into dominator and dominated.

between people. 'Thou shalt love thy neighbour as thyself' is the loving message of Christ. Love develops into an active ingredient in the integration and levelling of society; love was the name of the double projection of God unto man and man unto God, and—with the same name even though it is quite a different feeling—an expression for the special feeling between a man and a woman.

This became, as we shall see, problematic within the framework of ascetic self-realisation embedded into Christianity.

The road from being *seen* and *accepting one's shame* to establishing a reciprocal relationship and a *Mitsein* with an Other goes through phases such as *Love, Language, Masochism, Tolerance, Hate, etc.* according to Sartre. We shall focus on the role of love, as it is most clearly discernible and also focuses on both the *I* and the *You* and (under different conditions) creates both *individuality* and *collectivity*.

For the subject to be able to reconquer itself after having been turned into an object in the above-mentioned relationship of shame, it has to be able to "absorb the other" in some way. According to Sartre, this reconquest by the self of its being is realised when the self takes possession of the other's freedom. The strongest expression of this is love. If the self makes itself loved by the other, then the self can be certain that the other in his being and freedom becomes dependent on the object of his love. Thus, the self ceases to be an independent object; it becomes a subject and a condition in the relationship with the other.

On Love

These projects put me in direct connection with the Other's freedom. It is in this sense that love is a conflict. We have observed that the Other's freedom is the foundation of my being. But precisely because I exist by means of the Other's freedom, I have no security; I am in danger in this freedom. It moulds my being and makes me be, it confers values upon me and removes them from me; and my being receives from it a perpetual passive escape from self.

Irresponsible and beyond reach, this protean freedom in which I have engaged myself can in turn engage me in a thousand different ways of being. My project of recovering my being can be realised only if I get hold of this freedom and reduce it to being a freedom subject to my freedom. At the same time, it is the only way in which I can act on the free negation of interiority by which the Other constitutes me as an Other; that is the only way in which I can prepare the way for a future identification of the Other with me.

This will be clearer perhaps if we study the problem from a purely psychological aspect. Why does the lover want to be loved? [---] To want to be loved is to infect the Other with one's own facticity; it is to wish to compel him to recreate you perpetually as the condition of a freedom which submits itself and which is engaged; it is to wish both that freedom found fact and that fact have pre-eminence over freedom.

[---] But if the Other loves me then I become the unsurpassable, [---] I am protected against any eventual devalorisation. I am the absolute value. To the extent that I assume my being-for-others, I assume myself as value. [---]

From this point of view, my being must escape the look of the beloved, or rather it must be the object of a look with another structure. I must no longer be seen on the ground of the world as a "this" among other "thises", but the world must be revealed in terms of me. In fact to the extent that the upsurge of freedom makes a world exist, I must be, as the limiting-condition of this upsurge, the very condition of the upsurge of a world.

I must be the one whose function is to make trees and water exist, to make cities and fields and other men exist, in order to give them later to the Other who arranges them into a world, just as the mother in matrilineal communities receives titles and the family name not to keep them herself but to transfer them immediately to her children.

Being and Nothingness, p. 366–369

Anyway, when Nicolaus Cusanus in *De visione Dei* stands up against God (albeit in a soft and vague manner); or when he puts himself as the necessary condition for the gaze of God and refuses to remain an *object*, he makes an indirect claim of being a subject himself, an authority of his own right capable of setting an agenda the Other also is dependent upon. One thousand years after the All-seeing usurped all the power and all the glory, we enter a state of balance with the previously Absolute Other.

Nicolaus states that man is no longer only a function of God, but that God is also a function of man; intellectually, as Creation would have no meaning if there would be no one to praise it; visually, dioptically: God is not only seeing, He is also dependent on the seeing of man. 'What else, Lord, is Thy seeing, when Thou beholdest me with pitying eye, than that Thou art seen of me? [---] I know that Your gaze is that maximal goodness which cannot fail to impart itself to whatever is capable of receiving it. Therefore, You can never forsake me, as long as I am capable of receiving You.'[41]

Thus the Lord in a visual, empirical manner becomes a slightly clearer subject-object, and the same happens, in reverse, to His servant. Nicolaus understands that this is what reciprocity entails, and soon his self-esteem knows no bounds. 'Man is God, however not absolutely as he is a man,' Nicolaus says. Or: "Man is a second God", as both are Creators. One of "natural forms", the other of "artificial".[42]

We can, in the gradual relativisation of the relationship to God, in the emphasis on reciprocity and how artists/craftsmen perceive "the changing structure of His gaze", see how man establishes his own self-worth. In his phenomenological analysis, Sartre maintains that: 'Thus to want to be loved is to infect the Other with one's own facticity.' In the historical context, we can see how many challenges his creator by acting like a creator in his own right, as a manufacturer of artificial worlds. The self-worth of man is resurrected under new forms when his *labour* obtains an actual worth in itself.

After a millennium of laborious toil and creating artefacts, the slave has become the master.

Thus, once again reason in some sense has been internalised (the first time it happened in philosophy from Heraclitus to Anaxagoras) in that man now perceives himself as a subject and bearer of agency to the extent that he knows that he has a god *within* himself. Finally, we can look more closely at the two epistemological events that mark the beginning and the end of the epoch during which man and reason were separated.

In *De civitate Dei*, Augustine asks what *genius* is. He finds that there are two answers: *genius* means either "ruler of all—i.e., Jupiter", or "the rational soul of every man". The conclusion that unites the two views would then be that "the soul of every man is a god", which Augustine finds "absurd"; it cannot be so; reason exists only in God.[43]

Petrarch, on the other hand, who a thousand years later lived at a time when human reason was once again making claims to knowledge, accepted the dualism that Augustine rejected. When his brother, Gherardo, criticised him for dealing only with worldly matters in his poetry, Petrarch replied that this was the case, but that there was nothing wrong with it as the inspiration of the poets comes from God; his genius is a gift from heaven.[44]

For 15th-century humanist, Lorenzo Valla, it was quite clear that God dwells in man; that the soul is a *homo deus*[45], while Nicolaus Cusanus in the same vein argued that man, as a true image of God, carried his god within him.[46]

The Madonna

Between Augustine and Cusanus, between the Byzantine Almighty and, for example, Cimabue's Madonnas, there is a long evolution that in its different stages marks how the human/servant from a humble kneeling position, slowly rises, stands up on his own two feet, in order to be able to look his master straight in the eyes. It is not a question of an antagonistic rising against his master, but rather a constructive one. It is through the manifestations that labour and toil create, and as a creator of artificial forms, that man gains a new self-esteem based on the realisation that he himself has the power to shape his living conditions; to change the world.

This power is not commanding, as the power of the master, but processing, as is necessitated by the status of the slave. It is through the use of knowledge *not* possessed by the master, the immediate knowledge of nature, that he finally gains essential knowledge of himself and becomes his master's peer.

In the great sweeping movement of renewal and change that is the civilisatory process, the centre of gravity of cultural innovations moved westwards. The symbolic forms of the Byzantine worldview were integrated in the symbolic language of the Romanesque Middle Ages and later on in that of Gothic art and architecture.

In their search for a legitimate expression of the changing conditions of life, philosophers and artisans replaced the expressions of the ruler's power already introduced during Roman imperial times with an interpretation that rendered the relationship between the human and the divine in a milder way. The marked subservience eventually, via steps such as the political and cultural achievements of the Carolingians, the economic boom in the cities of northern Italy, in the Île-de-France region, in Flanders, in the Hanseatic League and in England, gave way to a self-understanding based on self-activity, initiative and action.

Civilisation is taking a new turn, so to speak, from the West. The Neo-Byzantine art on Italian soil in the 1200s shows that this kind of imagery still adequately communicated life experiences even though shaped in a tradition weighed down by history. It is only the encounter in the free atmosphere of northern Italy, between the Byzantine of the South and East and the Western,

North and West of the Alps, that a new self-esteem reaches a visual expression. Up until the time of Bernard of Clairvaux (12th century), the images that carried the ideals of truth, beauty and reason expressed *raison d'état* and domination.

The images depict a ruling Christ and a crowned Mary (*Maria Regina*): the deputies of monarchical power that can only be invoked in sadness and lamentation and to whom only a plea for mercy can be addressed:

'To thee we cry, banished children of Eve. To thee do we sigh, groaning and weeping, in this vale of tears.'[47]

With Bernard, a cult of a *different* Mary than the Crowned One commences in Western Europe. It is a Mary who does not represent the ecclesiastical power to the same extent, who lacks the insignia of glory, but who instead meets the viewer on a more personal level, as *Mother* Mary or Mary the *Human*.

Marina Warner writes of the changing cult of Mary that 'this intensely personal love of the Virgin that welled in St Bernard's heart infused her cult after him with the same highly wrought and intimate sweetness. [---] Till now she had remained a remote majestic figure, used to define the complexities of Christological doctrine, or to symbolise the authority of the Church. [---] In the 10th century began the first stirrings of the adoration that transformed the Virgin from a distant queen into a gentle, merciful mother, "Our Lady", the inspirer of love and joy, the private sweetheart of monks and sinners, and the most prominent figure in the Christian hierarchy.'[48]

When man in this way rises up against his self-chosen Lord and Ruler, then iconologically, as we have seen, the Lord is diminished in size, power and authority. He takes on a new human dimension in that He is represented by a mother and a child. Instead of Christ Almighty in His overwhelming majesty, we are given an image of a completely different spiritual character: The Madonna and the child—the most defenceless of all human constellations.

The figure of Christ is no longer perceived in his unreachable greatness but instead in his vulnerable smallness. There is nothing frightening or judgemental in the gaze of the Christ child; both the child and the mother are gentle and innocent in their appearance. Severity is replaced by gentleness.

The love that man has always been supposed to envelop his father and Lord with, is at last met by reciprocal love. In a way, man is now reconciled.

The representative of the judging Father on Earth is thus replaced by the motherly mother; a figure of human origin and in that sense equal. The mother as a spiritual figure is a completely different counter-image and gives a completely different response than the All-Ruling Christ. The mother is an authority to which one can appeal; for whom the pious prayer of grace, the *kyrie eleison*, does not go unheard. Already in the *Deësis* above, Mary (and John) are inserted as the *mediators* of the cause of man before the Lord.

The servant has found an influential ally; he or she has gained an agent who could speak for him or her at the heavenly court. The gaze of the mother of God is a compassionate one, her countenance and gestures express *sympathy* in the original sense of the word: compassion, sharing in the suffering of another. And in the face of Her humility, the slave becomes free—and through his own growth the slave humbles the Lord and his representatives.

Thus, in a manner despised by Nietzsche but necessary for civilisation, man engages with his historical legacy, gradually leading to the reconciliation and equalisation of the depths and the gaps in the faculties of the soul, and the overcoming of his own inhumanity.

The cult of the *Mater Dolorosa* was on the rise at the end of the 11th century in both Italy, France, England, the Netherlands and Spain, and really started to flourish towards the 14th century.

The Crowned Madonna, Byzantine; *Maestà* by Duccio, c. 1310; *Madonna dell'Umilitá* by Masaccio, c. 1423 (cropped)

In this often passionate worship of an almost *human* Mary, the earthly feelings a mother could have for her son were gathered and subsequently shed in the holy sphere of that the worship of the divine implied. 'Through her sorrow,' Marina Warner says, 'the man or woman in prayer could feel the stab of loss and agony. The Virgin was the instrument mediating bafflement at the mystery of the Redemption into emotional understanding.'

'She made the sacrifice on Golgotha seem real, for she focussed human feeling in a comprehensible and accessible way.'[49]

The dethronement of the Madonna follows exactly the same pattern as the humanisation of Christ, and her importance grows as people hope and believe that they can gain a hearing and get her to intercede on their behalf before Christ. With *Madonna dell'Umilità*, the dethronement becomes literal, as the Madonna is now placed directly on the ground, without the throne or the regalia as in the *Maestà* images. (We shall return to one of these, the *Madonna* of Simone Martini in Avignon.)

Dioptics

During the time man psychologically (but also *de facto,* as a subject) perceived himself as subordinate, the visual image he has given of his subordination has been conveyed by his vulnerability as being *seen.* The gaze-direction has been a one-way relationship, moving from the image out towards the watcher. Analogously, the emotional and intellectual flow has been from God to man. Reason and will have resided with God; man's emotions and thoughts have been given by God (or the Devil), and his whole destiny has been in God's hand.

Trade, the mechanisation of work, the flourishing of city-states and the accompanying sense that it, to some extent, is possible for man to shape the conditions of his own life changes all this. The new city-states are not only centres of trade and crafts, but also, in accordance with the dynamics and norms that trade creates, are introducing ideals of equality—for vibrant democracies have never existed without trade and nowhere has large-scale equality existed without democracy.

Trade as an originator of values has been rejected by all aristocracies and true tyrannies, for the very reason that in the long run it equalises all *status*-based norms; including tyranny itself.[xviii] The money economy emerges from trade, and

---

[xviii] One of the most interesting encounters between these two incompatible values is recounted by the peripatetic philosopher and "cultural historian" Dicaearchus. In his book on Pythagoras, he relates how Pythagoras came to the city of Lokroi (Locri) while

thus also its characteristic reciprocal values, including manifestations of egalitarianism and formalised mutual recognition. For two merchants are obliged to regard each other as rights-holders and as equals, unless, if one follows Hegel, they instead prefer to kill each other and thus cease to be merchants.

The judicial-democratic foundation of the northern Italian city-states was broader and more general than that of the Greek city-states, because the *workers*, the holders of labour-*power*, were also stakeholders and legal subjects and therefore also negotiating parties in determining the value of the specific commodity they could supply. That is to say: they had a say in determining the *value* of their work. With the Constitution of 1293, political power in Florence passed to the middle class; the guild system became the conduit through which both the formulation of civic virtues and paths to social flourishing were channelled.

After the so-called Ciompi Revolt in 1378, *day labourers* were also given the right to form their own guilds and were granted the right to negotiate wage agreements. However, the result of the most radical reforms, The Divine Republic of the wool weavers and dyers (calling themselves *Popolo di Dio*— People of God—even in official documents; as they could not yet identify themselves as a distinctive *economic* class) lasted only a month, before the middle class fought back.[50]

Although, the proletariat would have to wait six hundred years for redress, the experiences derived from work and trade became trend-setting for the conception of what is rational, how to live a good life, and what was considered a moment well spent. The worker—the slave who literally values himself— becomes the originator of the metaphysical values of the new epoch. With *work*

---

fleeing from Kroton. There he was met at the city limits by a delegation, who kindly but firmly informed him that it would be more appropriate for him to go elsewhere. One admired, the delegation allegedly said, Pythagoras for his wisdom, but one was satisfied with the present conditions and had no desire for change – Lokroi was Spartan-minded at the time and initiated a monetary economy only in the 3rd century B.C., while Pythagoras with his own active efforts, had probably been involved in introducing coins and standardising weights in Kroton in the 5th century BC. His whole philosophy of quantifying the universe can be seen (and in my opinion should be seen) as an intellectualisation of the principles that emanated from trade; *that everything corresponds to a number*; everything is translatable into a numerical value. As his contemporary sources also inform us of. Thus, in a society like Lokroi, with its status economy and concomitant primitive barter, "Pythagoras would certainly have had a disturbing influence", as Guthrie posits in his *A History of Greek Philosophy,* Part I, Cambridge 1 962, p. 178 n.1.

as the basis for dealing with reality, man's expectations are logically transformed to include activity in *this* world, which immediately is reflected in the theoretical and visual interpretation of existence.

A new metaphysics takes shape that breaks with Platonic idealism and Aristotelian conceptualism and makes the actual, real-world and nature the object of scientific attention, while image-creators begin to provide visualisations of *real*, physically unified worlds.

The difference between Athenian and Florentine citizenship is defined by the fact that the slave has now attained recognition and his work has acquired a value. The former was related to property; the latter meant having a job. In Athens, one was a citizen if you owned land; in Florence you had to be a member of a guild. In Athens, self-esteem and subjectivity were submerged in the jurisdiction of a household (wife, children and slaves) and a property.

In Florence, on the other hand, they flowed from the pride felt in—and the right to value the results of—one's own work. *Homo politicus* had become stateless; *homo faber* had taken power. This is also the decisive point in assessing the fundamental similarities and differences between ancient and modern high philosophy; between ancient and modern image-based self-understanding. One is rooted in the virtue of ruling, the other is linked to the values of technical work.[xix]

[xix] Aristotle explicitly discusses this matter in *Politics* (1 277b-78a). A citizen is rightly a person who has the right to participate in the government of the state, Aristotle says. But should the working class (the free workers) also count as citizens? Not at all, for if they are included it is impossible for all citizens to show civic spirit, and this is only attained by knowing how to *rule*. Craftsmen and labourers are even worse citizens than peasants and shepherds because "there is no room for moral excellence in any of their occupations". (*Politics* 1319a) The peasants, at least, had servants and the shepherds had sheep to exercise "moral excellence", i.e. power over.

Cimabue: Santa Trinità Maestà, 1290–1300, Giotto: Madonna Ognissanti, 1306–1310

People no longer turn to God—or not only to God—for advice and consolation, but seek it in *consciously* self-created instances. The great merchant of Prato, Francesco di Marco Datini (c. 1335–1410) expresses some of this double "bookkeeping" or reference when one reads the motto written on his account books, i.e., "In the name of God and profit". Where the reference to God obviously aims to appease a harsh and unknown destiny, while "profit" is the name of the interpersonal, "objective" yardstick by which the traders measure each other's personal initiative, strength and ability to survive as a trader.[xx]

Giotto

In painting, the fault line between the tempered Madonna-figures of the *ofthalmos*-relation and an advanced iconographic *di-optical*-relation goes between a master and his student, between Cimabue and Giotto and can be dated

[xx] Later on, Descartes makes this personal *ingenium* the foundation of scientific speculation, which is why Descartes' philosophy only ostensibly is individualistic since, like the rate of profit, its measure of truth presupposes a collective inter-subjectivity, called "objectivity". While at the same time the God as a reference is erased from the advanced self-consciousness. Still in the 1620s Galileo could express himself in the "name of God and truth", two hundred years later God is no longer needed. The mathematician Laplace's answer to Napoleon when asked why God is not mentioned in his book is rightly famous: "Sire, I did not need this hypothesis.'

to around the year 1300. There are many reasons to give the new century the honour of engendering a new era. Dante is a child of the 13th century and of medieval times, Petrarch of the next.

Cimabue and Duccio painted in a traditional "Greek" style, while Giotto, Simone Martini (a student of Duccio) or the brothers Lorenzetti represent something completely different. In the 14th century, the Italian city-states were set on their paths towards becoming powerful forces both politically and culturally, and the breakthrough of the Renaissance in art and architecture would surely have been quicker if not for the significant setbacks that accompanied the Plague of 1347–1350. But nowhere can the signs that a new self-understanding is being established be seen as clearly as in the case of Giotto.

Giotto: *Christ driving the Money Changers from the Temple*, 1304–1306

In the large frescoes of Giotto, there are two simultaneous changes to the "gaze". On the one hand, there is a cessation of eye contact between the beholder's gaze and the gaze of the subject of the image (which, by virtue of its position and initiation, represents a deeper form of "seeing"). Instead, the images create a dramatic space of their own, and the drama is depicted dioptically. The figures of the subject turn their gaze *inwards,* towards each other, with an often dramatic, sometimes almost explosive effect.

As if from nowhere, Giotto creates an art that depicts people looking and confronting *each other*. For the first time in painting[xxi], the intentionality of the

---

^{xxi} Greek plastic art displays an intense agonal and dioptic energy, especially in the many battle scenes, which in itself is significant, since it was in battle and war that the human

gaze creates an *internal* context to the image. It dramatizes the event, connects the pictorial subjects with each other through intentional approaches of approaching or distancing that charge the images with a frozen narrative; with a frozen purposeful activity.

On the other hand—and this is the second change—the image space and the viewer's space merge. If images as *icons* previously were a kind of porthole or peephole through which God or his representatives looked down on people from the inaccessible heights of another reality. From Giotto onwards, the pictorial space becomes a window through which people can view beings like themselves that are moving and acting in familiar spaces.

A distance, and at the same time, a new closeness is created. The vulnerability that stems from the experience of being constantly seen is replaced by a kind of distance when the image no longer has a direct psychological impact on those who, in a broad sense, worship it. The emotional charge of the image diminishes drastically. On the other hand, a possibility of identification lacking in the icon is created: the space of the viewer and the space of the image are now essentially of the same kind and visually and ritually are continuously merging with each other. (We shall return to this in more detail in the section on naturalism.)

Pietro Cavallini: *The Birth of the Virgin*, 1296–1300; Giotto: *The Mourning of Christ*, 1304–1306

dignity of the Greeks was decided. For as it is said of war in Heraclitus: Some it makes into slaves, others it makes free. Diels-Kranz: *Fragmente der Vorsokratiker,* frgm. 22B53.

Giotto's contemporaries immediately took notice of Giotto's art and identified it as something new. In the *Decamerone*, written just over ten years after Giotto's death, Boccaccio lets the narrator state that Giotto 'in his paintings reproduce nature with such striking similarity that one could almost doubt that they are executed by the human hand.'[51] Alberti writes[52] about the lost mosaic *Navicella* that Giotto lets each apostle 'with face and gestures express clear signs of a troubled soul in such a way that each exhibits different movements and positions.'

And one hundred and fifty years later, Vasari has something similar to say about Giotto's frescoes in the Upper Church of Assisi; that their figures exhibit 'wonderful variations in gestures and attitudes.' Giotto managed to express *i movimenti d'animo*, the movements of the soul, in his paintings. People exclaimed "they are so natural!". Perhaps people would have exclaimed "they are so spiritual!" about the images of earlier paintings.

A comparison between the mosaic *The Birth of Mary* made in *buona maniera greca antica* by Pietro Cavallini in the 1290s[xxii] and Giotto's frescoes in the Scrovegni Chapel in Padua a few years later show a clear difference in how they perceive Man: while Giotto's figures seem able to reach outside themselves in their intentions and actions, and can *relate to each other* when interacting or counteracting, Cavallini's humans are *enclosed within themselves*, or rather, as passive, static tools of a spirituality outside themselves, are enclosed within their relation to God.[53]

The iconic picture was superior in spirituality, soulfulness and power—all of which the viewer was almost entirely lacking of. And as the relationship to the icons was essentially non-visual, experiencing them also belonged to a different dimension than that of seeing: it belonged to the spiritual dimension. The relation to the icons was characterised above all by a feeling of passivity, introspection, or perhaps more generally: by a sense of reverence.

Nevertheless—and we shall see more of this later—icon art is also "naturalistic" in a broad sense; it also depicts the true nature of reality, such as it appeared to the best interpreters of the time.

With Giotto's works—and it is perhaps worth pointing out that they filled the same kind of pictorial space as the icons, i.e., the walls of churches and chapels, and were thus similarly dedicated to a greater task than that of "disinterested contemplation"—the spiritual moment, like the gaze and the

---

drama of events, turned *inward* into the image, thus neutralising itself. The majestic *benedictio latina*-gesture with which Christ Pantocrator blesses the congregation, Giotto always turns inwards towards the believers *inside* the picture[54], thus consuming the "power" of the gesture on the *picture* itself.

Giotto: *Christ entering Jerusalem*, 1305–06

There arises, as a parallel to the change in the relationship between proximity and distance described above, a *historical* distancing and a historical approaching: the blessing of Christ is no longer present in the room of the onlooker, but applies to the *time in the image*—when Christ was alive. But at the same time, The Holy Land and its people are made into a Tuscan landscape, populated by ordinary Tuscan people who are like me and you and the man in the street or the woman harvesting sun-ripened grapes outside the city walls.

The change in the visual representation of the self through the dioptical images, means that the self's affirmation of its belonging in the world no longer passes through the superiorly inaccessible and absolute (as with *Christ Pantocrator*), but via the equal. Thus there is both an internal and an external change: the representative with adjudicating authority and outward power turns inward, towards its peers. Thus the effects of power are neutralised and the observer is set free.

Before we continue, I would like to reject the proposition that the Renaissance, in any reasonable manner, would be a creation of antiquity. The Renaissance has very little to do with antiquity. The Renaissance is the expression of a clearly self-created cultural identity and primarily concerns the handling of wool. Wool, wool and more wool. The Renaissance is homespun and whole wool with a later element of silk brocade.

Giotto and Masaccio who created the visual codes were largely uneducated in regards to the classical codes. So was Leonardo, who despised Platonists and those glorifying antiquity. One of the few contemporaries that Leonardo respected, Nicolaus Cusanus, was not a Platonist either, and primarily his own man, and only secondarily a Pythagorean. In some sense, it is meaningless to speak about "Platonism" in science after the nominalist turn; Platonism and nominalism are incompatible.

To the extent that ancient knowledge exercised an influence on the late Middle Ages and the Renaissance, it was essentially something unsuitable that one had to get rid of. Those who claim that the Renaissance is a loan from antiquity have very difficult questions to answer: why wasn't the Renaissance conceived in Constantinople? Where the contact with Greek culture and classical languages was uninterrupted? Or in Athens, where the remains of antiquity literally did exist and the knowledge of languages also was there.

With this, I don't want to say that the relation between antiquity and the Renaissance would be uninteresting or already solved—quite the opposite! But the framing of the existing questions have to be reworked and the simple narrative of cultural transmission has to be reconstructed. The question that must be answered is: Why did a readiness to appropriate the ancient form language in both art and literature appear in Northern Italy in the early 1300s? Why did Dante and Petrarch relate to the phenomenon and to the city of Rome in two completely different ways?

Both had the same things in front of them, but saw two completely different things. In other words: what was it that got men in Florence or Padua to realise that they could make cultural forms more than fifteen hundred years old their own? Naturally, because the Florentine or Paduan way of life exhibited fundamental similarities (but also fundamental differences) to Athenian or Republican Roman life. These are the similarities (and differences) that have to be targeted by research. This also means that an investigation into the genesis of the Renaissance cannot avoid reflecting over the problem: what made antiquity classical?

The relative freedom of the observer is but a counterpart to the actual fact that the citizens of the free cities now could act as spiritually independent agents and acting beings, but only so long as they could rely on each other. The members of the commune found their strength in *themselves*, in the collective, in an internal interplay or counter-play, and in a jointly directed effort to gain wealth and success. The power of the *icons* was needed no longer.

Instead, the institutionalised interactions within councils, guilds and other corporations became the political and economical foundation of the newly found *autarchic* self-esteem.

Arnolfo di Gambio, who began work on the cathedral in Florence, a job that Giotto later took over, held the distinguished title of *capomaestro del nostro comune*. *Nostro comune*—our commune or municipality—was the proud expression of a genuine *we*-feeling and marked belonging to an environment of shared opportunity, characterised by vibrant commercial activity, construction work and forward thinking. But also, as Dante in particular got a taste of, of rivalry and infighting.

The same happens in the motifs of painting. The picture is no longer an affirmation that God is the Lord, but rather confirms what is already true in the community, i.e., that the people find their mirror images and their strength in *each other*. The direction of vision is thus radically broken and is directed towards an equal *within* the frame of the painting. The drama within the painting is reborn. Giotto's figures act as *dramatis personae* within the unity of the image; the motives for their gestures and actions are given by impulses and moods within themselves.

Or vice versa: the gestures, the directed interest, the participation or rejection; everything that his contemporaries found so convincing and so "natural", indicates that the characters are acting on their own inner motives. Vasari says of Giotto that he ceased to paint *occhi spiritati*; demonically mastering eyes.

Instead, according to Vasari, he depicted emotions. Emotions that now emanated from the people themselves, from the interaction, from the extant, present conflicts or causes for both joy and sorrow. Nicolaus Cusanus also declares that the criterion for good art now is that the figures have internalised their soulfulness: If a painter paints two pictures and one is lifeless but is of closer likeness to its motif and the other is of less likeness but more alive, i.e., such that it appears to be capable of acting on its own, the latter is regarded as being more perfect.[55]

This is by no means self-evident. Freedom can only be reproduced by one who possesses it. Or the statement can be made even stronger: only one who possesses freedom of action and of spirit can *identify* it. Only those who *can* be free can recognise freedom as a positive value among other symbolic forms that materialise the self-reflection of other life forms.

Therefore, the Renaissance is fundamentally not an abstract rebirth of forms that have, as it were, lain dormant over the centuries, but a genuine recognition of ways of expressing freedom, such as dialogue or emotional interaction, during a time when the foundations of *actual freedom were established* and actively sought a way to express themselves.

Comedy and Tragedy

This can also be ascertained by examining how the forms of expression of freedom have been "misunderstood" during times when actual freedom has been lacking. For example, it was impossible to translate the Greek word for "freedom" into any other contemporary Oriental language;[56] freedom without substance has no meaning. Nor was it possible to adequately translate the terms "tragedy" or "comedy"; they necessarily took place in the domains of freedom and did not survive the decline of democracy in any real sense.

The pyramidal society, the antithesis of freedom, can never set up an individual destiny as an equal counterpart to totality. The individual in a non-comedic system simply lacks psychology, subjectivity and freedom of action in our sense of the words—and above all the freedom to be a *handler*; to buy and sell.

When Arabic philosophers were about to translate the Greek words for "tragedy" and "comedy" (especially the translations and commentaries on Aristotle's *Poetics*), they encountered the problem that there were no understandable equivalents in Arabic. In a short story, Jorge Luis Borges gives us a glimpse of the gap that separated the conceptual world of the Greeks from that of the Arabs.

When the philosopher and Aristotelian translator Averroes (Ibn Rushd), whom Borges writes about in his story, finally finds he understands the meaning of the words, he interprets them as follows: 'Aristu (Aristotle) calls eulogy tragedy and satire, or curse, comedy. There are admirable tragedies and comedies abounding in the Koran and in the temple *mohalacas*.'[xxiii] The difficulty of

----

[xxiii] Borges in the short story *En busca de Averroes*. In his *Averroes' Middle Commentary on Aristotle's Poetics* (1986), Charles E. Butterworth is very critical of Borges' interpretation. And strictly speaking Averroes expresses himself more precisely. In

translating the Greek terms was not primarily linguistic, but went much deeper than that.

Neither the Arabic culture nor the medieval one for that matter had the political or cultural institutions that could have given the words "democracy", "freedom", "tragedy", etc. any meaning. Rather on the contrary, the dynamics of tragedy, defined by the conflict between the individual and the public, between the individual and "fate"; the critical frankness of comedy and the notion of "freedom" were either meaningless or in conflict with the values of the Muslim and the scholastic worlds respectively and in that sense were "incommensurable" with them.

When the basic psychological position was that of total submission to an autocratic jailor god, the only possible dramatic form that could be filled was that of flagellant suffering, which in the form of the *Passion Play*, gave this relationship a meaning, God/Fate a worthy counterpart, and the prisoner's feelings of faith, hope, despair and despondency an outlet.[xxiv]

That Dante called his great poem "Comedy" has been something of a mystery to scholars. Even though Roman literature interpreted the two dramatic genres in a corresponding manner to that of the Greeks (see e.g., *About Comedy and Tragedy*, attributed to Virgilian commentator Donatus), Church Scholars understood them differently or did not understand them at all. This shows that it was not a problem of translation, but a problem of transmission in a deeper sense.

The absence of an ancient culture, of ancient man with ancient problems, meant that there was nothing and no one that could have given substance and drama to this form of literature. But neither Muslim nor scholastic culture was

---

paragraph 8 which Borges interprets, Averroes mentions neither the Koran nor the holy scriptures, but writes, in Butterworth's translation, that "praise and blame are necessarily found in every comparison and narrative representation that occur by statement". (p. 67) But that does not make Borges' observation invalid.

[xxiv] One should note that passion as an experience of knowledge has an interesting conceptual background. The Greek root of the word, *paskhein*, often appears in Plato's writing and there it expresses a subordinate way of gaining knowledge that some translators consistently translate as "suffering" and others with "to be the subject of influence". The Greeks thus equated suffering with being an object. The Stoics on the other hand, made suffering and vulnerability a *primary* category of knowledge and by this measure made thinking more "slavish", whereas in the conception of knowledge that Plotinus advocated, the impressions of the soul were created as a "product of interaction between activity and suffering". (Drews 1 964, p. 221) As a historical phenomenon, passion links the Stoic principles of suffering and passivity (*passio* and *passivus* have the same root: *pati, "suffering"*) with the fierce Christian desire to be loved by God, thus filling passion with the sighs and the despair of unrequited love.

concerned with the actual freedom of the living individual, nor with the great questions of worldly freedom, and consequently did not understand them either. Dante, for example, who wanted to write in the great tradition of Greeks and Romans, is therefore forced to resort to etymology when he in a letter to Cangrande della Scala tries to explain why he called his poem *comedy* and what he meant with the word.

'The title of the book is: *Begins the Comedy of Dante Alighieri, Florentine in birth, not in custom*. In order to understand, you need to know that "comedy" comes from "komos" "village" and "oda", which means "song", whence "comedy" sort of means "country song". And comedy is sort of a kind of poetic narration, different from all others. It differs, therefore, from the tragedy, in matter by the fact that tragedy in the beginning is admirable and quiet, in the end or final exit it is smelly and horrible; and it gets its name because of this from "tragos", which means "goat", and "oda", sort of like "goat-song", that is, smelly like a goat, as can be seen in Seneca's tragedies.'

Albertino Mussato, a contemporary of Dante, writes that 'tragedians are actors who before people's eyes perform a lamentation of the past doings and omissions of villainous kings.'[xxv] However, with this definition, the *tragic* element itself, that sees the family (rather than the individual) as a rightful counterweight to the gods or fate, is lost. In general, it may be true that a sense of freedom in a, so to speak, lower form, never can understand one at a higher level.

Freedom is always a social product, drama is a literary representation of the inherent problems that accompany freedom, and consequently it can only have meaning in an environment where the conditions of freedom can be identified. Thus, only when a social and commercial setting based on equality re-emerged— the urban commune—the issues raised by the Greeks were once again perceived as interesting.

Ten years after Giotto painted the frescoes in the *Scrovegni Chapel* (inaugurated in March 1305), wonderfully perfecting not only his "dioptic" way of creating pictorial drama, but in which his colouring and his rendering of volume (the costumes, for example) find a tone and a natural elegance not seen since antiquity, another man active in Padua, Albertino Mussato, wrote a drama which is usually considered the first "modern" drama. Not since antiquity had

---

[xxv] Müller 1987, p. 44. Today the word "comedy" is seen as derived from *komos*; "a ritualistic drunken procession".

anyone experienced on stage what Mussato brings out in dramatic form in his *Ecerinis*: the hard-won realisation that what is human is actually made by man himself.

In his work, Mussato portrays the triangle of "personality", "conflict" and "fate" in a new way. In Greek drama, the counterpart of the individual is Fate, the collectively orchestrated imbalance that governs time and existence and whose inexorable hand it is impossible to escape. In plain language: it is the individual against the collective, and it is the collective that carries the day while the individual perishes.[xxvi] In Mussato, drama is not presented in terms of a general rhetorical atmosphere, but, according to Battisti, as a concrete clash or conflict between the characters.[57]

Well, Mussato hardly surpasses the ancient dramatic form (i.e., Seneca) in his stilted reading drama, but still he captures something unmistakably new. *Ecerinis* for example, unlike classical tragedy, is not about guilt and fate (how could it, when man *always* and under all circumstances is guilty), but about the secret of evil. *Ecerinis* is also unmistakably a bourgeois drama in the same manner that Giotto's dioptic art is a bourgeois art or the theology of Francis of Assisi is an urban religion; it is the *citizen* Mussato who speaks, and whose passion for the communal social project shines through in his warnings against tyranny.

Mussato wants to develop a civic ethic in order to educate urban culture, the *regnum hominis*, which now was struggling both against the divine order and against tyrannical forces in order to ensure the success of the bourgeois project of freedom in northern Italy. Yet, it is probably *evil* personified that ultimately emerges as the subject of the drama; the one thing that, in the figure of Ezzelino (Ecerini), possesses both power and will—even if things turn out badly for it. Ezzelino: 'Every man does his deeds freely./.../Let us conquer cities and towns near and far.'

'Verona, Vicenza and Padua are now subject to my will.'[58]

[xxvi] Charles Taylor interprets the Spirit of Art in Hegel's *Phänomenologi des Geistes* in the following way: "In tragedy [---] the individual character encounters fate not as something contingent and external, but as necessarily flowing from his action. [---] Each character embodies a basic value, that of the city or the family, which cannot but enter into conflict with the other once it is acted upon." Taylor (1975) p. 205 f.

The Vestiges of Antiquity

Another checkpoint on the road towards knowledge of the Renaissance is to see how the ancient sculptural remains and buildings were perceived before a real freedom was restored. A standard argument (besides the linguistic one) to explain the phenomenon of the Renaissance is to refer to the discovery of ancient sculptures and ancient architectural forms. This has to be a joke. This architectural residue had always existed, especially in Athens and Rome without there ever being a Renaissance.

Intellectually antiquity was also ever-present during the Middle Ages, in the form of Plato's and Aristotle's works—in an overwhelming manner.[xxvii] The same criteria apply to both visual and intellectual transmission: the Platonic body of the text was understood only to the extent that it conformed to one's own self-understanding. The Middle Ages did not perceive themselves at all as a middling age, but as a resigned continuation of antiquity, and one's manner of relating to the vast majority of the ancient forms of thought and art was resigned, dogmatic, and uncompromising.[xxviii] They simply did not concern them.

The vestiges (text, image, sculpture or architecture) of antiquity were, of course, ubiquitous to some extent, but from the point of view of understanding they resided at the same unattainable height as the Lord. One did not "understand" (as we understand) the dramatic form, one did not "understand" what the sculptures expressed; the agony or the will or the possibilities reflected in these forms of art simply had no spiritual counterpart in medieval viewers and they could therefore only see them as "sinful" or stand before them in mute wonder as before an alien being.

[xxvii] In the same way that an ancient Lord was constantly present. The most important philosophical reading besides the Church Fathers and the Scriptures was Plato's *Timaeus*, in which Plato introduces his famous Creator (*Demiurgos*) and his speculative cosmology, which was not difficult to reconcile with the Jewish myths. Especially after Neoplatonic mystics had made their own interpretations of Plato. Plato also makes these interpretations particularly easy for posterity as in "a sudden moment (*Timaeus* 37c) he brings the Demiurge to life as a father, proud and happy about his "child" and determined to make this "image of god" even more like its exemplar". (Thesleff 1990, p. 217)

[xxviii] The Middle Ages are an invention of the Renaissance – and still with Gibbon, *The History of the* Decline and Fall *of the Roman Empire* finally reaches its end at the inception of the Renaissance.

Dante, for example, saw Rome mainly as the holy city; the place that God had chosen to prepare the world for the coming of Christ. 'Rome was not important to him archaeologically [---] This reference to the city itself as a physical fact, to the walls and stones of Rome, is especially interesting in view of the total absence in Dante of the cult of "ruin-worship", that adoration of the tangible remains of the which would later find in Petrarch, so indefatigable an exponent.'[59]

Petrarch certainly thought highly of Rome—at least before he visited the city. When he later stands on the Capitoline Hill and in a letter to his friend, Giacomo Colonna, tries to sum up his thoughts and feelings, his reaction is not far from that of my niece, who, on a visit to Rome, wrote home to her parents: 'It is not as I thought it would be, but I think it's good anyway.' Petrarch writes: 'On the whole, I do not want to hide from you that what I am experiencing is the exact opposite of what I imagined. [---] Reality is always the enemy of renown.'[60] But the point here is not just that Dante and Petrarch *saw* different things, corresponding to the fact that one worked in the medieval interpretive tradition while the other stood facing the future. That one saw the remains of *spiritual* and the other of *temporal* and *productive* greatness—which at the same time is the difference between the ancient/medieval and the modern interest in knowledge. The point is that Petrarch, in his *preconception*, in an extension of the architectural and artistic manifestations he experienced in Avignon, Pisa, Genoa and Florence, had *constructed* a Rome in the same spirit.

That he expected to find, following his experience of a great cultural and economic boom, the same forms of greatness or grandeur in Rome and to an even higher degree, as Rome was unsurpassed. And the point could also be that it had to be people from Tuscany and Veneto, from Milan and Genoa, brought up in a commercially vibrant and politically active environment, who would be able to see that the same kinds of forces also had created Rome. That could recognise the *worldly* and *material* greatness of Rome.

A greatness with which they identified themselves to the extent that it rested on the same premises: freedom, self-consciousness, commerce, and a Republican spirit. This does not mean that the "discovery" of antiquity did not influence late medieval symbolic forms. It did. But again: it did so only when the foundations of a similar way of life had been laid, for as the Greeks already used to say: Like seeks like. Only democrats can fully appreciate democracy.

Every freedom only celebrates its *own* kind of freedom. And only freedom and democracy can represent the unifying signs and the cultural totems of freedom and democracy.

The values that advanced thinking would henceforth operate with and embody in insights and concepts were all potentially present in the transformation of societies and lifestyles that was underway.

The perception of reality as *dynamic*, the tendency to *quantify* phenomena, the *mechanical* analogies in interpreting events; they all had their origin in the seething and proud city-based bourgeois conception of existence; in the mechanical work of the factories, in the clattering processing of raw materials by the workshops into things, in the sluggish rotations of windmills and watermills that turned nature into power and innovation into convenience, in the restless counting and the constant calculations for profit and liquidity, in the curiosity about the foreign, in the spirit of discovery, in the geographical mobility, in the capricious relativity of profits and costs, in the unwavering objectivity of balance sheets and double-entry bookkeeping, in the speculation and calculation that went on day and night in banks and stalls, in squares and trattorias.

For, as Leon Battista Alberti says: "Money is the root of everything", and Villani: "There always is a market in Florence".

3 Nominalism, Individualism And Love Characteristics Of A Major and Profound Change

Let time be a quiet, almost imperceptible constant rain. Let the space be the conditions of life, culture—in other words: the attributes of time. It has begun to rain—time has made itself felt. It slowly drizzles, day and night. It rains imperceptibly, incessantly.

At first, there is no great change, except that what *is* appears more clearly. The fallen rain is soaked up by the ground, watering the enduring; nourishing what already exists and long has existed; that which is deeply rooted in the ground. The damp makes it lush and flourishing. But the rain continues to fall. The drops become bigger, the showers more violent. The water-soaked grass squelches when it is tread upon. Here and there small pools of water form.

Small rivulets are created. Soon there is water everywhere, even if the aggregations have different names: plashes, pools, puddles, swamps, lakes, brooks, streams and rivers. Eventually, the water joins together, grows in strength, rushes forth on a wide front, reaches one single direction, breaks through all levees and embankments and finally forms an enormous, rumbling tidal wave that washes away everything that has been before. Afterwards, nothing is the same.

The great change that swept across Europe and transformed the Middle Ages into the Modern Age, took place at all intellectual and emotional levels, simultaneously or successively. Sometimes the changes happened unnoticed, sometimes they had dramatic results. During the initial phase, the catalysts of change, the technological and commercial advances, initiated a golden age for the means of expression of the old culture. In the Île-de-France region, Gothic architecture was conceived as a tribute both to God as well as to man's limitless capacity to overcome earthly limitations.

In Tuscany's vibrant political and economic environment, Dante's poetry and Cimabue's and Duccio's Madonna paintings in the "Greek" style were created. In response to the increasingly unavoidable demand for a *natural science*, Thomas Aquinas fused biblical truths with Aristotle's physics to produce the most peculiar creation of scholastic philosophy: the *Summa theologiae*, which summarised contemporary knowledge on the *creating* and on *created* nature. In it, faith and knowledge, theology and natural science, spirit and nature, was united.

Neither feudal culture nor the church were able, despite their last, autumnal flowering, to withstand the unrestrained vitality of commercial activity. Just as an example: in the year 1293, the maritime tax alone provided the city of Genoa with three and a half times as much revenue as the total income of the French crown.[61] Even though the year 1293 was exceptionally good for Genoa, the comparison shows what the relative amounts were that liquid capital could generate in comparison with that which was tied to the yield of the land. Florentine bankers even financed wars between foreign countries.

Although, *this* was a high-risk venture that often ended badly for the banks, the example shows how a purely military and political power and a static, earth-bound pattern of life had to share space with, and later was overtaken by, a financially more productive mercantile sector. New values, hungry for life, in alliance with calculating mercantilism and entrepreneurial spirit, invaded all areas of thought and life; influencing and reinforcing each other until the Middle Ages were finally ripe to be swept away by the expansive power and audacious actions of the dawning Modern Age.

The phenomena which we are now going to consider bears differing names but are nevertheless deeply rooted in the torrent of change which during the late Middle Ages created a new platform for human activity, and which transformed both man's understanding of himself as well as the images that he created of others.

The three phenomena to be considered are *nominalism*, which did away with Platonic conceptual realism; *individualism*, which introduced a new conception of man when the ancient collective body politic or the medieval one whose true exemplar, God, no longer could assert his dominance; and *love*, above all love of *nature*, which redeemed creation from the neglect of the Greeks and the curse of Christianity.

Although, the three manifestations of emotional and spiritual life gather together quite different aspects of existence and life, they all have a common component in that all three highlight *the individual*, the actually present and concrete in its uniqueness. All are parts of "the water" in the metaphor above; elements in the great tidal wave of upheaval.

Nominalism and Individualism

The struggle over which level of the various aspects of existence should take precedence over the others, the conceptual or the physical; ideas or things, is the most important philosophical debate of the late Middle Ages. Plato, as we know, had argued that ideas are actually existing entities and that knowledge of the ideas or universals inhabits a primary position in relation to the opinions one can have about particulars, i.e., existing objects. That what one can essentially know about reality can be inferred from these universal ideas.

Aristotle's more nuanced position, which could be characterised as *conceptualist*, holds that universals are neither real nor merely arbitrary *names* as some sophists (and later nominalists claimed), but intellectual forms that determine the similarities between individual particulars.

Already among the Greeks there were defenders of a protonominalist conception of knowledge, who held that the names of things are merely arbitrary designations that can be changed if one so agrees, and that generalities are empty fictions. That the matter also was debated within Plato's Academy is evident from the dialogue *Cratylus*, which, however, does not give a clear answer to the problem of whether a name belongs to a thing "by nature" or by convention.

On the other hand, Plato did not need to take a clear stance for or against the two schools of thought in order to retain the purity of his theory of Ideas, since, according to Plato, ideas are not identical with mutable names or things, but rather their precondition.

During the late Middle Ages, however, nominalism, which in antiquity's "high philosophy" had appeared essentially as false or unreasonable, now becomes the channel which leads thought into what *we* consider to be a reasonable path. When Plato in *Cratylus* says that 'our friend Cratylus has been arguing about names; he says that they are natural and not conventional,' Francis Bacon finds the statement "curious".[62] However, Bacon is a late addition to the ranks of the nominalists, where the pioneering work was done by William of Ockham and others.

Long before Spinoza and Descartes definitively erased the central category of Aristotelian logic—teleology—from natural science, William had declared that 'motion towards an end is not real but metaphorical.' And concerning the concept of substance, he says that it is only 'a definition, a conception, or even merely a name.'[63] With Occam's razor, the Platonic and Aristotelian parallel world is cut off from the real one. A comprehensive and previously successful hypothesis thus becomes unnecessary.

For example, now only real, individual chairs and beds exist, the *word* bed is the name we have given to the actual beds and the word exists as such only to the extent that we use it in this sense.

Philosophical nominalism can be seen as forming the core around which a number of phenomena that all contributed to bringing the *particular* and the *individual* to the fore, out from the murky abstractions of the Greeks. Nature became the sum of individual things—and not the sum of abstractions that the Neoplatonists had called *the One* and the Christians had seen as a secondary function of God. Nominalism gave the experimental interest in nature an intellectual motive to investigate the particular and to surround the investigation with theories, as in the case of Roger Bacon or Robert Grosseteste.

Nominalism laid the foundations for a new approach to nature that later on also finds an expression in painting and literature. One example can already be noted here: Panofsky[64] has pointed out that the difference between the medieval and the Renaissance way of representing images is that the Middle Ages did it 'according to how the soul imagines it,' as Meister Eckhart says. A picture of a rose was made on the basis of a picture of a rose, therefore pattern books like the one by Villard de Honnecourt were important.

But the image of a rose did not need to represent an actual rose, instead it could just as easily represent a virtue or something else that the "soul can imagine". Only when a new relation towards nature had been established, image-makers could move from primarily painting objects from the spiritual world according to given patterns, and begin to attentively observe the world of the senses.

Since the nominalists emphasised the primacy of the singular and the individual over the general, the debate on nominalism was also important in determining the status of human individuals. Or rather, the opposite was true: nominalism as a philosophical movement was *made possible* by the emergence of individualism in society, when the most open minds dimly began to perceive the social, political and religious freedoms that the urban communities could offer. The symmetry between the social and the ontological level remained valid. It would have been impossible for Plato and Aristotle to define a human being in a general manner on the basis of common external attributes, since slaves were not human, even though their exterior often did not differ significantly from that of humans. (This fact annoyed many; and what was even worse: sometimes, because of their muscular appearance, slaves appeared to be more godlike or heroic and thus more *ideal* than fat and flabby humans.) In Plato's definition, therefore, a human or a man is an abstract. 'Either man is nothing at all, or if something, he turns out to be nothing else than soul.'[xxix]

In other words, with this definition, a being that does not rule over its body does not become a human being, which is why the slave by definition cannot be human. Seen in this light, Plato's theory of Ideas is nothing more than the *ideological* construction needed to hold together a system of knowledge that could not accept that individuals are equal even though they are, and which therefore could not base knowledge on individuals and individuality at all.

Subjectivity and Love

Both in the run-up to the Modern Age and in the corresponding interstice in antiquity, when the archaic currents were woven together into classical culture, an individualisation and personalisation of the human being with the focus on the phenomenon of *love,* took place. Love as the first manifestation of subjectivisation: be it Dante and Petrarch in the early dawn of our own time, or Sappho in archaic Greece. Love (or as a directed intention in which the self appears more clearly: the *longing* for the other) is one of the most powerful emotional expressions of the self.

Expressed love *is* subjectivity. Experienced subjectivity *is* an intensely experienced identifying and differentiating relation to the other.

[xxix] Plato*: Alcibiades* 130 c. Thesleff (1990) points out in his commentary that "the interconnection of identity with the soul does not occur so explicitly in other places in the Platonic collection of writings". − Plato also takes another, less idealistic position which, in accordance with the modes of operation of individualising dialectics, bases the definition on the "accidents" and not on the "substances" of the soul. According to this definition, man is roughly "a featherless biped". We can also notice here that Augustine *almost* follows Plato, but replaces the metaphor of ruling with a metaphor of work, (which is also mentioned by Plato as a stage on the path to the "true" view) when he says that "a man is a soul that *makes use* of the body".

In the way Homer depicts the heroes of the Trojan War, they appear strikingly modern, due to their individualisation and capacity to act. Their psyche, however, still lacks a self-determining substance; they are "top-managed" almost to the same extent as the people of the Middle Ages, even if the range of emotions is much greater in the ancient heroes because of the polytheistic conception of godhood.

Already in the first sentences of the Iliad, we encounter the—in this case devastating—effect of god-induced emotion; the *primus motor* that sets the narrative in motion: 'Who then among the gods set the twain at strife and variance [and] parted Atreides king of men and noble Achilles?'

As commercial activity begins to flourish, an actual freedom to act emerges, something that during archaic times fundamentally reshapes the long-established aristocratic ways of thinking and behaving. This change begins in the eastern Ionian settlements, where the image of the self changes immediately. In early literature, the change is clearly apparent. The warlike epic is replaced by the more subjective and emotional lyric poem.

In the lyric poems, poets had the opportunity to speak about themselves, to express their own values and to acknowledge themselves as a source and instrument of emotion. Through the internalisation of emotions, the notion of an individual and autonomous *soul* also creeps into the conception of man, which is reflected visually in the contemporary freestanding human sculptures. For the first time in Greek history, man is seen to stand freely, independently, without being part of a supporting, sustaining piece of matter. At the same time, in a spiritual sense, he has made himself an independent human being.

The Peplos Kore c. 530 BC *Ekkehard und Uta* 1250–1260

The next time the freestanding sculpture appears in similar circumstances, as a declaration of independence from God, the Middle Ages are already being transformed into the Renaissance in a commercial climate of lively trade and political egalitarianism, strikingly similar to that which developed in the Ionian city-states. Trade is based on private initiative, which in the self-understanding of the merchant is translated into the notion of a unified and demarcated *individual*.

This reflection of the real possibility of man to act according to his own will, and which man more or less lacked in both Homeric and medieval times, is given both a material and a conceptual expression. Materially, as the image of a freestanding, autonomous human being; conceptually, the focus is on the autonomy of reason and the relative freedom of the will. At the same time, the martial ideals that had emerged in the aristocratic circles around the Homeric or medieval courts became hopelessly outmoded.

The stiff-necked way in which, for example, Achilles exhibits with reference to his *arete*, his chivalric honour, would be very unproductive when bargaining or making contracts. A similar reversal of values took place when the medieval rules of etiquette under the concept of *courtois* were succeeded by correct bourgeois manners which were collected under the moniker of *civilité*, in which a *horizontal* or sociable modelling of affections asserts itself.[65]

In the work of lesbian poet Sappho (6th century BC), a distinctive and self-aware "I" breaks through the cracks of male patriarchal and hierarchical cohesion with tremendous force. Now it is explicitly *love* that makes the self aware of itself. And contrary to what is the case when Eros infuses his gift or curse into someone's body, in Sappho there is a flow of love *out* from the self as *longing* becomes the element that draws attention to the self and the other, as in this wonderful fragment:

The moon has set beyond the seas.
And vanished are the Pleiades.
Half the long weary night has gone.
Time passes—yet I lie alone.[66]

And even though Sappho also feels that love is attacking her as a blind force, the image of love is now not purely anthropomorphic, but she expresses her sense of its workings in a nature metaphor, as in the following stanza:

As a wind in the mountains
assaults an oak,
Love shook my breast.[67]

With the other as a mirror and love as a light, the self now sees itself for the first time. Sappho *invents* the self, in the same manner that Heraclitus, in the same region, would invent the soul a few decades later. And just as Sappho's predecessor, Archilochus, relativised and privatised morality[xxx], Sappho makes *taste* a personal affair. If Sappho had been a sophist, she could have complemented Protagoras by saying that 'what is beautiful is what one considers beautiful.'

But Sappho says it more beautifully (frgm.16): 'Some say an army of horsemen, some of foot soldiers, some of ships, is the fairest thing on the black earth, but I say it is what one loves.' As Bruno Snell says, with this sentence Sappho opens the way for the arbitrariness of personal taste;[68] a way that abruptly ends at the toll gate of Plato's philosophy of state.

Snell sums up the intellectual and mental innovations of the poets of the sixth century (BC) in the following words: 'The individual character of the lyric writer's experience led both to the discovery of the discord in his soul, and also

---

[xxx] The most striking example of the encounter between warlike aristocratic values and a morality relativised by commercial considerations is the story of the encounter between Archilochus and the state of Sparra. Archilochus, the archaic poet and mercenary, lived at a time when the money economy was rapidly and drastically transforming many of the Greek cities. But not Sparta, far removed from the trade routes and where warlike values therefore prevailed. When a young man from Sparta went to war, his mother gave him his shield with the words: "Come back with your shield – or on it." There were no other alternatives. According to Plutarch, this is how the story goes: When the poet Archilochus visited Sparta, the Spartans chased him out of the city when they found out that he had said in a poem that it better to throw away your weapons and flee than to be killed (a sign of a strongly marked individuality – the self is greater than the Cause). Archilochus had written: "One of the Saians now delights in the shield I discarded unwillingly near a bush, for it was perfectly good, But at least I got myself safely out. Why should I care for that shield? Let it go. Some other time I'll buy another no worse." The confrontation between Archilochos' commercial and relativistic view of wisdom and honour and the aristocratic and absolute values of Sparta is interesting. Here I will only mention some external characteristics that characterise what the commercial breakthroughs and the money economy brought about. The Ionian trading cities had 1: democracy, 2: a money economy, 3: city walls, 4: codified laws, 5: philosophy. All these institutions and phenomena all rest on agreements or conversations between people and express a strong self-consciousness in the form of a certainty that it is man who creates his own conditions. Sparta, on the other hand, lacked all this.

to the knowledge that intellectual and spiritual possessions are held in common. [---] But since the discoveries of the lyrists are matched in the creations of the visual artists as well as of the thinkers and the politicians, we may assume that these achievements of the great personalities are part of a larger historical process.'[69]

During the late Middle Ages, when emotionality re-emerged, love no longer focussed its attention solely on a general concept of God, but neither primarily on the self—for that had already been done—but towards a *you*. Since a special kind of individualism, to some extent, always had been implicit in the Christian sense of self, inasmuch as salvation from the beginning was an essentially individual affair, the unity of the self had, so to speak, already been established. The Greeks never reached such a point of individuality that they would have put the individual destiny of a man above the general interest.

Classical thought, when it is on form, is always subordinated to its condition of existence; i.e., the state. Christianity is different: its ideology is cosmopolitan, even world-encompassing. The highest universal was instead anthropomorphically projected unto the Lord, (and Christians did not, of course, oppose Him) but only as an *abstraction*. The strongest form of collective meaning thus existed only as an abstraction, as a *unio mystica*—which meant that people *actually*, in an unmediated manner, could establish living individual relationships with each other, when the freedoms to do so had been realised.

When this happened, love could also be directed towards real, actual objects, towards a living *other*, a *you*, even if these *yous* came to be embodied in poetic hyperbole by well-nigh unreal ideal figures such as a *Beatrice* or a *Laura*. I will continue on this strand of thought in the section on Petrarch.

As the register of emotions expanded in the "horizontal" interaction of equals without vertically detouring via the gods, the content of knowledge also becomes part of a discursive process of participating equals. During the build-up to the ancient period, Parmenides is arguably the last thinker to have to resort to god-given wisdom as a guarantee of the robustness of truth. After him it is the individual, human faculty of thought takes responsibility for truth. Above all this applies to the sophists.

In a manner broadly reminiscent of the transformation of the *ofthalmos*-relationship more than fifteen hundred years later into a dioptic one, the formation of truth and reason is now transformed from having been a *given* truth (*logos*) in Parmenides into a *dia-logos*; being a process in which the "path of truth" is formed by the invisible line created by the points where the arguments of the interlocutors meet. Plato then formalised the form of the dialogue in a way which, although it contains many internal tensions,[xxxi] still respects the equality and right of both parties to argue.

Incidentally, the late Middle Ages also had a development from the *logos*, from the knowledge that was instituted and given by God, to a *dia-logos*; a knowledge formed in discussion between people. Pierre Abailard (b. 1079) based his teaching on *disputatio* instead of the lecture form *lectio* that was usually used. *Disputatio* meant argumentation *pro et contra*, adopting personal positions, conflicts and their resolution, whereas a *lectio* usually involved reading aloud from given texts with associated canonical interpretations, without the involvement of the lecturer's own interests or opinions.

An almost genuine dialogue can be found in the radical philosophy of, for example, Nicolaus Cusanus or Galileo Galilei. But, as with Plato, the objections that do occur are too much of a rhetorical nature to genuinely create critical counter-arguments.

Francis of Assisi and the Love of Nature

If there is a trend in the development of truths, it is this: Truths are generalised. What used to be regarded as an all-embracing truth becomes a special case within a newer framework. The best example of this is the development of modern physics: Newton's "immutable truths" apply within Einstein's more general physics only if certain conditions are met. But even emotional content can, by all accounts, be generalised as part of the historical process. I am now thinking of love.

In its first socially active form, the one that contained the call that one should love one's neighbour as oneself, love bridged the gap *between* people, between master and slave, that slavery had created. In the next phase, however, love was generalised further. It became possible to love nature as well. Thus another

---

[xxxi] Of which only two shall mentioned: the objections made by the characters in the dialogues are not real objections but mostly rhetorical. Despite the generous form with two equal parties in discussion Plato did not accept that there could be many equal truths. If the truth exists, it is one and only one, but more often than not. The dialogues end in an indefinite nothingness. Plato can not move past the tension between the unifying logos and the dyad dia-logos gives rise to. He does not want to choose firmly between an individual or a general truth but is, as his thinking is constructed, obliged to affirm them both.

bridge between incompatible categories could be built. For love not only involves a strong focusing of the self on itself; it also contains a strong transcendental factor; love as transcendence, as the transcendence of the self, as the incorporation or establishment of the other as an idol. So now nature also began to make the claim to be such an ideal.

Interestingly enough, the conceptual extension of the knowledge interest towards nature took the form of an identification of Creation with the Creator. In Francis of Assisi, love is the force that starts bridging the gap towards the previously immeasurable evil of nature. Thus, a wave of boundless love directed towards the Creator could also pour out on Creation with its myriads of living and non-living things. 'With his new, Christian ideal of love, Francis of Assisi broke through and rose above that dogmatic and rigid barrier between 'nature' and "spirit".'[70]

In *The Canticle of the Sun*, the only known hymn that is certainly written by St Francis, God-created Nature is praised in enthusiastically pantheistic words.

Most High, all powerful, good Lord,
Yours are the praises, the glory, the honour, and all blessing.

To You alone, Most High, do they belong,
and no man is worthy to mention Your name.

Be praised, my Lord, through all your creatures,
especially through my lord Brother Sun,
who brings the day; and you give light through him.
And he is beautiful and radiant in all his splendour!
Of you, Most High, he bears the likeness.

Praised be You, my Lord, through Sister Moon and the stars,
in heaven you formed them clear and precious and beautiful.

Praised be You, my Lord, through Brother Wind,
and through the air, cloudy and serene,
and every kind of weather through which
You give sustenance to Your creatures.

Praised be You, my Lord, through Sister Water,
which is very useful and humble and precious and chaste.
Praised be You, my Lord, through Brother Fire,
through whom you light the night and he is beautiful
and playful and robust and strong.

Praised be You, my Lord,
through Sister Mother Earth,
who sustains us and governs us and who produces
varied fruits with coloured flowers and herbs.

Praised be You, my Lord,
through those who give pardon for Your love,
and bear infirmity and tribulation.

Blessed are those who endure in peace
for by You, Most High, they shall be crowned.

Praised be You, my Lord,
through our Sister Bodily Death,
from whom no living man can escape.

Woe to those who die in mortal sin.
Blessed are those who
will find Your most holy will,
for the second death shall do them no harm.

Praise and bless my Lord,
and give Him thanks
and serve Him with great humility.

In addition to praising the Creator and the heavenly bodies *The Canticle of the Sun* is a tribute to all of Creation; to, in turn, *air*, *water*, *fire* and *earth*, the elementary components of the cosmologies of the earliest Greek philosophers. As a philosophical treatise, *The Canticle of the Sun* is thus comparable to the considerations of the Ionian natural philosophers.[xxxii] The previously boundless evil of nature is de-demonised; even the devil pulled himself together, and could, under certain circumstances, start calling himself "beautiful".

Indeed, St Francis' contemporary, St Bonaventure, makes a remarkable extension of the concept of beauty when he allows that even an image of the devil can be beautiful if it faithfully represents its object.[71] Not only the natural but also that which is faithful to nature had acquired a value. Naturalness held becoming the content of the concept of beauty. Or as Nicolaus Cusanus said, 'All science and art are based on similarity.'

The basic idea of the sermons of Francis was that God and the World formed a unity. If we try to put ourselves in the deeply religious mindset that feels reverence in front of almighty nature, then we also realise that the new form of painting nature that took off with Giotto, and which to a large extent followed the footsteps and the spirit of Francis, does not imply a break with the old spiritual painting, but is merely an *extension* of it—and thus, as with all development, there is a further generalisation of the categories.

For if God and Nature have become one, to paint Nature is to depict the appearance of God. Just as nominalism gives primacy to the real over the ideal, pantheism creates the possibility to perceive the spiritual via the material— nature as God's intention in the world. The perspective is totally reversed, but from an expanded categorical point of view, everything remains the same.

That Giotto was close to the Franciscan movement, and primarily decorated the church chambers[xxxiii] of this order, is well known and almost seems obvious in the light of the fusion of spirituality and sensuousness they both sought. This

---

[xxxii] The same also applies to Nicolaus Cusanus. Both Nicolaus and St Francis were pantheists — the pantheism of Nicolaus had philosophical overtones, as when he writes (*De visione Dei* chapter 13) that God is infinity: "By this I understand him to be equivalent to existence." And both represent in their approach to nature a rather pre-Socratic attitude: Francis as a "meteorologist" and Nicolaus explicitly as a Pythagorean. But there is also another characteristic that likens the Franciscan movement to the earliest Greek philosophy: both are urban-based forms of thought that express the preform of a sense of individuality and a striving for freedom that later result in a "bourgeois" self-consciousness of the kind, that in Genoa, Florence, Padua or Venice triumphed over the static, literalist rigidity of scholasticism. Henry Thode claims that the Franciscan movement is a religion of the bourgeoisie and even an expression of a pre-Lutheran personal relation to God. (Thode 1904 p.60)
[xxxiii] Of which of course the frescoes in the Upper Church of Assisi; the church of St. Francis, are the most prominent. But also the lost frescoes and paintings of the Malatesta Temple; Rimini, the Bardi Chapel in Santa Croce; Florence.

is of course not the case, but it is hardly a coincidence either that early Italian painting which, from the 1300s onwards, sought itself a more naturalistic mode of expression, worked to a large extent in the spirit of the Franciscan movement. In the Franciscan Creed, the sensuous and the material took on a spiritual and sometimes mystical form that could give nature the dignity and status that a pictorial motif demanded in the context of the representation of the beautiful. As loved, nature is at its most beautiful, and only as beautiful it is worthy to be rendered as beautiful art.

4. A New Relation to Nature

Abbot Suger and the Gothic

At the very beginning of his great summarising work, *Summa contra gentiles*, Thomas Aquinas makes a slight emphasis on the content of the concept of "wisdom" (*sapientum*), which to some extent allows that even practical people can be called "wise". Thomas writes (I.1): 'The arts that rule other arts are called *architectonic*, as being the *ruling arts*. That is why the artisans devoted to these arts, who are called *master artisans*, appropriate to themselves the name of wise men.'

A little later, however, Thomas takes heed of Aristotle's authority by adding that "wise in general" (*simpliciter sapientis*) should be reserved for those who consider the ends and origins of the universe, since as Aristotle has said that the task of the wise is to consider "the highest causes" (*sapientia: cognitio rerum omnium per altissimas causas*). A person who could rightly be called "wise" in Thomas's view, and whose work he had certainly been in contact with, was Abbot Suger, head of the abbey of St Denis outside Paris.

If we wish to mark the date when the spirit of a new age was born, that definitively marks a break with the Greco-Roman, the 9 of June 1140 would be a suitable candidate. This was the date of inauguration for the west portal of the sepulchral church of St Denis, the reconstruction of which Suger had commissioned.

The event stands out in the history of architecture because here we can date the birth of a new style—the Gothic—in an exact manner, but also because the social and political motives for the change of the architectonic style are clearly stated by Suger. Moreover, not only from the transformation of the church chambers but also from the pride with which Suger signed his work, we can infer that a new sense of self is born and is given a distinctive material manifestation that has detached itself from the mental confusion brought about by the loss of the intellectual support points associated with the demise of the ancient system. The Romanesque style that preceded the Gothic took, as its name suggests, its form language from Roman architecture, especially in the way vaults and rounded arches were made. The Romanesque style with its dark and heavy vaults, massive walls and small windows give the impression that these churches were built as a bulwark against an evil and dangerous world; that they were spiritual havens for terrified people, shelters from the sins of the world, from whose windows the chorus *kyrie eleison*—Lord have mercy—wound itself like thin and inert incense towards heaven.

A very different openness, boldness and self-esteem are expressed in Abbot Suger's creation. Here, literally, the windows are opened towards the outside world. Possibly inspired by Neoplatonist light mysticism—Suger was a slightly later contemporary of the School of Chartres' foremost predecessor, Bernard of Chartres, and his brother, Thierry, or by the new relationship with nature announced by nominalism in the thought of Jean Roscelin or the aforementioned Abailard, Suger lets the light flood through the space of the church, with a form language totally his own and not borrowed from antiquity.

It is as if, for the first time in a long while, man has the courage to look God in His eyes, while at the same time opening the floodgates to reality and nature— the crown jewel of the Gothic style, the Saint Chapelle in Paris, consists almost entirely of windows! The construction of the Gothic cathedrals is like a gigantic production of symbols, in the spirit of the old but with new means; symbols that will eventually stand for, not for that of God, but for the greatness of Man.

In Abbot Suger, a new type of human being or a new human attitude emerges unmistakably, which would later be given the special label of "Renaissance man". In Suger, we find an inordinate and justified pride in the theoretical-practical work he has so successfully accomplished, and he self-consciously signs his creation: 'I, Suger, was the leader when it was completed.'

Suger was, therefore, not only the protohumanist Panofsky makes him into; he was the prototype of the Renaissance artist altogether, harbouring in his person not only a creative artistic ability but also an intellectual disposition. Here, then, we can see the beginnings of the reunion of work and thought, activities that for High-Greek philosophy were totally separate; a reunion which in its most favourable form gave rise to the art and the *joie de vivre* of the Renaissance.

Without being a philosopher, Suger—as Panofsky puts it in his comments on Suger's text—'placed him in the van of an intellectual movement that was to result in the proto-scientific theories of Robert Grosseteste and Roger Bacon.'[72] As an architect and church builder, on the other hand, Suger would have practically knowledgeable and theoretically insightful men like Alberti and Brunelleschi as successors. Viewing his work as a political strategist and in his efforts to strengthen the central royal power in Île-de France, Panofsky states that 'not without reason has he been called the father of the French monarchy that was to culminate in the state of Louis XIV.'[73]

In addition to the architectural design of the church and the artistic aspect of the furnishings, Suger went so far in participating in the practical work that he himself joined the workmen in the woods to select logs for roof beams when it proved difficult to find suitable timber, personally hand-picked skilled craftsmen and was probably responsible for some of the interior, such as the iconography of the stained glass, some mosaics, chalices, etc.[74] The planning included difficult structural design problems associated with the design of the new truss system, which, according to Suger, required "geometric and arithmetic calculations" to align the two church chambers with each other.

In other words, spiritual and physical work; theory and practice. Suger himself confirms this aspect of his work: 'relying upon the help of Divine mercy and the Holy Martyrs, [I] devoted my whole self, both with mind and body, to this very task.'[75]

To be sure, the mental part of the work contains the invocation of Divine Providence and the Holy Martyrs, expressed in the for post-slavery typical yet paradoxical pride in serving, *serving* the Almighty. But not only that: Suger goes so far in his emphasis on the material aspect of his work that he distorts some verses from Paul's letter to the Ephesians, where the church and the congregation are presented as merely *spiritual* communities.

Suger quotes, with his own additions in italics: 'Consequently, you are no longer foreigners and strangers, *he says* but fellow citizens with God's people and also members of his household, built on the foundation of the apostles and prophets, with Christ Jesus himself as the chief cornerstone *that joins one wall with another*. In him the whole building, *whether spiritual or material*, is, *we have learned*, joined together and rises to become a holy temple in the Lord. And in him you too are being built together *spiritually, from ourselves* to become a dwelling in which God lives by his Spirit, *the higher and better we strive to build materially.*'[76]

Among the reasons that Suger managed to attach a large part of the bishops of the Île-de France-area to his own bishopric of St Denis, this grand material manifestation in the form of a new church was certainly not without significance. In this way, Suger's political aspirations, theoretical insights and concrete practical work are joined together in a manner that we have to go back to the Ionian natural philosophers or perhaps to Pythagoras to find his equal. From here on onwards, thinking begins to renew itself.

But it is not only thinking that begins to reach new heights; it is also art, literature, and architecture. The higher and better *we ourselves* strive to build materially, the more we are joined in spirit in the dwelling of God, Suger said in the quote above. It is *we*, as humans, who build God's dwelling. *That* is the real substance of Suger's self-esteem; the feeling that we ourselves, by adding stone to stone to stone, can bring us closer to God. Thus the holy trinity between God, man and nature is not formulated—that would be done by Thomas Aquinas— but it is materially manifested.

Here, in a single epochal work, the spiritual subservience of man to the Lord is revealed as well as the constructural supremacy he, at the same time, has acquired over nature and matter. In the same moment, man has *de facto* come to know his own power, and has come to know the *means, instruments* and *techniques* he can use to experience this power. He has thus in fact freed himself from the power of the Lord by his own power, which is why *the god* can fade away and die at the rate that man's grip on nature becomes tighter.

Thus there is a paradox: as man builds ever higher and more majestic to the glory of God, the less he needs this God. This is the history of European self-awareness from Suger to Nietzsche, focussed in a single point.

Even in an opponent of nominalism like Thomas Aquinas, the demand that the theory of God must be supplemented by a theory of nature became increasingly inescapable. Marx has a formulation of how changes in thought relate to material production, which roughly is as follows: history forces a reconciliation between knowledge and material production. Material production in the golden age of feudalism reached a level not seen since the days of the Roman Empire.

'In the 12th century, a period of exuberant development broke out in western and southern Europe. In the cultural as well as the material field, a high point was reached in the years between 1150 and 1300 that was not equalled again till much later. This advance took place not only in theology, philosophy, architecture, sculpture, glasswork and literature, but also in material welfare.'[77]

And a bourgeois culture began to take shape, at first integrated into, later in competition with the feudal system. An expanding urban culture fuelled by work and a technological exploitation of nature and whose wealth derived from crafts, workshop production, trade in goods and money management.

In this situation, the demand for a theory of nature, on whose productive transformation all welfare was based, became more and more imperative. In philosophy, we notice how the pre-Thomists' interest in how creation is *ordered*—a Greek question—gives way to problems generated *actibus nostri*—by our actions (Nicholas Autrecourt). Roger Bacon wrote a draft of a *scientia experimentalis;* the beginning of a science that eventually, and increasingly demandingly in the works of later philosophers, would ask the question: *How* is matter actually constituted and *how* can it be manipulated; the matter and the nature from which we process and produce our goods.

The theory of nature Thomas needed, he found in Aristotle, this *praecursor Christi in naturalibus*, whose physics he adopted, but with the small changes necessary to adapt it to the Christian dogmas, and with a radical transformation of the whole Greek attitude to nature. Namely: the attitude already found in the ancient Israelite teachings and which became canon in Francis Bacon's thought, is also formulated by Thomas: 'Man has a natural dominion over external things, because, by his reason and will, he is able to use them for his own profit.'[xxxiv]

Thomas thus establishes the same trinity between God, man and nature that can be read into the powerful material manifestations of the Gothic: God's will is man's law but man is master of the external things. With the Neoplatonists, the light of thought and of clarity had streamed down upon the earth and man from above and above alone. To this idea, Thomas added that light and clarity also flow from below, "from the heart of things".[78] In terms of knowledge, the intellect is no longer satisfied with what it can passively *receive* from God. It must also know what it can actively *extract* from nature.

Man's dual relationship to the external world is thereafter dogmatically represented by two infallible authorities: God's *Bible* and Aristotle's *Physics*. It

---

[xxxiv] Thomas, *Summa Theologiae* II.2, Q.66, art.1. It can be interesting to compare Aristotle's and Thomas' theory of God. Aristotle's god was a lazy and idle god who did not even give himself time to think about Creation, while Thomas' God was a successful *working* CEO.

is rather ironic that Thomas' great synthesis between faith and knowledge, between Christian moral teachings and Aristotelian natural science, this synthesis of the major strands of thought that contemporised medieval thinking, would become the wedge that brought down the whole scholastic edifice of thought.

For, in asserting firmly that faith and knowledge were reconcilable, and that the dual authorities of Christ and Aristotle were infallible, any blow aimed at Aristotle's natural knowledge—and there would be many—was simultaneously directed against the Church. It is an expression of the fact that Thomas Aquinas was a true representative of his time that, while he joined its strands, he sowed the seeds of what would come. One could say, in the spirit of hindsight, that Thomas was too early with a new physics, or too late with the Aristotelian one. He would have needed a more modern physics.[xxxv]

But it on the other hand, did not need God; 'Sire, I had no need of that hypothesis' one could say with Laplace. Thomas certainly stood in the land in between, as the insightful steward of the spiritual heritage of two ancient personalities, but unlike Petrarch he stood with his back turned, and not with his eyes on the future.

Petrarch

Before we can bring together, the disparate but often intertwined threads of piety, emotion, thought-categories and social expectations into the point, or rather into the figure who, going by the name of Giotto, would reshape the rules of the sacred and the natural and thus pave the way for pictorial naturalism, we must first acquaint ourselves with a person of equal importance in terms of the literary representation, namely Francesco Petrarch.

The birth of literary naturalism is usually rightly dated to 26 April 1336, the day Petrarch undertook his famous ascent of Mont Ventoux. Located near Avignon, the mountain, at 1912 metres, is the westernmost spur of the Alps. In a long and lively letter to his friend, Dionigi da Borgo San Sepolcro, Petrarch recounts his experiences on the mountain, according to his own account on the

---

[xxxv] Here one could also mention that Galileo Galilei, who during the height of his career actually was in the service of the Church, sincerely believed that he would be able to provide the Church with a new natural science that would not contradict so-called common sense. The Church, however, did not believe Galileo.

day after the ascent—making it the first *credibly documented* mountaineering expedition in history.

The epistle is also a token of gratitude for the small handwritten edition of Augustine's *Confessions* that Petrarch had received from the Augustinian monk, Dionigi, and which he—and this is very important, both for Petrarch and for us—always carried with him.

The letter begins with a description of the preparations. Petrarch, together with his brother, Gherardo, stay overnight in an inn at the foot of the mountain, in order to be able to begin the ascent early in the morning. On the way up, they meet a shepherd who recommends a route, thus giving the impression that he has been up the mountain before—though perhaps not out of curiosity, 'because the mountain is there,' as mountaineers say, but out of necessity, to search for lost sheep, or for some other reason.

Once on the mountain, Petrarch first directs his gaze towards the Homeland, towards Italy. He sees the frozen Alps and the sky over the Motherland, though more with his soul than with his eyes. He is overcome by a longing for Italy. This "longing for Italy", a *unified* Italy is not insignificant. It is worth remembering that Petrarch's feeling for the country and its great past led him to become involved in Cola di Rienzo's spectacular attempt to unite the country, which, five hundred years before Garibaldi and Victor Emmanuel II, ended in complete failure.

Petrarch then spends a moment contemplating his own life, his deeds and his "shameful" love for Laura. Then he looks up again and looks to the west, without, 'because of the weakness of our eyes,' managing to catch a glimpse of the Pyrenees. To the south, however, he can see the sea of Marseilles, and below him, on the plain, he sees the winding Rhone.

Petrarch's travel reading, as I said, constantly included Augustine's *Confessions*. At this solemn moment, at the top of the rocky and inhospitable summit of Mont Ventoux, he takes out the well-thumbed book and opens it at random. He reads: 'Men go to admire the high mountains and the great flood of the seas and the wide-rolling rivers and the ring of Ocean and the movement of the stars, and they forget themselves.'

He closes the book, saying he is "angry with himself" for still admiring worldly things when he should long ago have learned, even from the pagan philosophers, that nothing is as worthy to be admired as the soul, beside whose greatness all else is small.

The first known mountain climb for the sake of the mountain itself, curiosity and discovery—Petrarch himself states curiosity of the mountain as the cause—ended in regret. It certainly seems like a literary construction that Petrarch invokes Augustine at this exact point, but if the episode is true, it can be (and has been) given enormous symbolic significance.[xxxvi]

Augustine and Petrarch stand at opposite ends of a thousand-year period of annihilation and silence. With Augustine, the desire for knowledge and curiosity were cut off, in Petrarch's time, the actual relationship with nature had intensified to such an extent that it was no longer possible to restrain curiosity about the secrets of nature. Petrarch finds himself in a very delicate situation: in thought he accepts the Augustinian virtues, but, as we shall see, he actually breaks with each and every one of them.

As befits a person on the threshold of a new epoch and with enough sensitivity to differentiate the conflicting impulses, Petrarch *wants* to live up to the demands of the old truth, but is unable to resist the new. Through the revealed, Augustinian truth, he constantly sees the clear empirical or sensual truth, the one that gives the eyes joy, the senses delight and the heart pride, and which he cannot resist in the long run. He haggardly notes, borrowing from Ovid: 'I see better things, and approve, but I follow worse.'

Augustine and Petrarch deal with the same questions, they try to determine the place in life for secular and divine love, the role of truth and the calling of man. But where the response to a divine love eventually supersedes all other considerations with Augustine, it is the worldly that ultimately wins the battle for Petrarch's soul. He can (like Augustine in relation to worldly pleasures) regret his passion for Laura; he can regret his curiosity about the secrets of nature, but he does not abandon them, instead he sublimates them into poetry about nature, the first nature poems in our sense.

'Petrarch's *pensare*-poems, which at the same time are both love poems and topographical poems, mark the origin of the idea of what poetry is, which we still regard as our own.'[79] But above all, Petrarch cannot reject the lure of notoriety. So if Augustine stands at the gateway to an epoch of meekness and renunciation and disavowal of the worldly, Petrarch stands at the other end, at the dawn of a pretentious, self-absorbed and ambitious epoch.

[xxxvi] That Petrarch actually stood on the summit of the mountain, having myself made the ascent, is quite clear, although it has been doubted by modern scholars. It is impossible to imagine the view from the summit from the foot of the mountain, and it is essentially as Petrarch describes.

Petrarch definitively abandons the Augustinian way when he allows himself to be lured by the temptation of earthly glory and exaltation, which at the same time clearly marks the emergence of a new subjectivity, a finite and secularly defined self is getting ready to take command. A subjectivity defined on the basis of the temporal and spatial, but with infinite claims. Thus, even Petrarch defies the Augustinian prohibition of gaining knowledge for knowledge's sake, even though he repents temporarily, he does not abandon the path he has chosen.

All the way from Homer up to the present moment, the problem of freedom has been related to death. "Better death than slavery" was the motto of the strong and the free.[80] The alternative of the slave is suicide, which can restore the freedom of the slave. This is illustrated, for example, by Euripides in the play *Hecuba*, where Polyxena escapes slavery by sacrificing herself and therefore gains freedom in the Underworld.[81]

Publilius Syrus considered it better to die than to endure the humiliation of slavery.[82] But since the slave as a slave has not chosen *that* freedom, slavery as a form of existence becomes an ersatz death or a life tainted by an indelible shame because of the constant certainty that death would be more honourable.

When the perspective then is reversed and *slave morality* becomes the norm, the other freedom, the freedom of the slave, i.e., freedom-in-death, begins to truly exist. Christ, who died willingly *for us*, has given *us* the real possibility of freedom. Every question is now framed *sub specie aeternitatis*; from the point of view of eternity. In Augustine, the promise of death's eternal freedom triumphs over the temporary nature of earthly pleasures. This is the perspective of freedom for a millennium. Only in the abodes of death can you be truly free. Petrarch's *Secretum*, a dialogue between Petrarch and Augustine, opens (of course) with Augustine saying: 'What are you doing? [---] Have you forgotten you are mortal?' But here death loses its grip as an argument, God begins to fade away as the absolute authority and primary ontological hypothesis, for from now on it is the worldly and that which is actually present that counts. Petrarch replies, in his vacillation between an older morality and a new sense of life, with Ovid's dejected observation and chooses, against his better judgement, the so-called broad road.[xxxvii]

[xxxvii] That the conflict between the secular and the eternal had sharpened is shown by the fact that confession as a means of releasing the individual from the inescapable conflict between the sin of the present and future salvation had been elevated to a sacrament at the Lateran Convention in 1215 .

The way in which Petrarch uses the Laura motif in *Secretum* signals that the battle is undecided, but if one is to judge Petrarch's thinking after his life, it is probably love for the earthly that prevails.

The choice for Petrarch to receive earthly accolades over heavenly came easily, as at the pinnacle of his earthly enterprise, he allowed himself to be crowned *poeta laureatus* at the Capitoline Hill on the 8 of April 1341. No such thing had happened in Rome for thirteen years (Albertino Mussato, who was referred to earlier, had received the same honour in Padua twenty-five years earlier).

In addition, he was granted the privilege of (in Gibbon's succinct phrasing) 'wearing, at his choice, a crown of laurel, ivy, or myrtle, of assuming the poetic habit, and of teaching, disputing, interpreting, and composing in all places whatsoever, and on all subjects of literature.'[83]

The Laura Motif

It is said that Petrarch possessed two portraits, made by the greatest contemporary painters, and that he lovingly kept these portraits side by side.[84] One was a Madonna by Giotto. The other depicted the beloved Laura, painted by his relative, Simone Martini. In his private little sanctuary of love, Petrarch thus placed the holy Madonna and the, for him, equally holy Laura side by side. Laura is often seen as an incarnation of Venus, the goddess of love, and Petrarch himself does not shy away from having his landscapes populated by pagan *amorini* and goddesses, but above all by Apollo and Daphne (dafne = *lauro*; laurel). However, it is at least as interesting to see Laura as a humanised Virgin Mary. In contemporary painting, the Virgin was already wandering among Petrarch's compatriots and in environments that he could easily identify as his own.

Thus, Laura could be an incarnation of the idea of the sacred. In this way, she would be filling the intermediary void in the triad *God—man—nature*. That this interpretation is reasonable is shown not least by the fact that Laura can be seen as, and by Petrarch himself was seen as, an aspect of all three parts of the triad: as the *aura* or *Light of the World*, as the living Laura, and as *laurus nobilis*, the laurel tree in nature.

Among the more protracted chapters in Petrarchan scholarship is the question of whether Petrarch's Laura really existed. There are ample reasons for doubt since even his closest friends doubted her existence. Boccaccio saw Laura as an allegory. When his friend Giacomo Colonna queried whether she was a real person, Petrarch indignantly replied:[85] 'How can you say such a thing? That I should have invented Laura's beautiful name in order to speak about her [---] when there is no Laura in my heart?'

No—'this Laura lives!' for how would it be possible to simulate love for so long 'without great effort.' Indeed, one can ask that.

Despite Petrarch's assurance, his love seems at least to me more like a simulation, even though following a successful recipe (which made Petrarch the greatest living poet of his time), than a deeply felt love.

One could perhaps agree that the first love-affair is real, but when, after seventeen years, he worships the same unattainable woman[86], and still three years later moans that 'For twenty years (o long, heavy toil!) weeping and sighing was all that stood to gain,'[87] I, at least, am prepared to agree with Gibbon and his sarcastic remark that it is difficult to be 'deeply interested in a metaphysical passion for a nymph so shadowy that her existence has been questioned; for a matron so prolific that she was delivered of eleven legitimate children while her amorous swain sighed and sung at the fountain of Vaucluse.'[88] The fact is that Petrarch, having taken the oath of chastity when he was ordained a priest, had (at least) two children by different women, so that his moral contestations over his love for Laura fall flat before he, at last, has time to utter them.

If Laura, as a literary figure, is not primarily an imprint of a living person, what does she stand for? She can as said stand for the central figure in the reformulation of the triad *God—man—nature*, which in Petrarch's time simultaneously and with internal interactions took place at all three levels and which changed all three: God, man and nature. Laura is the divine that has become human and the actual that has taken precedence over the ideal. Laura is also, and this she has in common with Dante's Beatrice, a deification of living man, of the living woman.

But while Beatrice possesses only this one dimension, Laura has three: She equates, if only for a moment, God, Man and Nature. She places herself beside the Madonna as an object of worship at the same time that the Madonna in contemporary imagery becomes human. All the emotional exuberance that human beings—let us say in the rush of "spring awakening" and a dawning sense of rash omnipotence that is the hallmark of youth at the moment when the supervision of the father begins to falter—since Bernard of Clairvaux had directed at the Madonna, was now focussed on a real human being.

Just as nominalism redirected the interest of knowledge from the idea to the real thing, so too was emotional interest assigned a real object. The worship of God as the highest idea of man was transferred to the worship of living and actual (wo)man. That the step made nevertheless is so small, is only a manifestation of what Hegel calls, within the historical process, "the necessary unity of concepts": in Petrarch's time, the Virgin Mary had almost been made human, and although Laura was not entirely an idea, she was at least an *idée fixe* for our poet.

And poetry, as in the case of Mussato, claimed to be "a second theology" and, as a philosophy, "a competitor to Aristotle". This was something Petrarch eagerly albeit ruefully agreed with.[89]

Laura – Madonna

The revolutionary example of the dethronement of the Madonna is the *Madonna of Humility* that the same Simone Martini who painted Laura's portrait had created in Avignon Cathedral. The dethronement is literal, because for the first time the Virgin is now placed directly on the ground, without the throne and without the insignia of power and glory on which she had previously always leaned on. The Madonna *is* of this world. Petrarch, of course, knew of this *Madonna dell'Umilità*[xxxviii] because he lived just outside Avignon.

That he sometimes calls Laura *la donna nostra* (our wife) and lets her sit on the ground (*seder la donna nostra sopra l'erba*) is certainly, as a poetic act, an expression of the flexible metamorphosis he allowed his adored one to undergo from form to form, but nonetheless remarkable in the ambiguity or "trimbiguity" with which he deliberately operated. The idolatry that later, in the wake of *Renaissance humanism*, glorified man and man's creation has its beginnings in this moment.

It is no longer the absent world and the absent man that is celebrated; it is the present.[xxxix] From now on, it is not the relation to God but to that of *nature* that

---

[xxxviii] The kinship between the word *humilis* (humble) and humus (earth) give her this earthy position. Also Francis of Assisi has this connection between earthiness and humility.

[xxxix] But once more I would like to highlight the peculiar continuity of the categories: the saint is made man and man at the same time into a saint. – In heretical folklore, as we know it from the village of *Montaillou* the peasants could discuss like this: "Do you believe that God or the blessed Mary are something – really? And I answered: "Yes, of

essentially determines the development of the categories of understanding and those of pictorial interpretation.

Laura – Human

Just as during the first breakthrough of individuality and self-awareness in the archaic Greek period, the strongest manifestations of the self are now being channelled through love. Petrarch even includes Archilochus in his catalogue of inspirational figures.[90] But in a way that perhaps is characteristic of how Greek individuality differs from the modern, Petrarch's sense of self primarily created not an *I* but a *you*—so does an ego that has been subject to the Christian message of love express itself.[xl]

In the first Christian act of devotion, love in a manner that follows the general mental pattern, is doubled. The Christian community, in the primary love of God, is united into a collective *subjectum*, into a community within which the individual characteristics of the believers are obliterated or subordinated to the commonality of being sisters and brothers in Christ. But *simultaneously* love has created a sanctuary for individual expression in the form of love *for the other*; for *thy Neighbour*.

The first rule of the Mosaic law that thou shalt "fear and love God above all things", is added to in the *New Testament*, with a new commandment that creates a basis for mutual love. The Apostle John writes (13:34), 'A new command I give you: Love one another. As I have loved you, so you must love one another.' So that as the mighty figure of the God of the *Old Testament* fades as human self-esteem increases, the space for love for earthly beings and earthly things becomes greater; emotionality flourishes.

This is true also for Petrarch. For him, love is primarily a passionately sustained and lifelong project directed towards a *you*. It is this chosen *you* that

---

course I believe it." Then Pierre said : "God and the Blessed Virgin Mary are nothing but the visible world around us; nothing but what we see and hear. As Pierre Rauzi was older than I, I considered that he had told me the truth." (p. 242) This text of the Inquisition is closer to Petrarch than we might suspect: The zealous Inquisitor Jacques Fournier later became Petrarch's Pope in Avignon under the name of Benedict XII.

[xl] A parallel, then, to the relation that enabled the discussion on *free will* to first crystallize in Christian

sociality, and then, as in Augustine, in a *negative* sense, as a denial. The negative is again the paradoxically positive!

makes the self appear unique and essentially separate from other *selves*, as Petrarch himself explicitly points out. Love has made him unique, *singular da l'altra gente.*

> *The eyes I spoke about so warmly,*
> *and the arms, the hands, the ankles, and the face*
> *that left me so divided from myself,*
> *and made me different from other men.*[91]

Laura — Nature

'Petrarch's topographical poems are love poems,' says Karlheinz Stierle.[92] But one could, on the contrary, also argue that Petrarch's love poems are topographical poems, so interwoven are the inner feelings and the natural manifestations of beauty. Where Laura goes, the world rejoices, is the message of Petrarch, as for example in these stanzas:

> *The green grass and flowers of a thousand hues,*
> *scattered beneath that ancient dark oak-tree,*
> *pray that her lovely foot will touch or bend them:*
> *and heaven with its clear and wandering sparks*
> *blazes around, visibly delighting*
> *at being made calm by such lovely eyes.*[93]

The landscape in Petrarch's poetry acquires such significance 'because the experience of the landscape and its beauty in its aesthetic intensity is comparable to a devotion to the beloved.'[94]

When Petrarch uses the absent Laura to enhance his sensitivity to the beauty of the landscape (a landscape that in a larger perspective, somewhere, in its continuous spatial extension, also includes Laura), it is—and this is something new in relation to the landscape—the same undertaking as when he stands on top of Mont Ventoux with his gaze looking both near and far. He looks out over the beloved but invisible Italy, and then looks down into his soul.

He senses the sea in the distance, and sees the river far below his feet. He sees the plateau to the west, but notes that the strength of his eyes is not good enough to make out the Pyrenees. Here, for the first time, we are given a curved horizon and a holistic perspective, with the self, its longing and its self-reflection, as the centre. With the relationship *I—you* (Petrarch—Laura) as an auxiliary construction, Petrarch spontaneously creates a poetic *central perspective*—the same as Giotto, equally spontaneously, and driven by the same general necessity created in the visual arts.

That which is modern in Petrarch's poetry is the way in which he unites the *I*, the *you* and the *world* into an emotionally and spatially interwoven whole. Petrarch stands at the dawn of the age when man comes of age for a second time; when he leaves his Father to begin his own life. It is the wave of emotions that afflicts *man(kind)* during his late teens that Petrarch captures and describes.

In a way that surely most of us recognise from our own youthful love, he calls the trees, the stars and the forests to bear witness to his love; he knows that the wind and the sun that surround him also caress Laura, therefore the sun and the wind and the meadow and the river and the landscape as a *whole*, is a bridge that puts him in touch with his beloved. And when he moves in areas where she is or where she could be or has been, he moves on holy ground, and all she has ever touched or may touch fills him with reverence because it puts him in touch with her.

The rapturous impressions of sight, the enjoyment of the eyes which Augustine so sharply condemned, bears witness for Petrarch to the existence of the sacred in nature.[95] Petrarch's love poems thus reflect a new way of seeing nature—a *love* of nature—rather than an antiquated interpretation of the theme of love. Petrarch is interesting because he adopts a circular horizon for his rapture; a panorama of nature *with himself at the centre*, that *somewhere (but invisibly) also contains the beloved Laura.*

Petrarch created something new and extraordinary—nature poetry—but wrapped, as so often happens with novelty, in something familiar—the *cansó* (love song) of the troubadour.

The de-demonisation of nature that took place when mythic stories gave way to philosophy in the 5th century BC is being repeated now, but in a different way because the circumstances are not quite the same. With the Greeks, the mutable diversity of nature was animated by capricious, boisterous, stern, jealous, fierce, tolerant, helpful or dismissive beings. In the Christian bipolar mythology, the essence of nature is exclusively negative. So perhaps Petrarch wanted to break the curse of the earth by making an archaic nymph of his adored Laura.

For if one interpolates the Greek conception of truth with the story of Apollo and Daphne, the following poetic story emerges: in the night of ignorance all beings are ensouled, the imagination can make a beautiful woman of a tree trunk. But when dawn approaches and the rays of the sun brush against her trunk, the moment of truth also approaches (in Greek, *aletheia*, truth, is the same as the visible—that the gloom is transformed when it becomes visible is thus an expression of an ancient Greek metaphor of truth) and she is transformed into a laurel tree.

To derive the name Phoebus Apollo from the sun's rays is nevertheless only one of several possible interpretations, but if we follow this line of reasoning, we see how Petrarch makes a holy trinity (which isn't too much considering what Dante did with his Beatrice) of the name Laura: l'aura, the radiance around the sun (Phoebus—the radiant one) or Aurora—the dawn glow; Laura—the woman and *laurus*—the laurel.

Perhaps the love of *nature in itself* was so unspeakably difficult to express, that he had to turn her into a being, into a woman. Petrarch's mortal sin is that he uses an earthly being to represent the highest object of love. In the space where the Christian duality of *Creator* and *created* was found—and this is also the central point of nominalist philosophy, and thus why nominalism and poetic and pictorial naturalism are parallel phenomena—he places an amalgamation of the Creator and the created in Laura and her wonderful milieu: nature.

Otherwise, one can hardly imagine Petrarch's twenty year old rapture for an embodied idea of love. According to Baumgarten, "Nature makes no leaps out of the darkness and into clear logical distinctions", and "The road from night to midday passes over the dawn".[96] Perhaps Laura is a nymph, an abstraction, who, in the rose-tinted seconds before the light envelops her and science's classifying eyes sweep over her and transform her into the plant *Laurus nobilis,* takes her last leap, still free, untouched and worshipped; as a being; as a guardian of the secrets found in the deep woods; as a favourite of the gods.

The love of St Bernard of Clairvaux, of St Francis or Petrarch are all parts of the same generative power that at one point in antiquity bridged the gap between man and slave and that now overcomes the aversion towards evil in nature. 'Alas, Love carries me where I do not wish, and I know my journey is towards her, so that I'm more annoying than before, to her who is the queen of my heart,' Petrarch sighs resignedly.[97]

That Petrarch is aware that his sin does not consist of violating the tenth commandment, in that he worships a married woman, but that he is violating the first in that he has reversed the gradation of creation, is shown by the admonition he addresses to himself in the figure of Augustine:[98] 'She [Laura] has distracted you from love of the Creator to love of one of His creatures: this has always been the broad way which leads to destruction. Petrarch: Don't be so quick to judge. Loving her has increased my love for God. Augustine: But you've reversed the right order of things.'

'[---] All created things should be loved for the sake of their Creator; charmed by one creature, you haven't loved your Creator as you should, but have admired Him for creating her, as if He had never created anything finer.' Here the parallel with the ontology of nominalism is obvious. The grandiosity of the moment when the gaze is turned away from God and towards man, lies in the fact that at that same moment man senses that it is *he* who is the Creator, but this time not as a *commanding* but as an *executive* authority.

It was this realisation, or this inkling, that forced through a new knowledge and a new visualisation of existence, because it—the conditions of being—had fundamentally changed.[xli]

The Idea Perspective, the Central Perspective and the Horizon

Hegel's view on the Greek understanding of nature, or rather lack of understanding, is that they *did not reach* nature with their concepts. According to Hegel, the concept of the master (in the master—slave or lord—bondsman dialectic) does not relate immediately to nature, it has no *concept* of nature, but relates immediately only to the conduits through which the good of nature is extracted, to the art of ruling or to politics.

The knowledge of the master is not based on a position of power in direct relation to the physical objects, but on a knowledge of existence as it renders

---

[xli] The legal measures against the Cathar heretics in *Montaillou*, which were carried out when Petrarch was in his twenties, resulted in extensive records that not only reveal the beliefs of the simple mountain people but also much about their way of life. For example, they were uncertain of whether it was the Lord or if it was dung that provided the coming harvest: "Some peasants considered that it was God himself who made the wheat "flower and swell". They thought the Devil produced hail, thunder and storms. But other peasants were equally sure that when crops flourished it was due to Nature itself, or to the fertility of the soil, or to the presence of the parfaits, (that is, heretics, translator's remark) or to human labour or to dung." Ladurie 1978, p. 293. And in his family chronicle, Leon Battista Alberti considers − for the first time in literature? − landed property as a productive asset.

itself through the interface of having power over slaves. The master has, as Hegel puts it, interposed the slave between himself and the objects. The master can thus behave (and must behave, in order to achieve his pleasure) in the same way as a gourmet in a restaurant: he can enjoy a delicious meal and show off his knowledge of the *names* of the dishes and wines, without having the slightest idea of the actual *process of production.*

He doesn't need that knowledge, only knowledge of the names of the dishes and how to *order* them. For the gourmet, the chef and waiter are merely tools for gaining pleasure. 'The master, however, who has interposed the bondsman between it and himself, thereby relates himself merely to the dependence of the thing, and enjoys it without qualification and without reserve,' Hegel aptly concludes. The same lack of qualification, i.e., the renunciation of the sweat and toil of labor, also characterizes the philosophical categories of understanding.[xlii]

The same detached relationship to nature is, not surprisingly, expressed in ancient art. As an example of how the conceptual correlation between thought and image resulted in peculiar, logical-visual symbolic forms, let us begin by considering the so-called *Nile Mosaic* in Palestrina—a Greek work from the 2nd century BC.

[xlii] Already Pliny the Elder criticised his compatriots for their inability to take responsibility for themselves, something that made them dependent on the power and knowledge of the slaves. "We walk with the feet of other people, we see with the eyes of other people, trusting to the memory of others we salute one another, and it is by the aid of others that we live. The most precious objects of existence, and the chief supports of life, are entirely lost to us, and we have nothing left but our pleasures to call our own." (*Naturalis historia* XXIX Transl. John Bostock and Henry Thomas Riley)

Although, the mosaic ostensibly depicts a landscape, its pictorial elements are not held together by "nature" but rather by "ceremony" or "history" in the form of a narrative or as a rendering of a known historical event. P. G. P. Meyboom has convincingly argued that the motif of the lower part of the mosaic is the annual flooding of the Nile, which was of vital importance for the formation of the Egyptian state and culture. The occasion was celebrated with an autumnal festival in honour of the Nile in the month of Koiak.

The Nile, personified as the god Osiris, was resurrected each year, swelled over the land—i.e., Isis—and impregnated her. From this conception, the Horus-falcon symbolically emerged, in whose form the legitimacy of pharaonic power coalesced. The upper part of the mosaic, on the other hand, shows the unknown geographical origin of the Nile, which was vaguely summed up as "Abyssinia". Meyboom concludes: the Nile mosaic does not offer 'so much a view of Egypt, or of a particular area, but a synoptic picture of the Nile flood.'[99]

Although, the Nile Mosaic is the image from antiquity that perhaps most closely *resembles* a landscape painting, the landscape plays no organising role in the image. Its natural elements are subordinated to the representation's need for clear and distinct images/ideas. In the Egyptian manner, the animals are depicted in profile or semi-profile and, to be sure, are often provided with a name tag. The tendency is thus for the individual elements of the picture not to be depicted as an object integrated into the landscape or into nature, but as "the conventional depiction" of the object; a house, a temple, a well, a boat, etc.

The objects are depicted from an instructive point of view; each thing presents its characteristics in such a way that one as easily as possible can identify it. We can also say that the pictorial objects are seen from a *general* conceptual point of view, as is mandated by the implicit Greek conception of collectivity; i.e., not from *one individual* point of view with the power to form a synthetic image of the viewed section of existence (as a modern individuality and perception of truth presupposes).[xliii]

[xliii] It is therefore misleading when Meyboom says that the picture is seen from a bird's-eye view. The viewer's perspective is a modern construction. Certainly there is a dominant direction of gaze downwards to the left, but one would require the combined vision of all the birds of Egypt to form the image of the Nile that is the subject matter of the picture.

Like the images on the wall of an Egyptian tomb, they stand as typical *representatives* of the *nomos* of these things, presented logically for their time; i.e., from the perspective of the *logos*.

A very important exception to these stereotyped images exists, however, and as we shall see, it is the image of man.

True nature in Plato's eyes was not what *we* would call nature, but true nature for Plato was that which was formed by the nature of ideas; of a hierarchical set of distinct and discrete ideas. Plato could not avoid borrowing expressions and analogies from the creation of concrete images to describe his abstract universe. Neither could visual art escape philosophy's way of perceiving existence.[xliv]

One could say that Plato stole both the privilege of defining the contents of beauty as well as the right to express anything relevant about the material world from the craftsmen, making beauty a non-material quality, while knowledge became an abstract, idea-based knowing. Both the beauty of, and the truth about the artefacts was detached from the actual objects and their concrete production, and became, under the new order, both the ideology and a legitimation of the logocratic state.

'I, Plato, *am* the truth,' Nietzsche says.[100] The Platonic *ideas* show, as in Egyptian imagery, objects from their *typical* side, as eternal and unchanging signs.

Plato's philosophy can thus be described as hieroglyphic, which could be another name for conceptual realism. Francis Bacon, who was not a bad historian of philosophy, divided the ways of denoting objects into *ex congruo* which he called hieroglyphic, and *ad placitum* which applied only by virtue of convention.[101] In Bacon's division, the theory of Forms would be hieroglyphic (Bacon himself, however, does not explicitly say so). While Nietzsche, who was at least as good an observer as Bacon, accused the philosophical tradition of Plato of its "egypticity". No wonder that Plato, insofar as he cared about the visual arts, admired the Egyptian.

Plato rejected art as an ideal-creating or idolatrous activity primarily on epistemological grounds, because it was *false* in the sense that it expressed a degenerate truth. It is best illustrated by the famous passage in the Tenth Book

---

[xliv] According to Cicero, *De finibus*, book I.vi, the conglomeration of thought and vision originates from Democritus: "The impressions, or as they call them, *eidola*, whose influence results not only in visual impressions but also in thoughts, [---] originate entirely from Democritus." There is more of Democritus in Plato than he wanted to admit.

of the *Republic* where Plato says this: 'Consider, then, this very point. To which is painting directed in every case, to the imitation of reality as it is or of appearance as it appears? Is it an imitation of a phantasm or of the truth?' 'Of a phantasm.' 'Then the mimetic art is far removed from truth.'

The artist then, like the epic poet Homer, is a "creator of phantoms", why 'it surely is fair to question him and ask, "Friend Homer, are you not at the third remove from truth and reality in human excellence, being merely that creator of phantoms whom we defined as the imitator?".'[102]

Epistemologically, Plato could (and had to) deprive the pictorial arts of their formative function, but the situation was still a bit problematic. Of the cardinal virtues, it was easy for the philosopher to usurp the right to define "the truth" and "the good", but with "beauty" it was more difficult. Since antediluvian times beauty had been deeply rooted in the pinnacle of material culture; the entwining tapestry of image, idol and ideal was so firmly rooted in religion, patriotism and everyday life that nowadays it is impossible to imagine Greek culture without art or art without the Greeks. It was not impossible for Plato. It was necessary.

And when he couldn't easily dismiss the appeal of *manufactured* beauty, the easiest step was simply to ban that kind of beauty. This should, however, not be taken too literally. As we shall see, modern science issued a similar "ban" on art, and on exactly the same premises.

It is not difficult to see that the "ban", which formally follows from an epistemological argument, actually is politically necessitated. For it is a repetition of Plato's *modus operandi* when he stole the knowledge of objects from the craftsmen. Ultimately, it is about who has the right to define what really is real. It is the *user* of an object, and not the maker, who is able to make the right judgements about the object, Plato argued. The core of Aristotle's logic expresses the same, for the modern reader, peculiar attitude.

Even Plutarch, who thought that 'it does not of necessity follow that, if the work delights you with its grace, the one who wrought it is worthy of your esteem'[103] could, thanks to this distinction, maintain the beauty of the object. In Plato, on the other hand, both the artist and the work of art are obliterated by the philosopher's ideological cleaver: there is no reason to admire either. For how could a dusty and dirty stonemason or a bronze caster, blackened by soot, slick with clay and soiled by beeswax, produce anything beautiful, true or good worthy of the admiration of a free man?

It was unthinkable for Plato. If the opposite, sophist position could have asserted itself with the same force (it did exist—but the question of what is "rational" has never been settled rationally); if the view that words are arbitrary or that beauty is a relative property of things had become more than marginally valid, then it would have required a broad consensus that objects first and foremost are brought into existence through the *making* of them, which in turn would have required a work ethic that did not and could not exist.

That kind of insight and that kind of ethic was impossible to assert in a political or polis-ideology whose continuity was guaranteed by the commanding authority remaining unchanged. And the knowledge structure of the command society of antiquity is based on the fact that whoever holds power also has knowledge of the *word* and of how the word becomes object. The word, concept or idea represents *logos* and the rational.

The definition of knowledge in the Platonic reality meant that to ascertain what an object *is*, one determined how the idea of the object related conceptually (and not, for example, materially) to other concepts or ideas. In Greek, to define is to delimit: *orizontai*; everything is defined through it being contained within the horizon of its idea. From this, we can perhaps better understand why man's visual horizon could not have been decisive for the way in which the interrelations of objects were to be understood.

It is because things were not determined with man as the measure and his vision as the horizon, but the other way around. The nature of a thing (or rather every category of things) is determined from an absolute and distant centre—its idea—but it appears in the world in the form which, so to speak, fits within its definition, or within its "horizon".

We shall see how this is exemplified by the Greek image of a chair. The image of a chair should, in order to satisfy the requirements of distinction and clarity of the theory of Forms, have four legs, a roughly square seat (to distinguish the chair from something "bench-like"; i.e., the "horizon" that idea of the bench fits within) and a backrest (so that the chair does not become a stool). Plato would also require that all four legs are depicted as being of equal length if, as is normally the case, they are in fact of equal length.

As he, in the *Sophist*, distinguishes between two kinds of *imitation art*. One he calls *likeness-making*, and the other *appearance-making*. Likeness-making happens 'whenever anyone produces the imitation by following the proportions of the original in length, breadth, and depth, and giving, besides, the appropriate colours to each part.' But not all likeness-makers proceed in this way. They produce *simulacra (fantasma)*, which distort and falsify the real dimensions and proportions of things.

'For if they reproduced the true proportions of beautiful forms, the upper parts, you know, would seem smaller, and the lower parts larger than they ought, because we see the former from a distance, the latter from near at hand. [---] So the artists abandon the truth and give their figures not the actual proportions but those which seem to be beautiful.'[xlv]

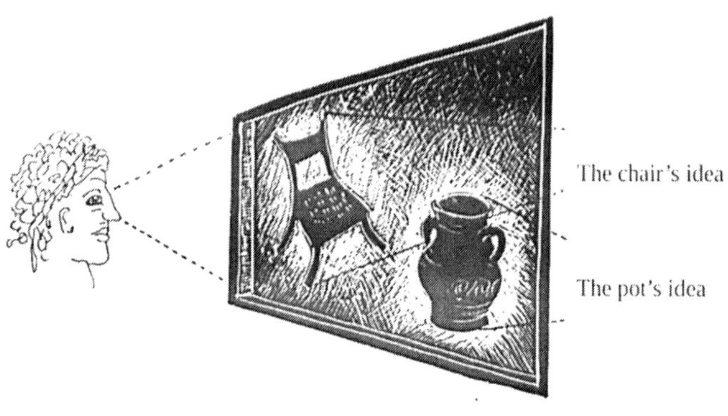

In accordance with the basic concept of conceptual realism, but in opposition to how the central perspective is constructed—with the self, the eye, as the centre and the edge of vision infinitely far away, the *idea perspective* shows, so to speak, the "horizon" or the defining characteristics of the concept at close range, while the centre of the object, its idea, is infinitely far away. Moreover, the ideas lack an organic connection between themselves. For the leading Greeks, there was no coherent material substratum to which the disparate and denominable elements of the world of objects could have been meaningfully included.

[xlv] Plato: *The Sophist,* 235-236. This example explicitly concerns colossal sculptures, which, because of the viewer's frog's-eye view must be made proportionally larger at the top than the bottom to "look real". In a comment on this passage Holger Thesleff says that Plato rejects perspectivism in art. This is of course correct, but Plato is not speaking about the *perspective of likeness-making* but about a *viewer's perspective*, which does not apply to the relation between the depicted object and the image, but to that of the image and the *viewer*.

The consequence is that the Greeks tended to represent each thing in an ideal form, as the conceptual definition suggests. If such a coherent material substratum *had existed*, its name would have been *nature*. But nature, as we shall see, *lacked* an *idea* (image) belonging to it and was therefore, unlike the objects, undepictable.

The way in which the idea perspective represents existence pictorially can perhaps become clearer if it is compared, in the following stylised way, with the depicting principle of the central perspective.

The objects depicted in a Greek painting are primarily connected with their idea, i.e., with their true nature, according to the Greek way of seeing; not with the kind of nature that is real to us. In a Greek painting, then, the "horizon" is in the foreground of the picture, while the truth of the "thing", the idea, is infinitely distant. The connection between the idea and its appearance is represented by the cones in the figure above. The pictorial objects are as disparate as their ideas are. The viewer of the Greek painting finds himself in a different kind of space than that which comprises the "idea-space" of the image. The image is the interface between the physical and the ethereal space on which the ideas are projected. The viewer of the image in physical space thus does not see visual representatives of physical nature, but of a conceptually coherent ethereal nature. This, incidentally, could be another formula for expressing Hegel's assertion that the Greeks did not reach nature with their understanding—what *we* understand as nature.

The projection of the central perspective is of a different, completely reversed kind. Now the image space and the viewer's space are basically the same, the image is a *window* towards the environment and not a projection screen. It is the individual human eye that has organised the image. An (imagined) shift of the viewer's position gives rise to an (imagined) shift of the pictorial elements. Nature appears in the image in its mutable, and not in its eternal form. (For how this relates to icon painting, see the chapter *Gold ground* below).

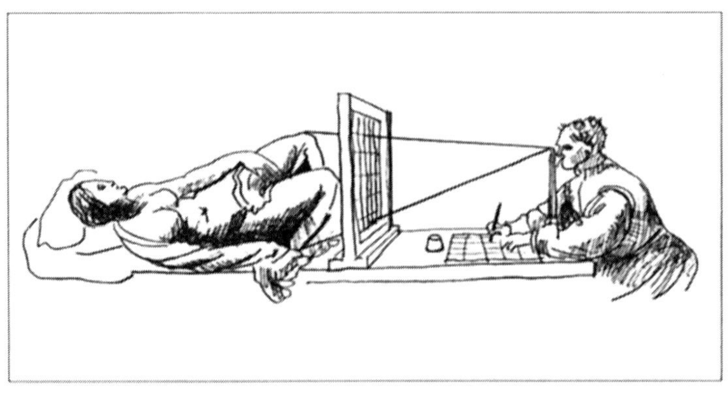

Central perspective (after Dürer)

The above examples are, of course, exaggerated and simplified, for in practice the Greek way of depicting creatures and things was a compromise between a species-typical and an illusionistic way of interpreting them. Foreshortening was known and used, but in such a way that each pictorial element became the bearer of its own perspective and illusionism generally was subordinated to the emphasis on the distinctive characteristics of each element.

How difficult it was to detach the formal perception of things from the conceptual and how persistent the latter view was, is shown by Lorenzetti's *Siena Madonna* from the 14th century, in which the same surface—a carpet on a floor—is given two separate vanishing points, one for the floor and one for the carpet, and thus appear to be viewed from different angles. And this at a time when certain rules of thumb for the central perspective already existed. Panofsky comments: 'The integrity of the material concept "carpet" is still stronger than that of the formal concept "complete plane".'[104]

The Image of Nature

According to a tradition dating back to Parmenides, the intelligible in Greek high philosophy was equal to the invariant. Both Plato and Aristotle held that adequate knowledge could only be obtained of that which could be affixed to an invariable quantity. Ideas were of this kind, statically invariant and eternally enduring. Real things, however, which were constantly transforming and changing shape, one could have no true knowledge of, only opinions or conjecture. Above all, this applies to all real things that are not artefacts, namely nature.

The Greek word for "nature"—*physis*—is at the same time the concept of the changing, the growing, the ever-varying, the organic and—in the tradition of Parmenides—closely linked with the notion of the "illogical", or, which later became the dominant connotation, the "evil".[xlvi] It would probably be a *contradictio in adiecto* to create the "idea" or "form" of nature, since nature is the absolute and subordinate opposite of the world of ideas.

And given the interplay of the categories of knowledge and the configurations of depiction, and above all in view of the conceptual and etymological unity of image and idea, the concept of "nature-image" as understood by the Greeks would collide with the absurd concept of "nature-idea"—a conceptual impossibility.

Nature in Greek thought is thus "illogical". Man could therefore not learn anything essential from it. There is an interesting passage in Plato where this relationship to nature is crosslighted. Socrates, in the company of Phaedrus, has wandered out through the city gates and follows the lush banks of the river Ilissos. Under a large plane tree that provides shade and cool, Socrates starts to exclaim a hymn of praise—probably the first in European prose—for the beauty of the surroundings. Phaedrus is surprised by this, knowing that Socrates rarely strays from the city.

This is because, Socrates replies, 'Forgive me, my dear friend. You see, I am fond of learning. Now the country places and the trees won't teach me anything, and the people in the city do.'[xlvii] Sixteen hundred years later, somewhere on the rocky shores of the Sorgue, Petrarch makes the exact opposite observation: *Le citta son nemiche, amici i boschi, a "miei pensier"*...he writes; (The cities are enemies; the woods friends to my thoughts...)[105] Thus the world and man have changed, from master to servant to a different kind of master: the Greek *polis-*

[xlvi] This ethical scale rests exactly on *the* premises that led Plato, for epistemological reasons, to condemn or neglect the value of knowledge involved in the production of the degenerate forms of ideas: the object and the image of the object. The "coming into being" (i.e. the creation of actual things) we have contact with and knowledge of through the body, Plato says, while only reason provides insight into "true being". (*The Sophist* 248)

[xlvii] Phaedrus 230 d: Neither does the landscape play a particularly big role in Greek literature: "To sum up in overly formulaic terms: In the Illiad, in Sappho, in Pindar and in most Greek tragedy [---] landscape, as a distinct element, does not play a part; and natural description is used, sparingly and briefly, as a direct metaphor for things human." (Parry, A.M *Landscape in Greek Poetry*; in Human lansdscape in Classical Antiquity 1996, p. 101)

man has become, in Petrarch's guise, *un cittadin de' boschi*—an inhabitant/citizen of the woods.

Once you understand that the Greeks perceived nature in this way, it would be unreasonable to demand of Aristotle, for example, that he should experimentally verify the theoretical conclusions he had reached, since *actual* events had a lower truth value than a conceptually determinable connection between things. What has been proved at a more general level need not, of course, be proved at a lower level. *Why* Aristotle understood things in this order is, however, the question we can and should ask, and one we must ask ourselves—as well as the question why *we* consider something to be true when it has been experimentally verified.

Galileo Galilei, in his *The Dialogue Concerning the Two Chief World Systems*, which precisely deals with the relationship between Aristotelian science and Galileo's experimental science, has an apt picture of the two different ways of conceiving existence.

The Aristotelian approach, Galileo says, 'seems to me to have great sympathy with a certain way of painting that a friend of mine used, who wrote upon the canvas in chalk: 'Here I will have the fountain with Diana and her nymphs; there, certain deerhounds; in this corner I will have a huntsman with the head of a stag; the rest shall be lanes, woods, and hills,' then left the remainder for the painter to set forth with colours; and thus he persuaded himself that he had painted the story of Actaeon, when he had contributed thereto nothing of his own more than the names.'[106]

A similar or an even greater vagueness in the pictorial expression of nature, that connects the active pictorial elements in Galileo's amusing example, is actually found in ancient painting or mosaic art, for example in the *Nile mosaic* mentioned above.

The Image of Man

With *man* the situation is different. Man was, if we still stick to Plato, an essentially *spiritual* substratum. Man was thus not essentially *body* or *nature* as in our time. If we take the Egyptian image of man as the starting point, it is easier to see what has happened in the rendering of images: In much the same way as the landscape of the Greeks, the image of *man* in Egypt is also additively constructed; six, seven parts, each presented from its *typical* side: a profile, an eye, an upper body, a pair of arms, a lower body, and a pair of legs with feet, where only the order is, so to speak, "correct".

With the Greeks, on the other hand, the sculpted or painted image of man appears in all its autonomous, unfettered—spirituality. This happens at the same time that man has given himself a *soul* and a *will* and has thus created for himself a hub for the self-integration of the faculties of the soul, which, in Homeric times, were still disparate and apportioned to the intervention and will of several external gods. With an autonomous soul as a command centre, man becomes whole and one; united by his own individual will.

He becomes a *personality*, both psychologically, legally and discursively—the opposite of being a type. Or, using the conceptual pair *idea—horizon*, one can say that man is now organised on the basis of his dominant point of view, from his idea—which is his soul—while the body is the envelope that encloses the soul and constitutes his boundary defined as a "featherless living biped".

Then, we can see the boundary conditions of Greek vision and Greek depiction more clearly: Man (i.e., the free man) is determined as a whole by a *logos*, a single organising principle, which harmoniously governs (or is to govern) him in all his parts. The objects, on the other hand, and to an even larger extent—nature, are composed of partly contradictory concepts.

The concept of "chair", for example, consists of both a unifying concept—the chair—as well as of conceptual parts such as "legs", "backrest" and "seat", without there being any difference of *domination*, as there is for man with the concepts of "soul" and "body", only a *disjunctive* difference between the parts, but it was not decisive for the leading Greek thinkers.

Egyptian man

The beings and entities that, so to speak, lie hierarchically between the free men and the manufactured things; the other elements of the set of "mortals" such as women, children, slaves and animals, could be a part of the human mode of representation to the extent that they shared the same conceptual "family tree" and, moreover, could be characterised as possessing a *will*, which in any case was secondary to the will of a man.

In this sense, painting in the Greek language was a *zografia*, a depiction of humans and animals.

In contrast, "nature" as the highest generality, both as image and as concept, completely transcended the horizon of Greek understanding. Likewise, antiquity lacked (nor could it have, because of the premises) a theory concerning the dynamic interrelationship of the objects, that could be viewed as satisfactory from our perspective—other than that of Aristotle, which *de facto* is primarily concerned with man-made changes. On the other hand, antiquity had a good eye for the dynamic and dramatic, not to say drastic, nature of both *societal* and *human* relations.

And, one should remember that the mythology of Greek religion possessed a naive and brusque sincerity, perhaps because it did not have the weight of all the hopes of a shattered empire behind it. There was no ruling principle in nature, neither of a monotheistic, spiritual nor of a material kind, which could have organised or *governed* nature in a manner harmonious with the Greek understanding of existence.

On the other hand, the Middle Ages, through a ruling God, and the Modern Age in its conception of an omnipresent mechanical *force*, possessed such self-integrating principles. With which we shall acquaint ourselves in the following section.

With the Greeks, the understanding of existence never really reached beyond the social and human, but within the framework of understanding and depicting the human it celebrated great triumphs. Free movement, interpreted through the concept of *force*, which preoccupied Leonardo and Galileo, would have had no meaning in a Greek context. On the other hand, they were extremely knowledgeable in expressing—through image or thought—the forms of the societal, free or unfree movement that fell under the concept of *struggle*.

The drama, the historical consciousness in various guises and the magnificent friezes all express this. Struggle, both as an internal and an external factor, determines the *raison d'être* of Greek freedom: in the external sense as the glorious and proud struggle of the Greeks for their freedom; in the internal sense so that, as Hegel puts it, the self-consciousness of freedom, its very psychological formula, is a confirmation that it has exposed itself to the struggle of life and death and passed the test.[107]

The conditions of this *agonal*[xlviii] existence are manifested as a stylised cultural code especially in the many gable fields and friezes of the temples, which kept the Greeks constantly reminded of the struggle that had been and had to continue to be waged for the sake of freedom, independence and national pride. It is the particularly Ionian theme of gods vs. giants; Lapiths vs. Centaurs; Greeks vs. Amazons, and many others. In fact, not a single temple was built on the Greek mainland during the 5th century BC that did not depict at least one of the above themes.

[xlviii] Jacob Burckhardt wrote in his *Griechische Kulturgeschichte* about *the agonal man*; the type of individuality formed in competition, struggle and contests with one's neighbour. The word *agón* meaning "competition", "struggle" originates in the word *agora* (square, marketplace) and covers the four aspects of competition that acquired their form in the sporting competitions (the Olympic Games), in trade, in the struggle for political favour (democracy) and in the philosophical discussion (dialectics).

And on the state of Athens' special talisman, the colossal sculpture depicting *Athena Parthenos* commissioned by Pericles to Phidias in the middle of the 5th century, which was to crown the magnificent renovation of the Acropolis, all three motifs were engraved and carved.[108] In this symbolic form, the heroic conditions of the city's creation and freedom were ever-present, in image, in thought and in ritual.

In addition, the Athenians had the stories in living memory (that was constantly being added to) of how they themselves, to ensure their own freedom, enslaved other peoples. Thus, they knew what an unfavourable fate might have in store.

The agonal theme is almost completely absent from medieval art, because the agonal feeling lacked a real meaning at that time, since submission was enforced unambiguously. The exception is of course, the struggle of man against Sin, often symbolised as Nature; as a snake or a dragon. The most famous motif of struggle is probably St George and the dragon.

Gold Ground

The rapprochement between spirit and matter, between body and soul, or tangibly, between master and slave, begun by the Stoics and further accentuated in Christianity, has an interesting outcome also in the pictorial representation. The totally separate levels of *idea* and *reality* in Plato's metaphysics are united in the further epistemological development, which is why it also eventually becomes possible to give an, albeit very vague, picture of a unified nature.

The Neoplatonist Plotinus, during the time of the imperial cult of the 3rd century, worked in the spirit of Plato but actually achieved something completely different than his master. Unlike his paragon, Plotinus gives the highest general category a name and an anthropomorphic connotation. He calls this highest entity *the One*. According to Plotinus, the One is Supreme and "necessity, law, to all". The Supreme, as the highest, has all other things as slaves. It is 'above all and is—it alone—veritably free, subject not even to its own law.'[xlix]

[xlix] *The Enneads* VI. 8.9-21. Or rather one should perhaps say that Plotinus only unilaterally revives the anthropomorphic god found in *Timaeus*, without affirming the contradictions and aporias present in Plato. The dialectics which are the essence of democracy and the engine that drives Plato are thus lost. For Plotinus' ontology is undeniably an ontology for subjects. The simultaneous genuflection before an actual Sun King (Gallienus) and before an imaginary one is no accident.

From the One, like the rays of the sun, the various levels of existence emanate down to the most insignificant parts of matter, which, however, are held together by or contained in the One, albeit at the very lowest level. Because of these markings, *spirit* and *nature* are not absolutely separated as they are with the Master, instead they are linked within the framework of Plotinus' consistent monism of the distinct levels; the hypostases.

This also has implications for Plotinus' aesthetics. Plato did not want to see art as an adequate expression of *beauty* and 'condemned it [painting] already in its modest beginnings because it distorted 'the true proportions' of things, and replaced reality and the *nomos* (law) with subjective appearance and arbitrariness.'[109] In Plotinus, however, the connection between the highest and the lowest is open, therefore beautiful objects can arise insofar as they possess 'a communion with that which emanates from the gods.'[1]

Beauty is the *logos* emanating from the Highest which takes possession of the corporeal. 'How can the earthly be as beautiful as the heavenly? It happens thereby, we learn, through participation in the form. For everything formless must assume a definite form or shape. As long as it has not received a sensible form it is ugly and excluded from the divine power of form; it is the generally ugly; but ugly is also that which is not wholly empowered by form and concept.'[110]

The bridge between the highest and the lowest, between the spiritual and the material, is even more clearly expressed in Augustine, and not only in his aesthetic view (the most beautiful and the ugliest) but also in his ethical programme (the master and the slave). According to Augustine, it is true that essential beauty is found only in God, but on the other hand there is no object in nature that would not have *at least some traces* (*vestigia*) of beauty. Thus, Augustine also transcends the dichotomy between spirit and matter and relativises the categories of knowledge, just as he in his ethical programme with the same argument condemns the dehumanisation of the slave.

Every individual is a part of humanity, Augustine says, because in every human being there are traces of God. The difference between spirit and matter,

---

[1] *The Enneads* I.6.3. Here, by the way, one can also discern how the concept of the theological has been conceived in symmetry with other categories (it could hardly be otherwise). In the same way as the master was out of touch with things, Aristotle's god has no contact with the actual, physical and empirical world. Aristotle's god is his own end and thinks only of himself. (Metaphysics 1074b) Plotinus' god on the other hand, is a working, formative actor, a causa efficiens.

between the master and the slave, between the Roman and the barbarian is no longer a distinction of type but a difference of degree—just as in Plotinus.

From Plotinus' theory of emanation and light-mysticism, the step to the icon and to gold ground painting is not a long one. A schematic figure may again serve as the starting point for how I aim to present the manner in which gold ground painting interprets and represents the higher realities. Placed on an axis, this figure would logically as well as historically be located in the middle between the idea perspective and the central perspective.

From the former, one derives the *oblique* manner in which the archetypes—the Holy Family or the saints—appear in pictorial form (e.g., that the sacred power of the originals is also projected into the image); from the latter, the integration of the space of the image with that of the (spiritual) space of reality. The properties of the image space are made present in actual space, which usually is a church. The icon allows the same spiritual nature to permeate both the image space and the space of the viewer.

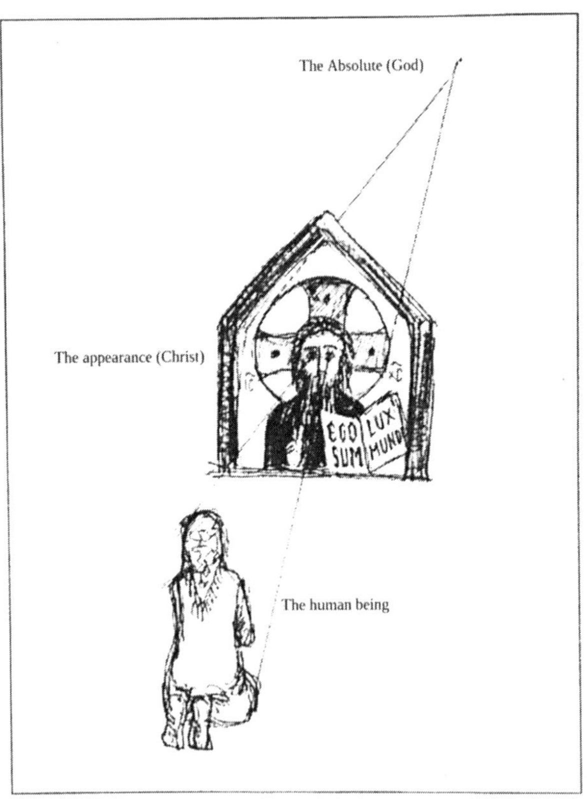

Here, as in the Greek image, the projection is directed from the ethereal sphere towards the plane where the images take shape. But now all parts of existence are incorporated in or subordinated to the highest governing principle, the One. In the Christian interpretation of existence, where the One is replaced by God, the same relationship applies: the highest entity—God—is the substratum which the other elements of existence are permeated by and are contained in.

Since the divine entity meets all the requirements of ideality, such as goodness, eternity and immutability, it can also be given an image. *The image* of the highest entity is made out of gold, that is, that which is the highest in real nature; the material substratum which best satisfies the requirements of eternity and immutability.

If we study the image above from the viewer's point of view (who, in accordance with the psychology of the *ofthalmos*-relation rather is the *observed*) another interesting thing happens. For unlike the Greek image, which, as it were, splits space into two essentially separate parts, the iconic image conveys a continuity; a flow of the same nature from the most distant idea—from God— via the icon out to the observer, the human being.

In this, then, the icon resembles the images that are subject to the conventions of central perspective, but the "flow" or the "relation of power" has a reverse direction and does not express that man has power over external things but, on the contrary, that man is subject to his Lord.

The similarity of the nature reflected in the original image and that which the viewer experiences in the space of the image is given by the fact that the image or the icon is sacred and that the experience of it is of a spiritual nature. Or one could say that the image has been delegated a *power* from above that also affects the viewer. Worshipping the icon is worshipping God. What one utters to the image is supposed to be perceived by its original, etc.

The space of the image and of existence has been synthesised into a communicating spiritual unity within which power and spiritual appeals are transmitted. Seen from the side, so to speak, the theological and psychological content of the image could be stretched out in the following way:

Eternity	manifestation	space
gold	image	the observer
God	The Son	the human being

The image of the gold ground assembles a hierarchical order between (at least) two ontological planes: the father and the son, the upper and the lower, and in the direction implied by the *ofthalmos*-figure: outwards from within. The Golden plane, the plane of God, is the infinitely distant one, against whose background the son, the mother of God, the apostles and sometimes also the Church Fathers emanate and take shape and form in their greatness, and from which revival, knowledge, love and the promise of salvation flow out to the observer, to the sinful and seen man.[li]

One can perhaps not move further than Byzantine art, laden as it is with mosaics and icons, towards anti-naturalism, and yet, I would argue that even though these paintings and mosaics have nothing to do with the depiction of nature in our sense, a historical constant is that art always produces images of the nature of *the essential*—that which is essential in its time; the really real.

Thus, the icon says something about the primary conditions of existence; it presents an (indirect) image of the nature of God, and thus the icon also tells us about man's perception of existence and about the limits of interpretation of said existence. Within the framework of depicting the sacred mystery, it would, however, be strange to include real *nature* in our sense, defiled as it is by the qualities of evil.

[li] It is in no way surprising that the ecclesiastical hierarchy repeats the heavenly; that a structural correspondence is established between them, as Pseudo-Dionysius already assumes in *Peri tes ouranias Ierarchias, peri tes ecclesiastikes Ierarchias*, On the Heavenly and Ecclesiastical Hierarchy; (see Cassirer 1927, p.9) and that the same pyramidal structure is transferred to the space of the image. As we can see the *image* of existence, as a fusion of Hellenic and Christian, is now also demonstratively pictorially hierarchical. Ernst Cassirer calls the worldview that emerged from the synthesis of Neoplatonic and Christian thinking *Stufenkosmos*. "The most important bequest of this speculation (especially of Neo-Platonism) to Christianity was the concept and the general picture of a graduated cosmos. The world separates itself into a lower and a higher, into a sensible and an intelligible world. Not only do these worlds stand opposed to each other; their essences, in fact, consist precisely in their mutual negation, in their polar antithesis. But across this abyss of negation a spiritual bond extends between the two worlds. From one pole to the other, from the super-being and super-one, the domain of absolute form, reaching down to matter as the absolute-formless, there is an unbroken path of mediation. The infinite passes over to the finite on this path and the finite returns on it back to the infinite. The whole process of redemption is included in it: it is the Incarnation of God, just as it is the deification of man. In this conception, there is always a "between" to be bridged; there is always a separating medium that cannot be jumped over but must be traversed step by step in strictly ordered succession." (Cassirer: 2010, p.9)

The Central Perspective and the Infinitely Distant Horizon

With the central perspective as the principle for visualisation, man is placed at the centre. In doing so, the order of the world is reversed in a way that is entirely analogous to the way in which the psychological self-image and the categories of knowledge have been renewed. The world no longer appears from the perspective of ideas or eternity, as in the Greek or medieval conceptions of existence, but on the contrary: the human eye becomes the point of reference for both knowing and depicting seeing. Thus Protagoras is finally vindicated, triumphing over Plato: *man* has become the measure of all things, with all that this means.

The central perspective seems to presuppose the fulfilment of three conditions—conditions which, incidentally, are not independent of each other: 1: That a reciprocal individualism is established; that is, that I am equal to you, that my perspective is equal to yours so that we can accept each other's view of the world. 2: A nominalistic ontology, which is perhaps the same as Panofsky's demands for "a substantial world". 3: A continuous conception of knowledge and of space with an infinite horizon of knowledge. Of these conditions, 1 and 2 have already been dealt with to some extent.

There remains, then, the spatial and epistemological continuity, the one that claims that the same qualitative conditions must apply from here to eternity, ruling out the existence of any absolute "outside", or the division of everything into an "elementary" and a "stellar" world, as Aristotle assumed.

Panofsky is probably correct in his notion that space was unified into a continuum for the first time in Christian Neoplatonic mysticism. Panofsky justifies this notion through the manner in which the metaphysics of Neoplatonism conceived light as a homogeneous fluid. The next step towards a geometrically uniform, continuously representable world was, to follow Panofsky once more, the establishment of a "substantial and measurable world". The medieval spatial understanding still depended on the ethical notions of good and evil; topologically speaking the "world" was not uniform but split into qualitatively distinct places and directions. Sacred places were not comparable to "secular" or "devilish" places; the space above the moon was of a different nature than that below the moon; the direction "up" and the direction "down" had morally different connotations, etc. To overcome the disparate perception of places and directions in the world, it must first be de-qualified, i.e., *quantified*.[lii]

In this process, even if it is a conceptual process, one cannot ignore the *actual* quantification of things, of time and of space that both preceded and was simultaneously intensified at the same time as the new conception of space took hold. As an example of how the practical time-space conception got a numerical character, one can look at how the distance between two places took on a numerical value, as geographical distances due to the increase in long-distance trade became the subject of extensive calculations which could be expressed in terms of money.

The various entities inducted into the numerical included transport costs and, especially, risk calculations with accompanying insurance costs or profit expectations, i.e., as the price difference in the value of the goods shipped at the two locations. Space became money. That time also was quantified can be seen as a consequence of the fact that work carried out in the sectors where social renewal took place was wage labour—as opposed to serfdom, slavery and other forms of forced labour. Time became money.

The mechanical clock made sure that every hour of the day was of the same length. It is interesting to note that the first measure of rationalisation in *our* sense of the word that I am aware of, is when Brunelleschi, the dome constructor in Florence and the prime theorist of the mathematical-geometric central perspective, had a canteen installed at the top of the dome, so as not to waste so much time with workers climbing up and down the sloping ladders to eat and relieve themselves.

As an inversion of the divine perspective *sub specie aeternitatis* with the all-seeing eye at an inaccessible distance, the central perspective as a construction is a consequent spontaneous reaction to the contemporary inversion of the categories of understanding and the growing importance of the self as bearer of knowledge and as *subject*. That existence could be visually presented from a fixed and personal point of view or that scientists like Albertus Magnus and Roger Bacon could speak of *their* science[111], *their theoretical perspective*, is thus part of the same profound transformation.

[lii] A.J. Gurevich: *Categories of Medieval Culture,* 1985 p. 89, writes that the Middle Ages on the whole lacked a conception of space. For *spatium* meant "extent, interval", while *locus* meant "the place occupied by a particular object". According to Gurevich the abstraction *space* first arose in Gassendian and Newtonian metaphysics.

The enormous field scientists henceforth came to focus their attention on was the nature of the actual, from the eye to the edge of sight; from here to infinity.

The Greeks had discussed the possibility of infinity, and if you go back to the pre-Socratic, very much commercially inspired philosophy, before economic "liberalism" and unfettered commercial capitalism had been forcibly redeemed by Solon and turned into a socially subordinate activity, one finds that infinity—*to apeiron*—in Anaximander even appeared as a basic philosophical principle. Aristotle, on the other hand, dismissed an actual infinity (*energeiai apeiron*) because the concept was incompatible with the teleology in his thought.

But his position also had very clear political and economic reasons: the idea of infinity in the form of the principle of infinite increase derives, according to Aristotle, from commodity trade (*chrematistike*), whereas power has a limit because power has both an objective and an end. Similarly, economic activity that is subordinated to power—*ktetikes* or 'the art of acquiring property'—has an end, says Aristotle, because it gives rise to the kind of wealth that is a 'supply of those goods, capable of accumulation, which are necessary for life and useful for the community of city or household.'[112]

Commodity trade, however, has no end; it aims only at unlimited growth, and is therefore evil.

Between commodity trade and the management of wealth, the same contradiction exists as between an ontology based on infinity and one based on finiteness, and since their behaviour in history coincides with commercially expansive and restrictive periods, it is not too bold a claim to state that the actual (commercial) interests have in this form given rise to the theoretical positions. Aristotle's rejection of both the process of commercial infinity and the infinite horizon of knowledge is thus unambiguously related.

This has also been noted by Austin & Vidal-Naquet: 'By definition, Greek science has as its object what is finite, and the infinite is very precisely what cannot be an object of science. Now the 'art of acquisition' (*chrematistike*) in the second sense which Aristotle gives to this word, is concerned precisely with the infinite, and therefore belongs to non-science.'[113] Plutarch also makes a connection between the accumulation of money and the principle of infinity and claims that it was greed that destroyed the venerable political institutions of Sparta.[114]

And it is equally unequivocal, as we shall see, that Nicolaus Cusanus in his method of understanding, united the two elements which Aristotle expressly condemned; the tendency of the commercial process to grow infinitely *per additamenta* and the infinite horizon of knowledge. Ways of life, social expectations and the foundations of knowledge go hand in hand, always have, and still do.

Nicolaus Cusanus

In its chronological simultaneity, the link between the practical quantification of the world of things that trade gave rise to and the theoretical quantification of existence that science carried out, is very, very strong. During the first phase of logification, this tendency is evident in the Ionian natural philosophers and in Pythagoras. The late Middle Ages repeated the Ionian phase with some significant differences. The merchant Leonardo Pisano, better known among mathematicians as Fibonacci, noted in the early 13th century that 'money contains sums and sums create mental habits.'[115]

An even clearer intellectualisation of the commercial process is found in Nicolaus Cusanus.[116] A pervading insight of his is that 'Wisdom cries out in the streets,' i.e., that wisdom is found in those who trade in the streets and the squares; in the practical men who speculate and take calculated risks.[liii] Already in the first pages of the central work *De docta ignorantia,* he puts forward a theory of knowledge, which assumes that an *explanation* involves the comparison of quantities, i.e., that knowledge is attained by means of a comparative method of the kind that *valuation* implies: weighing, measurement, estimation of value.

'In every enquiry, men judge of the uncertain by comparing it with an object presupposed certain, and their judgement is always approximative; every enquiry is, therefore, comparative and uses the method of analogy.'[117]

And Nicolaus continues in the following Pythagorean manner, 'Every enquiry, therefore, consists in a relation of comparison that is easy or difficult to draw; for this reason, the infinite as infinite is unknown, since it is away and above all comparison. Now, while proportion expresses an agreement in some

---

[liii] One can compare here with Descartes who reproached the scholastic philosophers for not daring to take risks, who did not dare put their personal, spiritual venture capital at risk. "For it seemed to me that I could discover much more truth in the reasonings that each person makes concerning matters that are important to him, whose outcome ought to cost him dearly later on if he has judged incorrectly, than in those reasonings that a man of letters makes in his private room, which touch on speculations producing no effect." *Discourse on Method*, A&T ed. p.10, transl. Donald A. Cress

one thing, it expresses at the same time a distinction, so that it cannot be understood without number. Number, in consequence, includes all things that are capable of comparison.'

'It is not then in quantity only that number produces proportion; it produces it in all things that are capable of agreement and difference in any way at all, whether substantially or accidentally. That is why Pythagoras was so insistent on maintaining that in virtue of numbers all things were understood.'[118]

We see that Cusanus explicitly refers to Pythagoras, but we can also see that he noted that the symmetry that exists and should exist between ontology and epistemology is already established in Pythagoras and compelled him to interpret the world as a *valuable* space in accordance with the practical interests central to a merchant's worldview.

In Nicolaus' dialogue, *Idiota de sapientia (The layman on wisdom and the mind)*, the Layman (*Idiota*) has the book-learned *Orator* to take a careful look at what is happening in the square and to describe what is happening there—and then lifts his gaze to the sky so as to transfer the interactions of the marketplace to "higher" phenomena. The analogy is unambiguous: the interactions of the marketplace are to be the model for the interpretation of all of existence; the theoretical gaze—originating in the commercial procedure—is to cut through the sublunary and the stellar spaces with a similarly sharp precision.

Layman: Since I told you that wisdom proclaims [itself] in the streets, and since its proclamation is that it dwells in the highest places, I will endeavour to get you to see this point. But first, I would like for you to say what you see being done there in the Forum.

Orator: I see money being counted there; and in another spot I see goods being weighed; and in an opposite spot, I see oil and other items being measured out.

Layman: These are the works of that power-of-reason by which men excel the beasts. For brute animals cannot number, weigh, and measure. Look, now, O Orator, and see by means of what, in reference to what, and from what these [activities] are done, and tell me [what you find].

Orator: [They are done] by means of discriminating. Layman: Correct.[119]

The functions of the square or rather the market are thus carried out according to a quantitative yardstick that consists of counting, measuring and weighing. In his analysis of the dialogue on wisdom, Johannes Sløk says that measurement; 'to measure something—*mensurare*—is the actual function of the consciousness, the *mens* (Cusanus also implies that there is an etymological connection between the two words, which, as we know, there is not). It would be perfectly reasonable to relate this basic idea to Renaissance thought, and in particular to Galileo's definition of the quantifying measuring function as being the scientific method in itself.'[120]

Knowledge, then, for Nicolaus Cusanus, is based on comparison (*comparatio*): just as the merchant finds out about a commodity's weight by comparing it with standard weights and its value by comparing it with standard values (nominal coinage), science gains its knowledge by employing comparisons. Science thus finds the interrelationships of things, or can determine the degree of correspondence (*convenientia*) between one thing and another. Here one comes to think of Heraclitus—who also lived in a dynamic time of commercial expansion—and his gold-for-commodities analogy.[liv]

Because the conditions in the early Greek and the northern Italian trading cities in the late Middle Ages were in many ways similar, latter philosophy did not need to *invent* the abstract invariants that used the coin as model (since this had already been done), but could adopt them. Hence the interest in Pythagorean—and later also in Democritic—metaphysics, but also in Plato.

But even if Plato also mentions measurement as a method of obtaining knowledge, the difference between Plato's and Nicolaus Cusanus' method of measurement is enormous and actually contains a completely opposite aspiration: In Plato, the function of measurement was always *normative*; in Nicolaus, it was always comparative. By an exact science, Plato meant a science that determined the measure of things in relation to an absolute value. Even relative concepts such as "more" or "less" were not acceptable to Plato in their relativity, because he did not accept actual *relations* as the basis of concepts.

Plato absurdly demanded an absolute concept of "more"—the idea of "moreness". And therefore, infinity as a notion could not be included as an element in any meaningful form of knowledge. Infinity, which is "moreness" as an actual principle, was for Plato, like nature, something that could not be affixed to any concept, it was *alogos*, unreasonable, and therefore belonged to the repulsive sphere of the irrational.

With Nicolaus, it is the other way around: the starting point is arbitrary, knowledge is *relative*, man is the one who postulates all measures. Nicolaus

---

[liv] Heraclitus: All things are an exchange for Fire, and Fire for all things, even as wares for gold and gold for wares. frgm. 22

Cusanus is, at his most consistent, in the endeavour to mathematicise and quantitatively determine the conditions of existence in his *Idiota de staticis experimentis* (*On Experiments Done with Weight-Scales*).[lv] Here he gives the impression that there is hardly anything in nature one could not determine by means of the weight-scales. Mass, time as well as space can be represented by a numerical value in Nicolaus' method—but also all sorts of other things.

For example, the aspect of the phenomenon of *motion* defined as velocity, he examines in what we would today call s-t-coordinates. The motion is a boat's journey through water, the distance s is the length of the boat and the time t the time it takes for the boat to pass an object thrown from the bow (i.e., the principle of the log). The scales are needed to measure the amount of sand (or water) that has passed through the hourglass during the passage—thus obtaining a measure of time! Besides "natural" time (the time between sunrise and sunset), Nicolaus also makes use of a form of abstract time.

Aristotle never achieved an equally advanced understanding of motion, but it should be added that he was never looking for it either; mechanical or *local* motion isolated as such had no meaning for him. In this respect, Nicolaus only has one predecessor in history, and that is Pythagoras. Both lived at a time when the monetary economy was young, both united unashamedly (the hallmark of transition!) what we consider "mysticism" and what we regard as "rationality" into a peculiar mixture, and both generalised as a cosmological principle the *ratio* found in bookkeeping, logistics, and commerce far beyond what we today consider "rational".

Nicolaus was well aware of this affinity: 'Pythagoras, noting that no knowledge of anything can be had except through distinguishing, philosophised by means of number. I do not think that anyone else has attained a more reasonable mode of philosophising.'[lvi]

[lv] Jaspers does not care much for Nicolaus dilettantish scientific experiments; their fame rest on false foundations, he claims (*Nikolaus Cusanus,* 1964 p. 61). I do not know. How much light can one expect a single light to spread in an otherwise compact darkness? Nicolaus's odd little text about measurement of mass, time and space is interesting, not because it is a precursor to Galileo's physics, but because it shows that there existed a pressure to numerically scrutinise the existence that the economic revolution had given rise to. Without any knowledge of its utility, a useful social principle was transformed into an ontological one. The meaningfulness was given by the fact that the method possessed a potent social meaning, while the true dividends came much later.

[lvi] Except myself, he might have said. He nevertheless adds Plato just in case. "Because Plato imitated this mode, he is rightly held to be great."(*De ludo globi,* II.109 Transl. Jasper Hopkins). However, Plato's philosophy is something quite different, and at its

Nicolaus Cusanus' relativistic view of how knowledge is formed is already built into the premise—measurement—for which we just saw the model. Nicolaus himself realised that the starting point for measurement is conventional and thus, in a sense, arbitrary. Faced with the threat of this methodological indifference, Nicolaus argues that reaching the "unit"—the unit of value, the kilogram, the litre, the metre, the second, etc. happens on its own accord, because of the inner (false!) connection between *mens* and *mensura*; because consciousness and measure are essentially the same thing. In this way, the *constructed* once again becomes the *natural*.

So, even though Nicolaus recognises that the derivation of the scientific method he presents inevitably causes it to relapse into conventionality and voluntariness, he still claims that it is rational and universal. Thus, from the very first moment of the new science, a contradiction makes itself known, between individual and general knowledge, between will and reason, which in the course of history was to be papered over in various ways—for example, as Descartes' "God" or Leibniz's "pre-established harmony"—and which would eventually dissolve its "natural" validity.

It is also precisely in this field of tension between *individuality* and *rationality* that a new, individual-based approach and a new perspective on seeing and conceptualising is laid upon the world. The central perspective *is* this field: the individual point of view against the infinitely distant horizon.

Henri Poincaré, with whom we will have occasion to become more deeply acquainted later, at a time when naturalism and the central perspective are already well on their way *out* of history, and when Euclid's geometry is only one of an infinite number of *possible* geometries, elegantly dissolves Nicolaus' dilemma by quite bluntly claiming that 'It is not nature which imposes [time and space] upon us, it is we who impose them upon nature because we find them convenient.'[121]

---

core it has nothing in common with that of Nicolaus.

5. The Instrumental Perspective

The way the Greeks represented their environment as disjointed entities, both in visual and theoretical representation, was already partly blurred in the Neoplatonist conception and more or less disappeared in the Christian, unified way of perceiving nature. This was not because there was any compelling spiritual necessity within the Jewish tradition to perceive nature in this way, for every flow of thought is formed in dialogue with the practical possibilities or difficulties that are present at the moment when it asserts itself.

'Truth is the daughter of time, not of authority,' as Francis Bacon said. And after all, man is such a clever animal that he is able to invent rational reasons for everything he wants to do (Benjamin Franklin).

The compelling reality facing late antiquity was that slave production could *no longer* be generalised. Neither *intensively*—through a more efficient exploitation of slaves, nor *extensively*—through larger numbers of slaves. The classical form of reason had reached its limit. The solution to this dilemma was the dismantling of the values of mastery in a true postmodern fashion, and that a new approach formed around the ability to be subservient, to be a servant, to work, to actually shape things, eventually took its place.

The changed circumstances changed the interest of knowledge. Nominalism had directed attention to that which is the object of the intervention of the hands, not of the thought; to actual things. The aim of science now becomes, as Francis Bacon later put it, 'to rule nature through one's actions.' And that nature is no longer the same as it was before.

The nature, on which nominalism focussed its interest, was the nature that made itself known through its *accidents*, its sensual or actual manifestations, and not, as in Aristotelian physics, through its conceptual *substances*. But at that stage, another problem appeared, which perhaps may be expressed in this manner: The new relation of nature that was being established as part of the nominalist critique of ancient philosophy, focussed its attention on the *surface* of nature without yet possessing a new concept of an underlying nature.

It was still the scholastic nature, composed of Aristotelian and Neoplatonic elements, and when considered a cosmological-ontological construct, it was an anthropomorphically interpreted totality. It was an *organism* permeated by an intellectual spirit or *soul* that wielded *power* over everything. The contradiction encountered by the first concretisation of a new relation to nature could therefore be said to be a contradiction between form and content. On one hand, an operative, experimental principle of interpretation was established on a *material* nature.

On the other hand, this principle was applied to a nature that was essentially infused and guided by *spirit* or *soul*. The interest of knowledge was thus redirected from what had previously been the conceptual nature of things (the *substances)* towards the *accidents* or the things-in-themselves. But before a corresponding, *material* concept of substance had crystallised, the search for a new nature was indeed like *alchemy*; a practice without theory; a purposeless experimentation without an overarching meaning.[lvii]

During some periods in human spiritual history, one can discern how man, in raptures about his new intellectual tools, uses them in a way that tells us a lot about how scientific thought patterns are formed. One such period is that which saw the birth of Pythagorean philosophy. The success of trade created a justifiable confidence in that counting things was profitable and led to success; such as assigning things a numerical value; comparing quantities with each other when expressed in quantitative measures such as weight, quantity or value.

Pythagoras caught this general commercial spirit and transferred a socially successful order called *kosmos* to the totality of everything (also called *kosmos*), by famously asserting that "*everything* is number". It is interesting, however, that Pythagoras (or his disciples) not only applied his mathematical formalism to conditions that *we* perceive as legitimate and useful, such as geometry or musical harmony, but also tried to determine the numerical values of justice, the soul, thought, etc.

[lvii] The word "substance" is difficult and interesting because it has undergone a similar transformation, in the same way and for the same reasons as the word "subject". After having had mainly an abstract, idea-based rendition in Aristotle, the concept of substance is mainly associated today with the materially enduring.

This was something which already Aristotle was surprised by, but which the Pythagoreans apparently found to be quite in order, because the project had been at least *partly* successful.[122]

Alchemy

A similar extension of socially valid principles into the domains of thought is found in the late Middle Ages. On one hand, we have a direct parallel to the Pythagorean epoch in the commercial boom and its influence on, as we have seen, for example, the thinking of Nicolaus Cusanus. But unlike what happened in antiquity, the concrete *form of work* would now also have a decisive influence on the shape of both thinking and of general values. The knowledge derived from handwork never had a deeper influence on Greek thinking because it was associated with slavish, unfree values.

But now slavery as a successful form of production had already been tested, overcome and reconciled with history.

By the 13th century, the arts and crafts had assumed such a role in the transformation of society that the success of cities now rested largely on success of their craftsmen—as mentioned, one had to be a member of a guild to be considered a citizen of the city of Florence. The art of transforming and refining matter had proved its practical, social usefulness. Since success is contagious, the craftsman's process was also taken as a model for scientific activity.

The result could have been an experimental science in our sense right from the start, had it not been for the fact that the *nature* of the experimental interest was different. The nature available to the experimenters was given by classical and Christian concepts. It was a nature filled of angels and demons, of good and evil spirits, and ultimately ruled by an all-encompassing world soul.

The nominalists had moved the objects towards the core and thus made them accessible to experiment and work, but a context of meaning between objects that could harmonise with experimental work and with the mechanical-technical craft practice was still lacking.

We call those enthusiasts who, without "knowing" what they were doing (due to a lack of a coherent interpretive strategy) were engaged in this kind of research somewhat disparagingly, *alchemists*. But then, we should remember that the *method* is indeed correctly derived from a successful social activity. Alchemy was perceived by its practitioners as a *scientia de transformatione metallorum*; and as a productive and useful "science".[123] The "irrational" element of alchemy is due to the fact that the nature it was supposed to manipulate was still spiritual and animate.

The reality the alchemists had access to had not yet been redefined according to the successful concepts of manufactories, mills and workshops. It would still take quite some time. Even Leonardo da Vinci, who had grasped the principles of technical-instrumental science more clearly than most, and saw man as a set of muscular forces and levers, perceived the earth as an organism. As did Giordano Bruno.[lviii] It is actually possible to determine quite precisely when nature acquired its modern mechanical character.

Sometime between 1596 and 1631, i.e., between the first and second editions of *Mysterium Cosmographicum*, Kepler in fact abandoned his notion of nature as a *divina animalis* (a divinely animated being) and gave her instead a mechanistic interpretation as an *instar horologii* (as clockwork). At the same time, he gave the central cosmological concept the character of work: The expression of the heavenly *anima* (soul) was changed in the 1631 edition to *vis* (force).

In his 1609 treatise on the planet Mars, Kepler writes that the true causes (*verae causae*) are physical causes. Theoretically, the god who previously had listened to the prayers of Man no longer had a place among the celestial spheres, but had been transformed into a steel spring, into force or pure energy. Such, then, was the nature available to Galileo (although he was not *allowed* to use this interpretation), and thus the conditions for him were quite different. Now the form and the content of the research corresponded perfectly.

Alchemical "research" is thus, like the Pythagorean mathematisation of the world, an example of what happens to thought when new social practices have been successful but have not yet succeeded in harmonising theory and practice into a unified ideology. The new *operational* relation to nature which in the investigative practices gave rise to a primitive and disoriented experimental *practice* (e.g., Roger Bacon) lacked an adequate mechanistic *theory* that would have united action and result into a functional unity.

Alchemical experimentation used a mechanistic-manipulative concept alchemy is more *production* than verification—but superimposed it on an essentially *spiritual* nature. Indeed, the ecclesiastical tradition still required

---

[lviii] However, Bruno is vacillating on this point: for example, he says that "nature is nothing but the force which is implanted in things and the laws in accordance with which they accomplish their processes". (*De immenso* lib. VIII chap. IX)

unaconcezione miracolistica della natura—a "miraculous" conception of nature (Gregory)—and a spiritually and organically interpreted ontology in order for *its* doctrines of the different levels of existence to harmonise with each other.

An example: the Eucharistic problem of transubstantiation was a first-order question for scholastic ontology.[lix] At the priest's *command*, the bread and wine would actually become the flesh and blood of Jesus. For this to happen, it was not necessary to have a belief in the "naturalness" of miracles, but rather an epistemology of conceptual realism.

The mystery of transubstantiation, although a scholastic phenomenon and an outgrowth of the conceptual realist strain, and so obscure in nature that it could only flourish in the medieval gloom, is perhaps the most striking concrete example of how what I have called command philosophy interprets existence. What happens when the priest commands the bread to become flesh is the following:

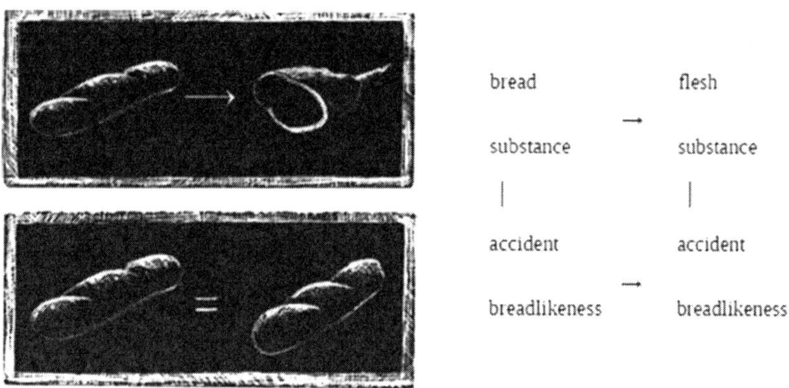

At the priest's command: *Hoc est corpus meum*, the bread substantially becomes *de facto* flesh, since the substantial is conceptual and superior to the accidental. That the bread *apparently* is unchanged is of no consequence, since, according to the consensus of Greek opinion, our minds are unreliable as a criterion of truth or verification and therefore cannot make judgements on matters concerning the substances. The accident, the breadlikeness, thus persists,

---

[lix] Galileo suffered from this dogma as late as the 17th century. The trials against him were mainly about
the atomistic theory of matter (which Galileo advocated and which would have overturned the dogma of transubstantiation) and not the heliocentric worldview. See Pietro Redondi: *Galileo eretico,* 1987.

but this is not essential, since the concept of breadlikeness is now a different one, that is, flesh.

Such was the Greek-Scholastic reality. Arabic science, on the other hand, which did not have to bear the whole burden of classical education, could, as *al-kimia*, capture the activities that had recognised the usefulness of an operative view of nature directed towards the accidents of existence that could be instrumentally processed and manipulated, but not yet commanded.

Unified Space

Although, the leading philosophers of antiquity rejected perspective foreshortening as a correct means of transposing a three-dimensional space onto a surface, the method was used to create *illusions* in the theatre—and remember that it is precisely the illusory that Plato condemns. Vitruvius claims in his *Scenografia* that a linear perspective was used in one way or another in the scenography of Aeschylus' dramas. In a probably quite correct way—although the central vanishing point was probably unknown—vanishing lines and other auxiliary constructions were used as scenographic tools to create the illusion of depth in *architectonic* backdrops.

And Lucretius had noticed that actual buildings as a pictorial scene have a vanishing point in the distance: 'Although, a portico is of equal width, and rests on columns of equal height throughout, still when we look from the end down its whole length, top, sides, and bottom shrink to a tapering cone; top joins with bottom and right side all with left, till they contract to a conical vanishing point.'[124]

When Aristotle models the concept of *cause*, he patterns his endeavour on man-made things. Similarly, both Vitruvius and Lucretius, in the context of the principles of imagery, speak only of *artefacts*; not, for example, of circular horizons or views of nature. In Hellenistic vase painting, one can find many examples of craftsmen who strove for a perspectivistic rendition of buildings—interestingly enough, a large part of these paintings depict theatre scenes—but not of nature. We can, therefore, conclude that, also in terms of seeing, antiquity did not "reach nature".

Then comes the thousand years of divine perspective, with man not as seer but as seen; not as subject but as *subjectum*. When Giotto again makes man the starting point and centre, the result is at first little more remarkable than, for example, the paintings we know from Pompeii and Herculaneum,[lx] except in one respect: spatial unity is now conveyed not only by architectural elements but also by "natural" ones.

But Giotto treated nature in the same way as the alchemists in his pictures, by feel, so to speak, according to certain rules of thumb and without an overall theory. Thus, he pictorially reproduced the *surface* of things, without knowing their internal, geometrically constructible relationships. This would be rectified about a hundred years later by Alberti and Brunelleschi.

Giotto and the Natural

We shall begin by considering a fresco that is part of the series of episodes from the life of St Francis that Giotto painted in the Upper Church of Assisi. The picture shows Francis giving away his cloak to a poor man—who later turns out to be Christ. The square image is divided by two diagonals into four triangular fields consisting of the "city" in the upper left corner, "heaven" in the centre, the "monastery" in the upper right corner and the living creatures in the foreground. We see that Giotto has placed Francis' face at the intersection of the diagonals, exactly between the secular city and the spiritual monastery.

The shapes of the landscape towering on the sides create a directional arrow of the blue of the sky that focuses attention on the centre of the picture, where an *istoria* (an epic or mythical act) in the classical sense is unfolding.

[lx] About the most famous suite of paintings of natural character, the so-called "Odysseus landscapes", Janson, for example, says that "Its unity is not structural but poetic." The reference against which the artist has played out the pictorial motif is not "nature" but "a story". The exception to this is "The Garden" from Livia's villa in Primaporta, which does not prevent Janson to say, as an overall assessment of the ancient conception of space, that "The absence of a consistent view of the visible world should be thought of, rather, as a fundamental barrier which differentiates Roman painting from that of the Renaissance or of modern times." H.W. Janson: *History of art* 1962: p. 187.

Giotto: St Francis Giving his Mantle to a Poor Man

The stylised landscape of Giotto's fresco represents something more than being merely background or filler, as usually is the case in ancient painting. Nor does it participate in the course of events for demonic reasons—as, for example, a stormy sea could be seen as an expression of Poseidon or of his will—but is there *in its own right*, in its own neutral pertinence, to mark the place of man in relation to the earthly and the heavenly, the secular and the spiritual.

For Giotto has placed Francis' eyes in the plane of the horizon, which at the same time marks that the viewer is on the same level as the saint, sees the same thing as the saint and in fact faces the same choices as the saint. 'The consequences of this choice of viewpoint are truly epoch-making; choice implies conscious awareness—in our case, awareness of a relationship in space between the beholder and the picture—and Giotto may well claim to be the first to have established such a relationship,' says Janson.[125]

The discovery that there is a spatial relationship between image and viewer—or rather between the depicted, the image and the viewer in a way that Dürer, for example, illustrated with his square pattern or which Alberti and Brunelleschi formalised geometrically—also marks the fact that nature is now on the same terms pictorially as the artefacts, incorporated into the sphere of possible phenomena with which man has a visually harmonious relation.

It is uncertain to what extent Giotto had become acquainted with antique painting before he himself appeared as a painter. Gosebruch mentions that he *may* have seen the mosaics in Santa Maria Maggiore (from the 5th century) and he *may* have known of the Virgilian illustrations of room interiors and perspective foreshortenings which are now preserved in the *Biblioteca Vaticana* as Cod. Lat. 3225.[126] It is not, in itself, decisive for the understanding of Giotto, since from the very beginning he surpasses ancient visual art in that; from the very beginning, he works with *overall views* whose different parts are related to each other in a way that is natural to us.

(And if the argument with the pictorial influence of antiquity would have any force, one must also ask why Cimabue did not innovate art. He had seen the same images, and a host of others besides.)

What little we know of Giotto's childhood and youth, at least, gives no indication of the assumption that he was instilled with any kind of literary learning and thus would have become acquainted with antiquity. His father was a simple craftsman, possibly a blacksmith. As a successful painter, Giotto seems to have been a practical and pious man.

He was also an enterprising businessman, a craftsman and unscrupulous creditor[127], all in one and the same person, who, precisely because of this, was able to embrace the progressive, energetic and active lifestyle of a new age without prejudice, and to give it a pictorial expression. So if the Renaissance in the visual arts had anything in common with antiquity, then Giotto was not a conduit, nor were the two other innovators of the visual language of that time: Masaccio and Leonardo.[lxi]

And if there is no link through them, we might as well stop searching and concentrate on that which is there. And that is the actual changes in the times in which they lived and themselves contributed to the reshaping of.

What is new about Giotto is not that he painted in perspective—spontaneously or according to certain rules of thumb so that each picture plane has an approximate vanishing point of its own. What is new is that he interpreted nature pictorially in much the same way as the alchemists explored it materially, i.e., "by feel", without an adequate *overarching theory* for what he did. What is new about Giotto is that he embraces nature on equal terms in the depiction, as a meaningful part of its *istoria*[lxii].

[lxi] Leonardo asks himself himself rhetorically: "Which is best, to draw from nature or from the antique?" (frgm. 486) He gives no answer but it is quite clear: the whole of his life's work is learning from nature.

[lxii] Etymologically, the word *istoria* also has to do with knowledge and exploration. Thus, the narrative in the image expresses the interest in knowledge in a visually logical form.

Nature, artefact, and man stand side by side, depicted according to the same principles. In this way, for the first time, nature, as an adequate framework for human activity, is made *visible*. If one wants to simplify the process, that led to the emergence of a new relation to nature in the way I have done above, by saying that the love that had been directed towards the Creator was generalised or rechannelled into a love directed towards creation, whereupon the knowledge interest that had been directed towards God could seamlessly be transferred towards nature (the expression "God's book" in reference to nature became common during this period), Giotto undeniably belongs to the first, "Franciscan" phase.

While Leonardo just as clearly belongs to a later, mechanistic-instrumental phase. Petrarch, as a nature poet, never made the leap to writing about his love of nature without first inscribing a saintly Laura into it. Neither did Giotto. He also placed himself between an earlier idealisation of God and a later idealisation of nature through the depiction of holy people and holy places as Tuscan vistas populated with ordinary Tuscan people.

In the promising zone between darkness and light, the Apollonian Eos emerges with rosy fingers in the form of a Giotto, a Petrarch, the moment before day breaks with its clear and revealing light. Petrarch understood his position, saying of himself: 'placed as I am at the boundary line between two countries and looking, at the same time, behind and ahead.'[128] Giotto could have said the same.

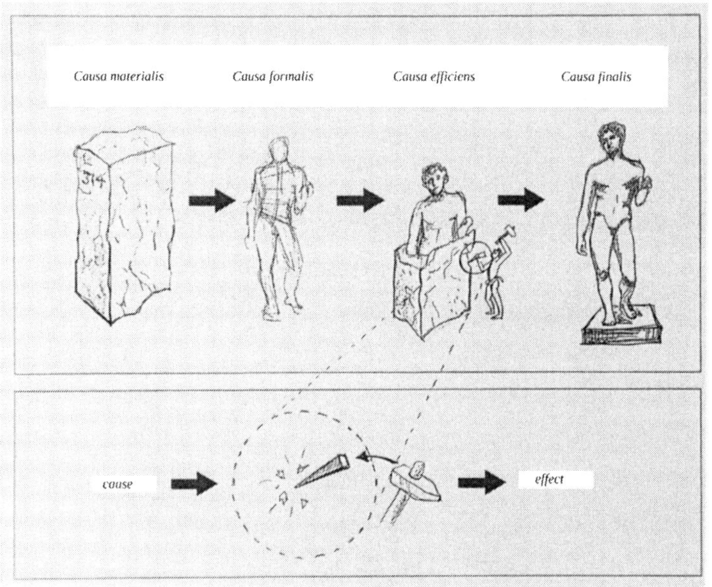

Aristotle's concept of causation vs. Francis Bacon's. Both are valid within a successful productive strategy; the former based on command, the latter on work processes.

Leonardo da Vinci

In a way not seen since pre-Socratic times, the means and forms of art and knowledge were conjoined during the Renaissance. The visual and the theoretical interpretation of the world strove towards the same goal, which now was a coherent, dynamic-functional representation of concrete, living reality. In the midst of this eruptive furnace of creative activity, of the rediscovered theoretical-practical interaction of the hand and the head in which the empirical has become the logical and the logical empirical, stands Leonardo da Vinci.

In his paintings, he completes and perfects the stylistic ideal of the Renaissance. An epoch, a static, earth-bound one, is about to end. A new age, with all the turbulence, dynamism and power of a new economy, a new method of production and a new way of thinking has begun. But in Leonardo's (and Raphael's) art, the static harmony and balance and serene repose of the old age reaches its pinnacle in a way never before or since surpassed.

But at the same time as, Leonardo, in his public career, with some few exceptions, carries out a type of painting oriented towards balance, harmony, serene gestures and facial expressions, that is to say, towards a statically perceived communicative intentionality, he fills his sketchbooks with disaster scenes, floods, torrential rain, drama, flash floods, panic-stricken warriors, screaming horses, victims desperately fighting for life in whirlpools and giant waves, cities collapsing in fire and dust. For Leonardo does not merely perfect, the static stylistic ideals of the past.

He also understood, better than anyone else, the techniques and instruments and restless spirit of progress that would eventually defeat them. And already in the next generation of artists, led by Michelangelo, the visual turbulence, action and drama would surge forth in full force.

What is bubbling beneath the austere surface of Leonardo's work is the knowledge that the world is a world that no longer has a goal, a purpose or a meaning. Of Aristotle's four-part model of causation, (figure) which for more than a millennium indicated the origin and source of existence, only one element remains, that which says that an effect has a mechanical, effective cause. Aristotelian teleology no longer applies to Leonardo. And it is something he has in common with his contemporary Niccolò Machiavelli.

Leonardo and Machiavelli

It has been common to perceive that the upsetting thing about Machiavelli is that his ideal ruler is totally devoid of morality. That he is not bothered and not allowed to be bothered by considerations of whether an action or deed is good or evil in itself. It is the effect, the impact of the action, that counts.

But it is precisely here that the courage of Machiavelli appears. The difference between, say, Plato and Machiavelli is exactly the same as between antiquity and the present: in his political visions Plato emphasises finality, the end goal, the *Republic*, and in this assessment, morality plays a part because it is the *good* republic that is desired.

Machiavelli, on the other hand, only sees the *means*, the *Prince*, that is, the state function's most efficient cause, its *causa efficiens*. Thus, Machiavelli applies the new way of thinking that has emerged from the change in the form of work that used to be a function of *dominating* (present in the ancient political economy) and now has been taken over by functions based on *processing*— which are the same as the content of the logical category *causa efficiens* (efficient cause) of Aristotle.

Machiavelli thus lays a new logical network over an old phenomenon, breaking up the teleological mode of consideration also for political thought, and thereby updating it to the level of contemporary natural philosophy, from which Aristotelian teleology was slowly but surely being eradicated.

Yet Machiavelli is the more ancient of the two Florentines, and Leonardo the more modern one. Machiavelli's ideal prince, Cesare Borgia, speculated using ancient figures as the model in medieval terms: friends, enemies and family ties; blackmail, deceit and murder; confiscation of territories and lands; useful alliances, strongholds and bastions. Cesare Borgia was a medieval politician with modern means and Machiavelli his prophet.

Leonardo da Vinci, on the other hand, was a modern technician who speculated on productive theory and had the future as his field of imagination. Machiavelli sought a workable formula for power. Leonardo a corresponding formula for force. But both are talking about the same thing: *potenza*. Machiavelli drew a picture of the technique of power—Leonardo of the power of technology. With which the Middle Ages were buried.

The Symmetry of Knowledge and Skill

In his person and in his activities, Leonardo unites the pinnacle of achievements of his time from three separate fields. A: as a technical-instrumental genius and inventor of machines; B: as a pictorial artist in the traditional sense but also, to an even greater extent, as a virtuoso in terms of visual interpretation and representation of mechanical functions, both organic and technical; and C: in terms of scientific competence and insight.

The productive expectations that existed in textile manufacturing but had not yet been given an autonomous intellectual formulation were the starting point for Leonardo's conception of existence and how it should be interpreted. The processes and procedures in workshops that transformed raw materials into useful products, but to which Greek philosophy had scarcely given a thought, in Leonardo give rise—with paradigmatic force—to an insight, that mechanical knowledge is the most useful and beneficial of all knowledge.

According to Leonardo, 'Instrumental or mechanical science is of all the noblest and the most useful, seeing that by means of this all animated bodies that have movement perform all their actions.'[129]

Leonardo makes an explicitly sociomorphic interpretation of the nature of reality (in the sense that it was the technical that transformed the social; Aristotle had made a similar point almost two thousand years earlier, but then the technical was an art of the *polis*) when he transcends the scope of interpretation of instrumental and mechanical events to *all* moving bodies. He starts from the craftsman's notion that there are instruments and mechanical tools with which to perform and facilitate useful work, and that there is a spontaneous, craftsmanly knowledge of the instruments and their use.

Then he transfers that form of intuitive knowledge of the craftsman to nature, in that he speaks of "all moving bodies", also natural ones. Finally, he states that the best way to understand these bodies is to perceive them as parts of a gigantic machine best described in terms of instrumental and thus clearly sociomorphic but fundamentally unnatural analogies. Schematically, the symmetrical relationship between the social level (A); the visual depictive level (B) and the metaphysical level (C) of Leonardo is summarised in the following figure:

A. Social level:

Mechanical work is; useful and successful; the knowledge of mechanical work is "noble".

B. Image level:

That which "happens"—the *istoria* of the image—makes itself known through mechanical causes. e.g., Moving muscles indicating anger or fear; as the effect of the blowing wind in nature, etc.

C. Metaphysical level:

The *cause-effect* relationship is mediated by a mechanical force.

Concerning Level A:

With his interest in machines and workshop processes, Leonardo directed his creative abilities straight towards the heart of the rationality of the new age, which can be described as an "intellectualisation of the industrial process" (Benjamin Farrington). In the torrent of technical drawings and illustrative "exploded-view drawings", virtuously executed in a way that even the Encyclopédistes could hardly surpass, the fully automatic machines that produce other tools are particularly noteworthy.

Right from the first phase of the machine age, reason finds as its task to contribute to what in modern productive practice has become the only meaning of the word *rationalise*.

In his book on Leonardo, Serge Bramly writes that 'His contribution to technical progress was eventually absorbed into the technical advances of his age. But there are some spectacular inventions (or improvements in design) that cannot be taken away from him, in particular his textile machines (which seemed to him to be more useful, profitable, and perfect than the printing press): machines for spinning, weaving, twisting hemp, trimming felt, and making needles.'

'He was unquestionably a mechanical genius—and indeed a prophetic one—anticipating the industrial revolution in the sense that his 'machines' (including tools, musical instruments, and weapons) all aspired towards systematic automation.'[130]

Leonardo produced a lot of practical work for the welfare of textile manufacture, the branch of industry that more than any other single factor was the engine of the Renaissance, and a field in which he made around forty inventions and improvements that Kenneth G Ponting describes in his book on Leonardo's textile machines.

If the Tuscan bankers and textile contractors had not been so interested in investing in the old Roman spirit of *status,* lavish palaces, luxurious villas and sumptuous church buildings, but instead, had invested their profits productively in new work processes and technologies, there would have been nothing to prevent the industrial revolution from starting in northern Italy and on the basis of Leonardo's visions. Instead, it was England that received both the credit and the textile production.[lxiii]

[lxiii] These "what if" arguments are of course superfluous. What has occurred to me is perhaps the following: In examining the role of Protestant ethics in the rise of capitalism one should perhaps also take into account that the southern boundary of the spread of the Protestant revolt quite closely follows the northern border of the old Roman Empire, that once also had been the border between slavery and "freedom". The ascetic, industrious and status-free ideal is perhaps nothing more than the ingrained safeguard of personal freedom of preslavery – to some extent the same ideals as Hesiod propones.

Leonardo da Vinci: *Image of a storm*

Concerning Level B:

Long before Descartes and the philosophical notion that man is a machine, Leonardo applied a mechanistic interpretation of humans and animals in his depictive programme—that certainly had philosophical ambitions. The "essence" of a thing is determined by Leonardo by the way that it is constructed and technically functions. In order to, for example, correctly depict a human being (*questa figura strumentale dell' omo*), Leonardo requires knowledge of his skeleton, of muscles and tendons and the way they work, the layers of fat and skin and how they behave, etc. Man is the sum of the construction of him.[lxiv]

The instrumental interpretation or unmasking of the wonders of nature is even more evident in the following observation by Leonardo: 'The bird is an

---

[lxiv] In the section entitled COME AL DIPINTORE E' NECESSARIO SAPERE LA INTRISICA FORMA DELL' OMO (frgm. 489-90)Leonardo writes : "I say that first you ought to learn the limbs and their mechanism, and having this knowledge, their actions should come next, according to the circumstances in which they occur in man. And thirdly to compose subjects (storie), the studies for which should be taken from natural actions and made from time to time, as circumstances allow," This should be compared, of course, with Plato's view that man is the incarnation of a command function.

instrument functioning according to mathematical laws, and man has the power to reproduce an instrument like this with all its movements.'[131]

But it is not only that which is living that requires a mechanistic interpretation in order to be adequately accessible to the depictive understanding. Any phenomenon in nature that deviates from a static or dead state of rest has a mechanical cause and must be represented as the result of this cause. 'Every effect is the direct result of its cause,' Leonardo writes, and 'nothing in nature happens without a cause (*sanza ragione*).'[132] For example, in depicting a storm. Leonardo, for the most part, a man of few words and precise in his descriptions and utterly mute when speaking of himself, suddenly becomes expressive when there is talk of floods, storms and disasters, in other words, when there is talk of large-scale production in the segment that in Leonardo's workshoplike interpretation is deemed "the work of nature" or "the work in nature".

'If you wish to represent a tempest consider and arrange well its effects as seen, when the wind, blowing over the face of the sea and earth, removes and carries with it such things as are not fixed to the general mass. And to represent the storm accurately, you must first show the clouds scattered and torn, and flying with the wind, accompanied by clouds of sand blown up from the sea shore, and boughs and leaves swept along by the strength and fury of the blast and scattered with other light objects through the air.'

'Trees and plants must be bent to the ground, almost as if they would follow the course of the gale, with their branches twisted out of their natural growth and their leaves tossed and turned about. Of the men who are there some must have fallen to the ground and be entangled in their garments, and hardly to be recognised for the dust, while those who remain standing may be behind some tree, with their arms round it that the wind may not tear them away; others with their hands over their eyes for the dust, bending to the ground with their clothes and hair streaming in the wind.'

'Let the sea be rough and tempestuous and full of foam whirled among the lofty waves, while the wind flings the lighter spray through the stormy air, till it resembles a dense and swathing mist. Of the ships that are therein some should be shown with rent sails and the tatters fluttering through the air, with ropes broken and masts split and fallen. And the ship itself lying in the trough of the sea and wrecked by the fury of the waves with the men shrieking and clinging to the fragments of the vessel.'

'Make the clouds driven by the impetuosity of the wind and flung against the lofty mountain tops, and wreathed and torn like waves beating upon rocks; the air itself terrible from the deep darkness caused by the dust and fog and heavy clouds.'[133]

What Leonardo so superbly sketches in image and in words is the modern form of agony, where the mental state is not, as in the emergence of ancient subjectivity, symbolised by the struggle between anthropomorphic agents, gods vs. Amazons, etc., but is represented as man vs. nature. The drama transcends the familiar schemes of ethnic and clan rivalries, as Fate now is given an all-encompassing natural form.

Less dramatic but equally clear is his advice for how the artist should depict the wind: 'In representing wind, besides the bending of the boughs and the reversing of their leaves towards the quarter whence the wind comes, you should also represent them amid clouds of fine dust mingled with the troubled air.'

'[---] All the leaves which hung towards the earth by the bending of the shoots with their branches, are turned upside down by the gusts of wind, and here their perspective is reversed; for, if the tree is between you and the quarter of the wind, the leaves which are "towards you remain in their natural aspect, while those on the opposite side which ought to have their points in a contrary direction have, by being turned over, their points turned towards you."[134] Again, what can be perceived and depicted is the result of mechanical action.'

Concerning Level C:

Leonardo's outline of a natural philosophy is sparse and haphazardly scattered over a large body of text. We do not know exactly to what extent he planned to publish them. The few times he sat down to summarise his studies of nature, his stays at the writing desk were not extensive. Soon enough other interests took over. So Leonardo's thoughts on nature were not available to his contemporaries, nor to the men of the scientific breakthrough (Bruno, Galileo, Francis Bacon) a hundred years later.

One can only speculate about the influence Leonardo's ideas would have had if they had been known among the scholars of the time. In any case, it would probably have been quite substantial.

On the other hand, Leonardo, in his position as an outsider, was not obliged to take into account the prevailing scholarly squabbles, but could unashamedly throw the thousands of years of the Greek-scholastic idea of science into the dustbin where he believed it belonged. That opportunity was not available to scholars who wanted to announce their research findings in the much harsher ideological climate of the Counter-Reformation a hundred years later.

Nowadays, there is no reason to leave Leonardo's name aside when reviewing the pioneers of the new science. He belongs to them, as much as he as an image maker belongs to the elite of artists. And he does so by virtue of his insatiable curiosity about empirical reality. How it mechanically *functions*.

Major epistemological breakthroughs are sometimes transparent in the sense that the thinkers who are involved in enforcing them, reveal their extra-theoretical motives and thus also their deepest motivations in their choice of concepts and analogies. The very first philosophy of ancient Ionia is of this kind. In the absence of a philosophical tradition, and consequently, of philosophical concepts and theoretical abstractions, thought had to create them with the help of words from the practical everyday world.

In the choices it made, early philosophy reveals its symbiosis with the commercial and democratic aspirations out of which the Western model of civilisation would later grow.

The same transparency is found in the thought of Leonardo. But now the basic concepts are not submerged in democracy and commerce—for such abstractions already existed—but in the pandemonic but extraordinarily useful clatter of the workshops. And these he knew like the back of his hand. For Leonardo, the technical tool, the machine, is a strong or even compelling metaphor for the events of existence, and he expresses this in such a way that an undisguised originality lingers in his images and metaphors.

We can see in his texts how he orientates himself towards a workshoplike interpretation of existence; how, starting from the practical potential of the workshop that he knew well, turns towards all of existence, with an unlimited and unknown potential, but that was nevertheless possible to get a grip on using a similar interpretive strategy that in workshop conditions paired intelligence with practical, productive utility. The mechanical ingenuity of the machine becomes an image for nature, and its processes of change are perceived as a product of something akin to a workshoplike process.

Consequently, the world that Leonardo regards as the real one is essentially a material world, whose principle of movement and change is *force*. This is evident, for example, in the following textual fragment: 'Force, with physical motion, and gravity, with resistance are the four external powers on which all actions of mortals depend.'[lxv]

Admittedly, Leonardo's views are easily distorted when translated into a modern physical language that possesses the clear distinctions and definitions that Leonardo lacked. What is clear, at any rate, is that with observations such as these, he stands far above the scholars of his time, and that it is Leonardo's technical-instrumental ingenuity that makes these remarkably stripped-down and purely physical insights possible.

Also in another respect, Leonardo deserves to be mentioned as one of the greats of natural science: He consistently emphasised that it is the sensory observations that form the basis of sober knowledge. 'All our knowledge has its origin in our perceptions (*pricipia da sentimeti*).'[135] And the primary human sense for Leonardo is sight. To this we shall return.

Leaving Leonardo's "three levels" behind, let us delve deeper into his thinking and his works. He claims that there is a (reverse) symmetry between nature and interpretation. 'Although nature commences with reason and ends in experience it is necessary for us to do the opposite, that is to commence with experience and from this to proceed to investigate the reason.'[136]

When Francis Bacon, some hundred years later, formulates the principles of the new science, which later more or less explicitly formed the basis for the exploration of nature, Leonardo's visions are not far away. Bacon writes: 'What in operation is most useful, that in knowledge is most true.'[137]

[lxv] Leonardo: *The Literary Works of Leonardo da Vinci,* frgm. 859. When looking at the original text, Leonardo almost sounds like Anaximander: *colle quali tutte l'opere de' mortali ànno loro essere e lor morte.* Of course, Leonardo still has a long way to the Newtonian insight that *force* and *weight* are equivalent, because he sees them as qualitatively distinct phenomena: "weight (*il peso*) has body (*é coporeo*); force does not". (frgm. 1113 B) And from this follows, in accordance with the Platonic dualism between body and soul that: *forza è una virtu' spirituale, una potenza invisibile.* Leonardo is thus not completely materially mechanistic. That, physics, as mentioned earlier, would only become with Kepler and Galileo.

Giotto: *Navicella* (reconstruction)

As a painter, Leonardo praised only Giotto and Masaccio as his predecessors, both of whom were commended for breaking the lax habit of copying their masters and instead boldly explored nature[138], while the only thinker he has, as far as I can tell, been influenced by is Nicolaus Cusanus.[lxvi] As we have seen, in his writings Nicolaus formulated an analogy between the quantifying and measuring functions of the market and the way reason, in his view, ought to operate.

But he also showed conversely, that the ideal figures thought perceives in its operations as objectively given are *human constructs*; results of human work. In *De beryllo*, for example[139], it is said that the geometrical circle has primacy over the natural one in that it is produced by the human spirit (*mathematicalia fabricat*) and that the spirit therefore possesses full knowledge of it, i.e., of the procedure of its construction and the principles of its production.

And this is the principle of full knowledge in general; full knowledge of a phenomenon is obtained when we interpret it in accordance with the way in which the phenomenon is produced.

[lxvi] Leonardo had first-hand knowledge of Nicolaus' philosophy thanks to Paolo de Pozzo Toscanelli, who in his youth had met Nicolaus in Padua. Toscanelli had also been Verrocchio's and Brunelleschi's teacher of geometry, and possibly also a cartographer for Columbus.

For Leonardo, it is not the commercial processes that give direction to the optimal development and design of existence, but the ingenious work of machines and instruments. In his eagerness to fly like the birds or dive like the fish, Leonardo, as we have seen, equates them with technical constructions. Also in visual representation, a mechanical-instrumental relation prevails.

When Giotto wanted to depict a storm in one of his most famous works of the time, the mosaic *Navicella* in Rome, he represented it in two different ways. On one hand, he depicted the storm in the traditional way as two deities with swelling cheeks blowing air. But as a true discoverer of new worlds, Giotto used not only the animated but also the naturalistic form of representation. The impression of a storm is also given by the billowing sail, by the terrified apostles, and by the apostle at the stern struggling with the sheet of the sail.

Such a double solution no longer sufficed for Leonardo.[lxvii] God as the origin of something had become unfashionable. When Leonardo turned to *his* god to finish the day with an evening prayer, he went about it in a business-like tone: 'Thou, O God, dost sell us all good things at the price of labour.'[140]

Subjective and Objective

Leonardo still has great difficulty in distinguishing between what *we* perceive as subjective and as objective; between what is manifested primarily as an individual perception and what is the result of human action or occurs without human intervention. This is a consistent feature of Leonardo; his conceptions of the premises of knowledge constantly oscillate between that which is primarily valid for emotions and individual perceptions, and that which concerns the "workings of nature". As an example of Leonardo's way of confusing things that we perceive to belong to different classes of phenomena, we can mention his plans to create a book on anatomy.

It would have been about: birth, the child, the man, the woman, "laughter and its causes", "weeping and its causes", killing, flight, terror, murder, and other things we think of as disparate elements that seem to have little to do with anatomy.[141] For Leonardo, however, something *objective* was what one could create a *pictorial object* of, or, in a more modern mode of expression, which could be depicted through a (camera) lens.

[lxvii] The same is true, for example, of Leonardo's image of the saints. Their holiness would no longer appear from a halo, but would appear as an inner, spiritual virtue.

Since it is possible to create a pictorial object that depicts both laughter and horror, they were objective for him in the same way that Ginevra de' Benci or the town of Imola were objective, and belonged to anatomy in so far as both laughter and horror appear as a result of the work of muscles and tendons.

The visible, or seeable, as the expression of truth was spontaneously already given in pre-Socratic philosophy and was applied in the literal sense of the word in the tradition of natural philosophy (such as e.g., the notion in Hesiod that knowledge of a thing is the same as an enumeration of all its visible parts). Such was the truth until the Eleatic turn in philosophy, when concrete seeing was replaced by abstract seeing and concrete truth with an abstract truth—although the words that were supposed to express the new conception (*theoria, aletheia*) remained the same.

In the turn towards a new interest in nature in the late Middle Ages, it is again the part of existence which can be perceived with our senses that the ability to understand and conceptualise is directed towards. For Francis of Assisi, his affirmation of nature meant that all sensory impressions could provide an equal confirmation of a divine truth. The song of a bird, the scent of a rose or the delicate shifts in the colours of its fragile petals were all examples and evidence of God's spiritual presence in nature.

For Francis, a single fragrant rose transcended all theological abstractions. The natural became exemplary and explaining became illustrating. This can be inferred from the prominence of *optics* in Roger Bacon's natural history. When brother Roger, also a Franciscan monk, wrote his *Opus majus* in the 13th century and in which he laid the foundations of an experimental science, the word "optics" still meant "the science of seeing".

'It is possible that some other science [than optics] may be more useful, but no other science has so much sweetness and beauty of utility. Therefore, it is the flower of the whole of philosophy and through it, and not without it, can the other sciences be known.'[142] The first step of knowledge is not related to the spiritual, but to the "seeable"; that which is made visible.

Humanity is now leaving an ancient settlement because it has become unsuitable. New vistas are opening; man looks out towards horizons whose contours are preserved only as an indistinctly recorded memory of the distant times when he moved to the places he is now moving away from. And the orientation, the determination of place, is again primarily done with the help of the eye. The world that sight can perceive is the first world—though not the only world.

The link between the intelligible and the visually representable culminates in Leonardo—and therein lies the secret of his enormous versatility and his theoretical-practical genius. Leonardo is at the heart of scientific development, he can, with the pathos of the certainty of serving the truth, claim that "painting is a science"[143] in the same way that geometry is a science because both make use of lines, surfaces and bodies, or in the same way that astronomy is a science because both use perspective and observation.

Indeed, he might even argue that painting is philosophy, since both deal with bodies in motion. We live in the world of the eye, Leonardo says, and light is the brush of God. The world of the eye is the same as the world of thought because we can have a reliable thought about everything we can see but not about what we cannot see. With this strong belief in the possibility and necessity of visualisation, it follows consequently that a large part of Leonardo's writings deals with solutions to optical problems and techniques concerning perspective. Optics has become a kind of surrogate epistemology—with both seeing and knowing operating on the terms of optics.

Even a hundred years later, Francis Bacon, in demonstrating how the inductive method works by examining the phenomenon of *heat*, tends to conflate what *we* consider to be heat with what *looks like heat*. That is, he lists all the phenomena that emit light, from the sun to fireflies.[lxviii] It would take until the 18th century and men like Celsius and Fahrenheit before the phenomenon of heat was de-visualised and the determination of heat became a purely quantitative and dispassionate instrumental procedure of reading off a measure.

We can also note that Leonardo—among a thousand others things—planned to write a book on "water in itself". But he would not have thought of treating such problems, so central for later physics, as "force itself" or "motion itself". As they are not primarily visual.

The distinction subjective—objective along the lines we consider natural only gained conceptual stability with the English empiricists who divided the

---

[lxviii] That he therefrom succeeds to crystallise a concept of heat that defines that heat is motion has nothing to do with a modern conception of heat. Bacon was an insightful but frustrated protagonist of a cause of the future, but as an experimenter he was a bungler (in comparison to Galileo, for example). Which again shows that the pragmatic element of science is not conveyed through an immediate success or benefit, but through an imagined, expected societal one.

world's changing and multifaceted appearances into *primary, objective* and measurable qualities such as mass or speed, and *secondary, subjective* qualities such as colour, taste or shape which could not be given any interpersonally measurable value.

The splitting of the world achieved by empiricism is different in principle from Plato's division of existence into a primary part and a secondary part. And what happens to the role of the image also does not lack a parallel in antiquity. During the Renaissance, art and knowledge went hand-in-hand, men like Leon Battista Alberti, Filippo Brunelleschi, and Leonardo da Vinci could belong to the vanguard within both.

The new ideals of knowledge and visualisation that since the time of Roger Bacon and Giotto based themselves on *experience* did not at first distinguish between different qualities of the senses; they were all equally primary. Reality appeared as it did to the best observers: as a visually representable whole. In the same immediate way that the archaic Greek perception of truth indicated that the visible was the true, the real in the pre-empiricist natural theory was that which could be experienced with the senses, without distinction.

Later, for epistemological reasons, and in a way that is thus fully comparable to Plato's devaluation of art's function of meaning, the qualities of existence that art conveys were separated from those that it is believed that science should convey. For Plato, the actual existence of objects themselves was a matter of second-rate importance; for Locke the same applied to the colour, form, smell, taste, etc. of objects. Locke called those qualities *secondary*, while the *primary* qualities were the mass of objects and the relative velocity of these points of mass.

Existence seen with this constraint, instrumentally mediated by measuring apparatuses, was considered more objective and therefore more "true" than that which art and our senses could convey. "Sensuality" was once again given a scientifically disqualified meaning, just as in Greece. From now on, natural science and the depictive arts are once again forced to go their separate ways. A special kind of knowledge—the knowledge about art—was at the same time given room to develop. Art in the modern sense had seen the light of day.

But at the same time, the brief and fruitful encounter between the work of the hand and the work of the head was cut off again. Knowledge once more became technical-instrumental, ideological and the bearer of values that served a certain way of life. By *ideological,* I mean that knowledge, because of its utilitarian nature, produced a cut-through existence, declaring that the part that could be linked to a useful practice is more essential than the other part and that it had its notion of this constantly confirmed by the authorities and categories that *had established and maintain this order.*

But when the original connection between subjective and objective, between primary and secondary, between form and content—which still is magnificently united in Leonardo—was cut off, a new mystery arose: how could the processes of nature and the technical-instrumental understanding of it overlap each other so well.

The great sceptic David Hume solved this problem by asserting that there 'is a kind of pre-established harmony between the course of nature and the succession of our ideas; and though the powers and forces, by which the former is governed, be wholly unknown to us; yet our thoughts and conceptions have still, we find, gone on in the same train with the other works of nature.'[lxix] One wonders where Hume's famous scepticism suddenly went.

To say that Plato's theory of Ideas is ideological is, of course, a tautology, but the idea that it is structurally in harmony with and borrows its originality from the command structure of slave society and functions as its ideology in the aforementioned way, I find difficult to refute. (Francis Bacon, who had the honour of dealing with the Athenian mindset, with Plato's ideology and Aristotle's teleology, had a very clear opinion on this point.)[144]

That the scientific-technical strategy that Francis Bacon energetically propagated and which was perpetuated by scientific societies and later on by polytechnic universities has a similar function as a "productive force" is equally clear. Its function is also power-related: it both legitimises and maintains power over nature. And as all successful thinking, the scientific reaches a level of exemplarity that makes all other thinking which would like to be successful, to orient itself towards its ways of working.

Even philosophy, for as Wittgenstein says (in *The Blue book*): 'Philosophers constantly see the method of science before their eyes and are irresistibly tempted to ask and answer questions in the way science does. This tendency is the real source of metaphysics, and leads the philosopher into complete darkness.

[lxix] David Hume: *An Enquiry Concerning Human Understanding* 1993, p. 36. Thus, Hume does not note that the "pre-established harmony" is actually the result of a long historical process. But already the next phase of thought – Hegel – would take up history as an element of understanding and thus relativise the notions of "pre-established" and "eternal".

I want to say here that it can never be our job to reduce anything to anything, or to explain anything. Philosophy really is "purely descriptive".'[145]

Regarding the Greeks, it could be said that they constantly had the politico-legal method in mind, which was the strength of classical philosophy, but also its blind spot. Everything they saw and everything they could see and achieve with their method, confirmed both the correctness of the starting point and the result. And these were, then as now, the good, beautiful and pleasant life.

The conception of what is a valid and relevant truth now detached itself from the immediately experienced in accordance with the criteria of objectivity set by empiricist philosophy and became abstract truth. The truth that was now sought was that which could be reached by means of instrumental interventions (weighing and measuring). That which could not be accommodated within the instrumental perspective became uninteresting, or it was simply not seen.

This methodological blindness is the hallmark of technical instrumentalism, in both its ancient and its modern form. Efficiency means limitation. Another characteristic of intensive production is its self-consciousness. The instrumental character of production, with a *tool* interposed between the (collective) subject and its basis of existence, creates the distance between the two that enables the subject to discern itself as subject and thus creates the *actual* abstraction that is the prerequisite for theoretical abstractions. An autonomous tool seems to be the basis for an autonomous, reflective intellect.

For the subjectivity of modern technical instrumentalism, the starting point is, of course, Descartes' conception of the status of thought and of the self. For Descartes, man is the subject and nature the object. (With this dichotomy, he justified the use of nature with the same argumentative strategy that Aristotle used to justify the exploitation of slaves). Descartes did not, however, create such an isolated and atomistic individual subject as is often assumed.

This is because he, as an underlying condition of true knowledge, required that what one knows, one should be able to perceive and communicate clearly. And what can be clearly perceived, according to Descartes, are proportions and objects that can be expressed quantitatively and which can be conveyed through the language of mathematics. But this requirement is not as unconditional as Descartes thought, but instead a result of a long theoretical-practical process and thus, considered as a starting point, already coloured by the expectations of the circles of people that had felt how the winds of change blew in both commerce and manufacturing.[lxx]

Descartes admittedly starts from a solitary and doubting *ego*, but inasmuch as he cannot doubt that the doubt itself is real and true—for then he would be incapable of doubting—there must undoubtedly be *something* that is true, and if *something* is true, there must be, according to Descartes, *something* that guarantees this truth, something that compels the *ego* to believe that truth exists. Descartes calls this guarantor God.[lxxi]

Descartes' renewal of the process of knowledge thus consists of *two* steps: Firstly, *doubt* places the starting point of knowledge creation with the individual, but since that action alone would result in unproductive solipsism, the second step, *faith*, builds up general truths that the learned community can embrace. Descartes thus provides a pattern for the formation of a discursive truth consisting of the elements of subjectivity and objectivity, and the binding agent, the medium of discourse: the artificial mathematical-geometrical language.

And although, the construction is transparently conventionalist—true is what one believes to be true, what one recognises and agrees upon as truth on the basis

---

[lxx] The first actual stock exchange was founded in 1632 in Amsterdam, a couple of years before the Discours appeared. It now became possible to buy (and sell) expectations, profit expectations pinned on the future. Among the more spectacular events during its first years was the so-called tulip crash of 1636, when the price of tulip bulbs after extensive speculation (which created bulb-hysteria in an entire population) suddenly crashed. Descartes makes the kind of ingenium that concerns itself with the practicalities of life the model for intellectual activity in general. "For it occurred to me that I should find much more truth in the reasonings of each individual with reference to the affairs in which he is personally interested, and the issue of which must presently punish him if he has judged amiss, than in those conducted by a man of letters in his study, regarding speculative matters that are of no practical moment, and followed by no consequences to himself, farther, perhaps, than that they foster his vanity the better the more remote they are from common sense; requiring, as they must in this case, the exercise of greater ingenuity and art to render them probable." (Discourse on the method, I)

[lxxi] In the writings of the pious cardinal Nicolaus Cusanus it was said that the World is a contract, while God is absolute. Descartes "borrows" the authority of God in order to install an absolute secular truth with His help – the objective truth. Or one might say that Nicolaus' coincidentia oppositorum – The World and God – in Descartes' position merge into a non-contradictory unity so that the assumed contractive – World – in its essence, is given an absolute status. As an intermediate form between God as the absolute truth-giver in scholasticism and e.g. Nietzsche's epistemological relativism without God, Descartes' deity is necessary; instrumental reason must, in order for the ecumenical goal of "progress" not to fade away, believe in the illusion that its categories are "natural". One thinks that Descartes' motto *larvatus prodeo* is linked to this: He believes in science alone, but he gives it the face of God.

of the premises—it is given in the form *God-given*, or *absolute natural truth*. Or rather, because it simultaneously acknowledges its conventionalist starting point in that the truth function expresses itself as a process, it takes the form of an aspiration towards truth; an infinite approximation towards the unattainable limit which is the absolute.

Descartes' subjectivity, then, is really a preform of Hegel's dialectical notion that the subject is subject only insofar as it is confirmed by other subjects. The subjective becomes objective when it is confirmed by others. Truth is true only insofar as it is confirmed. The modern project is thus a collective project like the ancient one, but with the difference that the intellectual collectivity of the classical period was, so to speak, "natural" and ethnically based, whereas the modern one is discursively constructed, conscious, and capable of universal realisation.

I repeat: Descartes' (philosophical) subject is not a solitary, isolated and merely doubting subject, for it is by definition a collective subject, since it presupposes objectivity, i.e., the subject is a subject only as long as it can intersubjectively communicate its positions and have them verified. It is not a collective subject in the same closed, ethno-political sense as the Athenian, since it is based on a strictly personal commitment and responsibility, but within the framework of the two instrumental forms of life, their task is the same; both constitute a necessary component in the maintenance of the collective project which Romans called *salus publica*, the welfare of the state or people.

It is important to keep in mind when we later approach what is called "subject erosion" in the modern or postmodern sense.

Therefore, it is perhaps logical that the relation to reality, which, after the cognitive division of existence of Locke or Hume moved towards an aesthetic attitude and created for itself its own concept of knowledge—*sensual knowledge*. And that this knowledge is a non-instrumental, individually perceived truth, as in Baumgarten, a *veritas individus*[146] and at least seemingly the expression of a far more radical subjectivity than the Cartesian one.[lxxii]

The two approaches, the objective, Cartesian, with the scientific method as its guiding light, and the subjective, aesthetic one, encounter each other in an interesting way in Kant's writing on judgement (*Kritik der Urteilskraft*). Here, one could say that Kant puts the epistemological nobility that art once carried on

---

[lxxii] But also the aesthetic community works, to a certain extent, as a normative collectivity based on formalised aesthetic communication.

its shield to the test. But he does so with weapons borrowed from natural science, which long ago distanced itself from the elements art used in describing a world that during its heyday had been very real indeed.

Kant and the Concept of Beauty

Faced with the epistemologically induced valorisation of the importance of the measurable world, art was degraded again, in the same way as in Plato and for the same reasons. Not that art in any artistic sense became less valuable, except as an expression of a possible "truth". In a way that brings Plato to mind, Kant, in his *Kritik der Urteilskraft,* "steals" the definition of what art accomplishes from the artists and makes it his own.

It is thus not the maker's but the viewer's relation to the work of art that Kant expresses when he says that *beauty* is what surrounds an object which, during uncommitted *observation,* gives rise to a feeling of pleasure. (§ 5) One can be fairly sure that artists from Goya to Cézanne or van Gogh wouldn't have recognised their aspirations in such a definition, since art and its result—beauty—for them was a supremely ethical and *committed* project; a duty and often a torment that they did not undertake out of *freedom* (as Kant says) but out of an inner *compulsion.*

Art is disqualified because its most essential quality—beauty—lacks *concepts,* i.e., concepts that according to Kant would be conformable to scientific discourse. On the other hand, one can have *opinions* about art. This conflict gives rise to Kant's famous antinomy on art (§ 56), where he in the *thesis* states that 'The judgement of taste is not based upon concepts; for, if it were, it would be open to dispute (decision by means of proofs).' While the *antithesis* reads: 'The judgement of taste is based on concepts; for otherwise, despite diversity of judgement, there could be no room even for contention in the matter (a claim to the necessary agreement of others with this judgement).'

Kant resolves the antinomy (§ 57) by showing that the word *concept* is used differently in the thesis and the antithesis. For the concept to be precise, the antinomy should be formulated as follows: 'The thesis should therefore read: The judgement of taste is not based on determinate concepts; but the antithesis: The judgement of taste does rest upon a concept, although an indeterminate one (that, namely, of the supersensible substrate of phenomena); and then there would be no conflict between them.'

Kant's antinomy thus expresses that art may be subject to reasoning, but that knowledge of it in a higher, scientific sense, is inaccessible. It also expresses that truth in general has become detached from visually revealed truth (beauty) in the manifestation of things, in that the former has been bestowed with the primary elements of existence, while beauty has been given the secondary ones (colour, form). In this sense, the judgement of taste was no longer based on the degree of precision or conceptuality attained by the judgement of truth.

But a small remnant of reality remained for the judgement of taste to hold on to—that which Kant calls "the supersensible substratum of phenomena". (We shall return to what this might mean when we arrive at the time when beauty ceases to be the basis of judgement for the pictorial relation to reality.) Kant thus moves towards broadly the same terms as Plato, who had discovered that the categories associated with the instrumental praxis of the time, i.e., the art of ruling, were expressions of *episteme,* or true knowledge, while those that were not were merely expressions of conjecture or opinion; *doxa.*

It is worth keeping in mind, however, that regarding the concept of beauty, Kant was primarily speaking of *natural beauty* and not *beauty of art.* For example, he says (as an echo of Plato; § 48) that 'a beauty of nature is a beautiful thing; beauty of art is a beautiful representation of a thing.' But Kant then overlooks the fact that natural beauty is the *result* of a centuries-long process during which artistic beauty (which must also include both beauty of poetry and that of gardening) has set up an ideal way of looking at life—an ideal that now was re-reflected in the concept of natural beauty.

So in a historical perspective, the opposite proposition is actually more valid: natural beauty is, if not secondary to artistic beauty, at least dependent on it. *Beauty as conception* is a way of seeing and understanding that art has implanted in mankind, slowly and with great effort. "Nature", as said, is a peculiar invention of man.

6. Denied Instrumentalism

Now that the forms of thought that emanated from both ancient and modern technical instrumentalism have been given some outlines, it is time to return to the two post-instrumentalist, postmodern periods in history which, in a decisive manner, *deny* instrumental values. Previously, in Chapter 2, I dealt with the philosophical confrontation with the high philosophy of antiquity, which resulted in thought taking up the cause of the slave and identifying with its conditions of life.

In image reproduction, a similar movement is taking place, towards a brutalisation of the image of the master, including elements of disgusting realism, while the instrument/slave is suddenly and unexpectedly *glorified*. The sculptors also felt the cultural currents that were undermining the old and which, in turn, would pave the way for something new. We will now examine this in more detail. Then it's time to tie it all together in a big bag of thoughts that holds our own tumultuous and chaotic times.

Heroisation of the Instrument

In the shadow of the sovereignty of free philosophical thought developed in antiquity, a remarkable thing happened; the *artist*, relegated to the status of manual labourer or craftsman, was the person who could, so to speak, formulate the knowledge of the social *as a whole* in his work; who had access to the totality of existence, since art both contained a component of labour and had an interpretative or knowledge function.

As a result, art could become *truer* than thought—a paradoxical turn of events that has an equally interesting parallel in our time. The theme of post-Aristotelian philosophy, that the slave, at least from the perspective of eternity, is equivalent to the free man, appears in visual art as a concrete statement: the slave is given the same proportions, and spiritually, the same human greatness as the free man. The slave has thus already become human in art, and sometimes more than human: the slave even becomes an ideal or a hero. The slave becomes an individual worthy of respect and compassion.

The Ludovisi Gaul (Copy. The original from 200 B.C.)

Attalus I's monument of victory over the Gauls, from 200 BC, with *The Dying Gaul* and *The Galatian Suicide*, (*The Ludovisi Gaul*) expresses the heroism, the exaltation and the dignity the artist found in the actions of these barbarians. (This group may also include the somewhat lesser-known *Kneeling Gaul Defending Himself*, which is kept in the National Museum in Athens.)

In all three sculptural groups, the depicted Gauls—non-humans who, according to Aristotle, deserve no better fate than to become slaves—find their greatness, however, only when encountering the majesty of death, even though on this side of eternity. Their greatness rests on the fact that they *refused* to submit, that they chose *freedom*!—the freedom of death, now!

We can now turn to Plato's epistemological reasoning about the truth function of art and say that Plato deprived the artists of the essentiality of their knowledge and their perception of beauty, because it was in the production of symbols in art that the truth about work and the truth about the social as a totality threatened to break through—and *de facto* did. Because of his social position and his practical disposition, the artist knew work and its conditions, and he could, moreover, due to reasons of tradition, give it a prestigious expression.

As mentioned earlier, in both archaic and classical times art had been idealising; aesthetics had an essentially ethical task of providing society with human ideals (this is also embedded in the etymological root of the word). Man was supposed to look up to the idols, to the depicted heroes and gods.

This was at a time when the patron goddess of the Athenians was still being celebrated as the patroness of *craftsmanship*, while Hesiod's praise of work was still being heeded, and before the onslaught against the kind of *arete* (virtue) derived from concrete work initiated by Xenophon had taken hold as a general prejudice. For Plato, it was absolutely inconceivable that a craftsman could produce ideas, let alone ideals.

Xenophon complained in his time that it was too difficult to distinguish a slave from a poor but freeborn man by how he *dressed*; he believed that different insides would be reflected in different outsides; that freedom would be *seen*.

Aristotle goes a step further: somewhat indignantly, he exclaims that since it is once and for all the case that the slave naturally and by his nature is a slave, it is vexatious that nature should not at the same time also have arranged this division in a clearer fashion: 'if persons were born as distinguished only in body as are the statues of the gods, everyone would say that those who were inferior deserved to be these men's slaves [---] but beauty of soul is not so easy to see as beauty of body.'[147]

Yes, sometimes the slave, in all his athletic appearance, is more divine than soft and flabby Man! So if *appearance* (as is the case in art) should be used as a criterion of the human instead of the inner virtues of the soul; if love was directed towards the beauty of the body instead of the soul; and if the somatic were to stand in harmony with the spiritual and give a true picture of the excellence of man, it would appear that the slave stood above man and that man was inferior to the slave!

This was, of course, impossible. Therefore, all bodily ideality had to be denied, the actual had to be devalued, the absolute primacy of the soul had to be postulated, and the content of art had to be emptied of meaning. But when Athens had thus thrice denied its mistress Pallas Athena's special protégé, *craftsmanship*, and thrice denied the works that the pride of the gods—*fire*—could produce, she lost her totem, her greatness, and subsequently her future.

Within the framework of traditional, Athenian-classical taste, it must therefore have seemed a shock to see un-humans, barbarians and peoples who deserved no other fate than enslavement, in the elevated place where one was accustomed to find gods, demigods or heroes. In the place where in the aesthetic or religious experience of the *polis,* one traditionally expected an idol, an exalted object to be worshipped, the inhabitants of Pergamum found a barbarian, a creature intended primarily as an *instrument* or a tool!

In this way, the realisation of the essence of technical instrumentalism appeared through a back door, via the unexpected glorification of the *instrument*. And Pergamum occupies no peripheral place in the history of Hellenic civilisation, on the contrary. During their golden age from the 3rd to the 2nd century, the Attalids saw themselves—correctly—as the true heirs of Athens. Not only did they take possession of the philosophers and artists of Athens, but also of her patron goddess, *Athena Nike*, who was given a seat on the Lydian acropolis.

And not far from the place where the Gauls were given their posthumous tribute, the altar of Zeus was erected with its famous frieze, where the heroic fighting spirit of the Greeks found its most vivid and dynamic sculptural expression. Vagn Poulsen has called the Pergamum altar frieze 'the greatest show of force of Greek sculpture,' but he adds that 'on closer inspection, however, one realises that exhaustion is nearing.'[148]

From Pergamum, the cultural relay baton passes directly to Rome, since Attalus III, probably to the great surprise of the Romans, bequeathed his empire to the future capital of the world in 133 BC. This gave the growing empire not only access to vast Greek cultural treasures—including the famous library—but also a dynastic link with ancient Troy.

The Laocoön Group.
Late 100s BC.

According to legend, the Trojan Telephus founded Pergamum, while Aeneas escaped the swords and lances of the Achaeans and, in the words of Virgil, was 'forc'd by fate [---] [to] The Latian realm, and built the destin'd town [---] From whence the race of Alban fathers come, And the long glories of majestic Rome.'[149]

The most remarkable manifestation of the connection between Pergamum and Troy, which later as a marble copy was to attract great attention in Rome, is the so-called Laocoön Group. According to legend, Laocoön had warned the Trojans about the Achaeans' parting gift, the Great Horse, and had thrown his spear at it. Afterwards, when he went to the beach to make a sacrifice, he was attacked by two sea serpents, which devoured him, his father and his two sons.

For the fact that he was right in the matter was no excuse for violating the sacred principle of respecting the gift of a guest.

The Laocoön Group has been called, among other things, "the swan song of Pergamum"[150]. However, as I see it, the Laocoön Group stands for much more; it marks, admittedly somewhat belatedly, the demise of the whole classical idea of freedom. In the archaic sculptures, we saw the signs of how man slowly and hesitantly entered a freedom that he himself had created. Now we find ourselves at the other end of the road, at the slope down towards the evening, where external circumstances once again grab a hold on man; on that which had been a form of fragile self-determination and a personally defined sense of self.

Laocoön's futile struggle against the snakes is, at the same time, the death struggle of the Athenian way of life. That it takes place on foreign soil and in a foreign guise is nothing but a sign of the strange survival of ideals and human hopes. But when they perish the culture with which they have been associated also dies.

The *"rigour mortis"* that then enters the visual arts is a mute commentary on the restoration of monarchical principles that simultaneously took hold of thought and politics. Not even republican Rome succeeded in creating its own cultural code, instead appropriating the Greek one as an outer garment—something already initiated by the Etruscans—as they had not genuinely internalised the principles on which classical culture rested.

In Laocoön's death throes, a remarkable bridge is built across three epochs: from mythical Troy, via a monarchical Pergamum with Athenian dreams and ideals, to the centuries of servitude in which the Snake—*evil incarnate*—had completely devoured man.

There was a cartoonist in the US sometime in the 1910s or 1920s who made fun of modern art on the grounds that it created a world that *was impossible to live in*. It's an interesting argument. It would be unpleasant to live in the angularity of Cubism or the nightmarish world of surrealism. But one could actually say the same about an *artworld* that heroised the slave. It would have been unpleasant for a free Greek to live in a city where the slave was the hero and work the virtue.

Yet the reminder that this is necessary appears in art and in the philosophy of the Stoics. Hegel has aptly called the form of consciousness that agonises over the situation when it is impossible either to accept the state of things or their solution, *the unhappy consciousness*.[lxxiii] When it is no longer rational to (according to the view of rationality of the time) rationalise. When—to put it in Hegelian terms—the realisation that the essential, i.e., work, lacked the means to express itself *as* or *in* an *Allgemeinheit*; as a valuable or valid generality. Plato and Aristotle believed—indeed knew—that it is *ruling* and its rational form, *the state*, that creates value and good conditions for the essentials of life.

The "unhappy consciousness" is unhappy because it assumes but does not itself comprehend its own generality; because it obscurely suspects but cannot conceptually crystallise the master-slave opposition in general, societally functional terms. In terms that contain the same conditions and meet on the same level. Among these impossible conditions was the task of mediating for example, the contradiction that existence (freedom) in a double sense implied non-existence: for the master, freedom presupposed the inhumanising that resulted in the slave; for the slave, freedom presupposed an encounter with real death.

Old Market Woman. Copy of a Greek work of the second century B.C.

The "unhappy consciousness" could therefore perhaps adequately interpret its own situation only in terms of the *self-denial* inherent in the Stoic indifference or in the sceptical inability to make up its mind; to be unable to choose sides. Artistically, self-denial is expressed in the unveiled *realism* that broke through in art and that strongly broke away from the elevated classical style— *Old Drunkard*, for example, originally exhibited in Pergamum, or the *Barberini Faun*, which possibly originates from the same place.

Another kind of corporeal realism linked to the denial of *polis*-rationality surges forth in Diogenes' subversive behaviour in the streets and squares of Athens.

With this Diogenes of Sinope, son of the moneychanger Hikesias, and therefore acquainted from birth with the relativity and ephemerality of money and values, 'the most dramatic moment in the process of truth in early Western philosophy [occurs]. While Plato's 'high' theory irrevocably cuts the ties to a material embodiment in order to tie the threads of argumentation all the more firmly to a logical fabric, a subversive variant of "low" theory emerges, splitting

---

[lxxiii] Hegel does use the term somewhat more narrowly – when discussing sceptical philosophy. But he also finds an "unhappy" element in Judaism.

the truth process into discursive-grand-theoretical battles and satirical-literary skirmishes.'

'[---] Diogenes desperately and hilariously defends himself against the 'linguisticisation' of cosmic universalism at the very moment when he acquires the scent in high theory of the vertigo linked to idealistic abstractions and the schizoid blandness of a thinking that only concerns the head. Diogenes opens the non-Platonic dialogue and shows that Apollo has another face, that of the satyr, the rascal and the comedian.'[151]

The Mentality of Slave Production

As a shaper of mentality, death is ever-present in the dramatic and dynamic state form that created slavery, but also in the static and retarding one that abolished it. An ideology such as the Athenian, whose concept of freedom is based on the effective exercise of power, does preserve—somewhere in its self-conscious superiority—the knowledge of the logic of submission and of the relative conditions of freedom. Athenian self-sufficiency knows that what it represses in its youthful arrogance is that it ultimately lives by mercy. On someone else's mercy.

The unhappy consciousness becomes a general consciousness in the moment when the subject is struck by the feeling that the principles on which it previously based its existence have been lost. In his "unhappiness", the subject turns to the source of his unhappiness, to the object of the exercise of power that created freedom, to the slave, where he believes truth lies. So, the elevation of slave-consciousness retains the category of freedom intact, but now it is the freedom of the slave, i.e., *death*, that is realised.

In the mental space between the ancient freedom to *rule* and the freedom of the new age under the aegis of *work*, lies a paradoxical and transcendent concept of freedom, which in its framework has the annihilation of the slave as a presupposition, but which, through perceiving service (e.g., church service) and work positively, results in a different kind of mastery.

Since it is impossible to briefly do justice to Hegel's subtle and terminologically extremely elusive text, I will reproduce a few long paragraphs from Charles Taylor's *interpretation* of the passage in the *Phänomenologie des Geistes* in which Hegel depicts the paradox of slave ownership and the sense of unhappiness the inability to intellectually reproduce the paradox produces.

'Hegel starts the dialectic of self-consciousness with the famous dialectic of the master and the slave. The contradiction underlying this is the following: men strive for recognition, for only in this way can they achieve integrity. But recognition must be mutual. The being whose recognition of me is going to count for me must be one that I recognise as human. The operation of reciprocal recognition is therefore one that we accomplish together. Each one, says Hegel, accomplishes for himself what the other tries to achieve in relation to him.'

'My interlocutor sees in me another, but one which is not foreign, which is at one with himself; but this cancelling of my otherness is something that I must help to accomplish as well. The contradiction arises when men at a raw and undeveloped stage of history try to wrest recognition from another without reciprocating. This is at a stage when men have not recognised themselves as universal, for to have done so is to see that recognition for me, for what I am, is recognition of man as such and therefore something that in principle should be extended to all.'

'But here we have man as a particular individual (Einzelnes) who strives to impose himself, to achieve external confirmation. This leads to armed struggle. And necessarily so, says Hegel. It is not just that men are opposed, since each seeks one-sided recognition; it is also that the risk of one's life is part of the very claim to recognition. We have seen earlier that self-consciousness is both a living being and somewhat more; somewhat more because it does not just undergo the life-process unconsciously, but is already beyond it in thought.'

'In the attempt then to win recognition of themselves as self-consciousness men prove that they are beyond mere life by showing that they are not attached to this particular living thing which is themselves, that their recognition as "beings for themselves" (Fürsichsein) is more important, that they will risk their lives for it. This struggle easily leads to the death of one or both combatants. And this obviously misses the goal.'

'Even if I remain alive in face of my dead adversary, I have won no recognition. My "negation" of him has been a natural one, as Hegel says, it is a simple negation as we saw earlier, whereas what is needed is a standing negation, one in which my opponent's otherness is overcome, while he still remains in being. The problem is thus that while each is pushed to put his life in hazard, to show that he is above mere attachment to life, this remains essential. The only outcome to the struggle which can even look like a solution is one which takes this into account.'

'But this is the case with the classical outcome of enslavement. Before it comes to the death, one side gives in, recognises its attachment to life, and becomes subjected to the other. The victor spares the vanquished in order to make him a slave. Both protagonists then preserve life, but in a very different way. The victor has won his point. That what is essential for him in his Fürsichsein, his own sense of self, and that life is subordinate. For the slave, however, it is life which is essential, his sense of self is now subordinate to an external existence which is beyond his control.'

'The full relation of master and slave has to be understood with third term, material reality (Dingheit). Master is related to slave mediately through this reality: the master subjects the slave through this command over things, at the limit through the use of a chain. But at the same time, master is related to material reality through the slave. The relation of the master to what surrounds him is that of a pure consumer; the hard task of transforming things and preparing them for consumption is that of the slave.'

'The master's experience is of the lack of solid reality (Unselbständigkeit) of things; the slave is the one who experiences their independence and resistance as he works them. But this outcome, although better than a fight to the death, is also vitiated as a solution. The recognition is one-sided; slave is forced to recognise master, but not vice versa. But for this very reason, the upshot is of no value for the master. His vis-à-vis is not seen to be a real other self, but has been reduced to subordination to things.'

'Recognition by him is therefore worthless; the master cannot really see himself in the other. Rather he is reduced to the parlous condition of being surrounded by beings which to him cannot be self-conscious; so that the surrounding world on which he continues to depend cannot reflect back to him a human visage. His integrity is thus radically undermined just when it seemed assured. But if this outcome is a failure ultimately for the master, for the slave it prepares the ground for ultimate success, and within the relationship a reversal slowly takes place.'

'The slave at least has before him a being who exists for himself in the master, even if this master does not recognise him. His environment is not reduced to the sub-human, as is the case with the master.'[152]

'Thus Hegel's notion here is that the slave becomes a universal consciousness through his work. Both the fear of death and the discipline of service were necessary.'

'The fear of death alone would have shaken him loose for a moment from the particular, but would have built no standing embodiment of universal consciousness. But work alone, uninformed by the fear of death, would have produced just particular abilities (Geschicklichkeit), not a universal consciousness of self. For what the slave achieves through his work [---] is the grasp of himself as free thought. He recognises in the power to transform things the power of thought, the power to remake things according to concepts, and thus universal models. [---] Only under the discipline of service would he have undertaken the work which has raised him above his original limits.'[lxxiv]

'The dialectic of the master and the slave issues in a higher stage, which Hegel identifies with the philosophy of stoicism. Through work, discipline and the fear of death, the slaves have come to a recognition of the universal, of the power of conceptual thought. And this is already to have won through to a certain freedom. [---] But stoic freedom is radically incomplete. For we are still dealing with a philosophy of slaves. Through their commerce with matter they have come to the intuition that thought is the basis of all.'

'But just as they cannot make over their environment, and particularly their society, in order to express this intuition—for a rational political structure and laws will only come at a later stage in history—so they are still incapable of working through their idea in order to show the particular determinations of their world as manifestation of universal, (in the Hegelian sense) conceptual necessity.'[153]

'In accounting for this collapse [of stoicism] and the derivation of the next stage, Hegel brings us through another historical philosophy, ancient scepticism. This he paints as the fulfilment of the basic idea of stoicism; where this latter considers the determinate content of things as irrelevant or inessential,

---

[lxxiv] Taylor, p. 157. Even if we now are close to the cradle of historical materialism, I would prefer a more concrete interpretation: the slavish or barbarian knowledge was on a non-instrumental level; it was a *vegetative* knowledge, conforming to the wisdom of life that grew out of a simple existence in which "the Lord giveth and the Lord taketh away". The encounter with the Greek form of efficiency certainly created the impression that it is man who works in nature and against matter, but in the perverted form that the *commanded* intervention implied. In this sense, Aristotle's observation about barbarian inferiority is correct, because barbarian self-understanding did not appear in an instrumental ruling form but in its general form was a submissive but not an enslaved form of knowing. – Slave consciousness must therefore mediate between the actual relation, that it is the master who has *organised* and brought everything about (and that the slave, in the face of death, has agreed to this) and the equally actual relation that it is material reality (and not the concepts) that is really real.

scepticism goes over to the attack and calls it into question. It is the polemical consequence of stoicism. But this just serves to point up more acutely the underlying contradiction.'

'For as embodied subjects, we go on living in external reality. We declare its non-being, it returns unceasingly and inescapably. So that in fact what we have is an oscillation between a sense of our own self-identity, and an equally acute sense of our dependence on a changing, shifting external reality. As fast as we call this changing reality into question in order to experience ourselves as immutable and self-identical, our own inner emptiness forces us to accept that we are embodied in the mutable and self-external.'

'But this oscillation occurs in a single consciousness, and putting these two moments together, we derive a new dialectical phase, in which the subject has to accept the fact of inner division (Entzweiung), in which the inner self itself is painfully divided, into an ideal immutable and self-identical being on one side and one plunged in a world of confusion and change on the other. This is the stage of the unhappy consciousness, in which the relation of master and slave, which stoicism claimed to have escaped, reappears, but now within the subject, in the relation between these two mutually incompatible sides.'[154]

The "strategy of retreat" (Taylor) of Stoicism in relation to Golden Age power-related thinking meant a *theoretical* "erosion" or weakening of subjectivity in relation to the category of *power*, while an equally theoretical generalisation of the concept of "humanity" (in parallel with the practical) based on the repatriation or internalisation of the experience of denied subjectivity guaranteed, so to speak, continuity in the historical process.

Against the extremely effective but limited project of technical instrumentalism, Stoic resignation posited a realisation of the conditions of a totalised but powerless existence. Autarkeia became ataraxia; self-control or power-over-only-oneself.

Realism, the de-heroicised man and even more the heroicised slave, is visualised knowledge of the Stoic situation: that both the master and the slave before are equal in the face of eternity. The image of *The Gaul Who Kills Himself and His Wife* is a recognition of him as a human being, behind the back of philosophical reason. Only he who dares to live is truly free; he can never be enslaved. Only in death can the slave win the master's respect, for only by his death can he show that he puts freedom above slavery.

It is precisely in this moment that recognition occurs—that which, according to Hegel, both crave. Only in death does the double recognition occur where the self-esteem of both master and slave meet.[lxxv]

In this context, the Pergamum Group is not primarily a tribute to the slave or to barbarism, but is, as a variant of a specific Greek theme, a tribute to *freedom*—nature and concepts, as we know, make no leaps. When Athenians and Macedonians in the Hellenistic empire could suffer the same fate, when chance proved to be a competitor to autarchic reason, the celebration of death became the form of freedom-worship that both Greeks and non-Greeks could unite around.

Freedom was still a matter of honour and an exalted reminiscence of what had previously been politically true—but freedom now appeared as freedom in the necessary and perverted form of death: eternal peace. And that was the form it had to take in the crucible where the irreconcilable was to be united. The heroic age had wagered death and received freedom as the result. When the result was spent, only a ghostly memory of the heroic effort remained. Freedom had died, but Death was granted the rights to decree an eternal life of freedom.

Later, of course, *The Crucifixion* would grow into an almost immortal symbolic representative of this singly accessible psychic generality charged with ensuring the memory of the possibility of freedom; the only general freedom in which the experience of both master and slave could yield to each other.

Dismantling Naturalism's Criteria of Understanding

The new science that gradually replaced scholasticism over the course of a few hundred years had, according to its first and most impatient proponent Francis Bacon, the explicit task of *enslaving nature*. In the introductory outline to his magnum opus *Novum Organum* Bacon makes his intentions clear: 'The end of our new logic is to find, not arguments, but arts; not what agrees with principles, but principles themselves: not probable reasons, but plans and designs of works—a different intention producing a different effect. In one, the adversary is conquered by dispute, and in the other, nature by works.'[155]

[lxxv] In one of his Essays Montaigne says that "A man who has learned how to die has unlearned how to be a slave" – a thought that all individual philosophies of freedom have embraced.

Bacon's explicit project was to make science relevant to the industry that had not yet been born, but whose forerunners in the form of the workshops of the craftsmen and the foundries and forges of the manufacturers Bacon understood the importance of. Bacon believed, that what he had to do was not to hold an opinion, but to do a job. And the intention was not to found any school or school of thought, but to lay the foundation for endless wealth and prosperity. Francis Bacon did not want something small: he wanted to create a new England.

To achieve that, the new science needed a new method of research and a new logic. Benjamin Farrington calls the inductive logic Bacon created, and which he used to gain dominion over nature 'an intellectualisation of the industrial process.'[156] And that is exactly what it is.

Just as much as Aristotle's causal theory or Plato's idealism relate socio-conformably to a society built on structures of command and oppression, so does the new logic interpret the given natural conditions according to the possibilities offered by machinal and instrumental interventions. And the more productive and more successful these manipulations are, the truer the theory behind them appears to be, and the more attractive the theory appears to be to fields of science not directly aimed towards the exploitation of nature.

The winner always writes the laws—even the laws of nature—and success is contagious. Naturalism as an interpretive principle extended across ever wider domains.

The pictorial aesthetic of naturalism means that nature is *captured* in its causal unity. This is particularly true of romantic naturalism: while the empiricists regarded nature as a huge store of raw materials to be inventoried and counted, the romantics perceived themselves as part of nature, which they expressed ecstatically in various enthusiastic tones. Romantic thought expresses that the self possesses a deep unity with all existence.

But no longer in the same way as in the mysticism of late antiquity or the Middle Ages, that man lost himself in existence and powerlessly ascended into the cosmic or divine unity that had been established. On the contrary—and this expresses the modern aspect of romanticism: the romantic self is a life-hungry, pretentious and self-conscious self that tries to *absorb existence in itself*. The self does not disappear, as in Christian mysticism, the self expands beyond all limits and swallows up all of history and the universe within its ecstatically universal soul, as is the case with, say, Beethoven, Goethe or Hegel.

Once naturalism was accepted, established and ingrained, when its heroic phase was forgotten, having become academic, it took on the character of a *preconception*—a valid rule of interpretation that was not questioned and was not allowed to be different.

But what had been the metaphysical presupposition of naturalism? It had, as we have seen in Leonardo or Francis Bacon, been the general recognition that technical work is useful. What happens with thought if it realises that the activities and scientific methods that have produced such great results have personal gain and greed as a precondition? Or even worse: if its results begin to prove *harmful*.

Many things happen, but in the case of knowledge, we will concentrate on three: 1. that knowledge is pragmatic; that it views existence from a perspective of *utility* 2. Thus, as a consequence, the knowledge that is most advanced claims that God is dead in Descartes' sense, i.e., that the *objectivity* postulated by Descartes does not come from God or nature but rests on human agreements about which things are beneficial to man. 3. And when objectivity changes, the conditions of subjectivity also change.

When the communication that guaranteed rationality and truth proved only to be a cover for a way of "lying according to convention" (Nietzsche), the unproblematic cohesion of an intersubjective community is destroyed. What remains are *individuals*, local folds of locally-based communication and rationality. What remains is a distorted and incompletely communicated *subjectivity* and a large amount of individual *points of view*.

In art, for example, the multi-perspectivism of *cubism* arises. And in the field of knowing, Nietzsche, at whose core all three of the above-mentioned aspects of the disintegration of the scientific paradigm lies, emerges.

Nietzsche and Revealed Perspectivism

In the notes Nietzsche left behind after his collapse in 1889, and which he had intended to compile into a volume entitled *The Will to Power*, there is an occasionally brilliant albeit unsystematic understanding of what happens when science allies itself with a particular mode of production or a certain way of life— more precisely, with the way of life that Nietzsche calls "the mechanical mode of existence".

According to Nietzsche, science becomes *perspectival*, i.e., it sets up certain narrow criteria for what is scientifically primary and relevant in all of existence, and at the same time becomes systematically blind to the views that are not constructed in accordance with the utility demands of production or the contemporary way of life. Each node of power sets up its own goals and applies its own perspective to the rest of existence, so that existence is in harmony with the genuine operations of power. This interaction as a whole results in what we call "the world".[157]

In Nietzsche's notes, we can follow how he, with gradually increasing clarity, formulates the insights that to some degree are the foundation of this book: that metaphysics is the mediating basis of a normative pattern of interpretation designed in accordance with the functioning of useful social institutions. 'We can comprehend only a world that we ourselves have made,' Nietzsche says. From that, it also follows that an *alternative* way of thinking needs an alternative way of life as a companion in order to clear the way for its claims of validity.

Ideas have always disgraced themselves if they have not been supported by strong interests, as Marx said. 'The categories are "truths" only in the sense that they are the conditions of our existence,' is the corresponding insight of Nietzsche.[158]

Nietzsche is, in the dual lighting I prefer to see history, a kind of Protagoras of the modern. In opposition to Platonic conceptual realism, many sophists—including the circles around Protagoras and Prodikos of Keos—argued that concepts are merely conventions (*nomoi*) and are not by, and do not exist in nature *(fysei)*. In 4th and 3rd century Athens, the objections of the Sophists were unsuccessful; it would be fifteen hundred years before the Sophists, who by that time were known as nominalists, were vindicated.

One of Nietzsche's most far-reaching insights is that *theories* are also conventional and that their truth value is pragmatically substantiated; that they too are *nomoi* and not *physei*. Nietzsche is, as I see it, a nineteenth-century sophist; relativist, sceptic, scourger of "eternal" values, and ultimately also a "loser" according to the general serious-minded academic opinion. Plato had argued that the substance of his metaphysics, *the ideas*, existed and were real entities.

Modern physics had argued that one of the basic substances of its model of the world—the world presented as a workshop metaphor—namely *force*, also exists unconditionally.

Against this notion, and perhaps most of all against the cogent form it was given in Kant's philosophy, Nietzsche attacked vehemently. 'The biggest fable of all is the fable of knowledge,' he exclaimed. 'One would like to know what things-in-themselves are; but behold, there are no things-in-themselves! But even supposing there were an in-itself, an unconditioned thing, it would for that very reason be unknowable! Something unconditioned cannot be known; otherwise, it would not be unconditioned!'[159]

Further: 'Logic is bound to the condition: assume there are identical cases. In fact, to make possible logical thinking and inferences, this condition must first be treated fictitiously as fulfilled. That is: the will to logical truth can be carried through only after a fundamental falsification of all events is assumed. [---] But what is truth? Perhaps a kind of belief that has become a condition of life? In that case, to be sure, strength could be a criterion; e.g., in regard to causality.'[160]

To want to know is to order things in a way that suits us, Nietzsche repeats over and over again, and what we have done when we think we know something is that we have imposed as much form on Chaos as is needed for our practical needs. Not "to know" but to schematise—to impose upon chaos as much regularity and form as our practical needs require.

'In the formation of reason, logic, the categories, it was *need* that was authoritative; the need, not to "know", but to subsume, to schematise, for the purpose of intelligibility and calculation. [---] No pre-existing "idea" was here at work, but the utilitarian fact that only when we see things coarsely and made equal do they become calculable and usable to us. [---] Finality in reason is an effect, not a cause: [---] The categories are "truths" only in the sense that they are conditions of life for us.'

'So what is man's eternal and noble search for truth? It is merely a case of an animal species that has discovered certain regularities in its observations '*so daß sie Erfahrung capitalisiren kann*' (so that it can capitalise on the experience).'[161]

Nietzsche called this connection between science and utilitarianism "modern decadence", while giving the painful and tragic insight that there are no "higher values" in the idealist sense; that it is not possible to put one's trust in value syntheses such as "truth", "meaning" and "coherence", the name *nihilism*. In its passive form, *nihilism*, according to Nietzsche, does not yet imply a denial of values that exist, but is rather an unfortunate psychological state characterised by a sense of emptiness, meaninglessness, inertness.

To overcome the unhappy state of nihilism, Nietzsche introduced the *Übermensch*, the active nihilist, who is aware of the worthlessness of values and their pragmatically conditioned content.

The *Übermensch* can be seen as a modern equivalent of the Stoic ideal of man. He is a human being who places himself outside the conformed ideals of life, or who is *forced* to do so because the formalised discourse that previously created unity, community, objectivity and reason has crumbled. Thus, with Nietzsche, the *modern* deconstruction of the dominant values of knowledge begins. Instead of denying the philosophy of the state as in post-Aristotelian philosophy, Nietzsche denies the contexts of meaning created by technology; what Nietzsche calls "mechanisation".

Despite the differences between the two eras, the result of the re-evaluation of values is perhaps somewhat surprisingly the same; it emerges as the demand for a strong and autonomous human being. The Stoic calm and the insight of the *Übermensch* are in principle of the same kind and an expression of previously meaningful foundations of understanding having been uprooted. In that state, man has only himself to rely on. One may well call the phenomenon "subject erosion" if one likes, even though it is rather the ecumenical goal, the demand for "objectivity" according to existing formulas, that is being eroded. [lxxvi]

At the risk of being tedious, this statement can be made even clearer: The Stoic human ideal and the *Übermensch* (or the fragmented existence of the "postmodern" subject and its discursive detachment from the instrumental-technical instance of rationality) is the way in which instrumental strategies dissolve at all, when they are no longer capable of producing continued confidence in themselves; when their form of rationality no longer can be universally generalised as for example, "more freedom", etc.

The dissolution of the Aristotelian collective *praxis*-ideal and the critique of Cartesian collective *objectivity* result in both cases in a philosophical reduction of the subject to itself, and a denial of instrumental rationality. When Nietzsche proclaims that "God is dead", it is not a matter of theology and the death of some

---

[lxxvi] The difference between the Stoic and Nietzschean ideals, however, is that the Athenian collectivity had been so natural, spontaneous, and unreflectively given in ethno-ethical terms, which is why its atomisation was expressed essentially ethically, whereas the Cartesian collectivity, undoubtedly as a result of its prehistory in which the Stoic/ Christian element is of crucial importance, is a universalistic and constructed collectivity created by epistemological components, which is why its collapse rather belongs to epistemology.

anthropomorphic deity. It is worse than that. It is a whole idea of science that is dead. It is the Cartesian god, who guaranteed truth, consensus and distinct perceptions, that has passed away.

It is *objectivity* that is dead; the unifier of the (polyphonic) consonance of the learned community. It is the belief in an unconditional and universal validity that has been undermined. What remains are only local practitioners of opinion formation, subcultural identifications, isolated discourses, diverse sets of limited perspectives, "mini-narratives". From Descartes' "strong" model of doubt *and* faith, faith or trust has been removed; all that remains is isolated doubt and the solitary self, while God and the Absolute have been lost.

When Aristotle's model of knowledge was stripped of the impudent teleological part, it resulted (at first) in philosophical sectarianism and self-referentiality. When one removes the requirement of objectivity from the Cartesian model, the result is in some sense the same.

Here we see the ties that drew Nietzsche towards the pre-Socratics. For Nietzsche did not merely reject the claims of Cartesian philosophy, he rejected all moral and cognitive notions that high philosophy had produced since Socrates. According to Nietzsche, Plato and Aristotle were decadent. Nietzsche therefore wanted to reconnect with the currents of thought that prevailed before Socrates and Parmenides, before the logical agreements and conventions had been made.

In pre-logical thinking, he found the non-decadent, Dionysian elements of life and sensuality that had to be reactivated and involved in thinking in order for a new form of understanding to take root. In the thinking before Parmenides, he believed, a freshness of life, vitality of youth and an invigorating rigour and coolness of dawn existed. Its language had not been clogged by logic, fixating *All* at *One*, its experience of the world was neither conquering nor conceptual; every event was unique, *every thing* appeared in an individual, unassailable form. An equally beautiful and tragic consequence of Nietzsche's longing for this fallacious originality, where grammar and communication finally cease to function, and where the individual becomes a solitary, reasoning uniqueness, is that his longing finally was fulfilled when he entered the completely private state that the Greeks called *idioteia*.

Before abstractions separated the essential from the tangible, perhaps the experience of the world (both in the history of the individual and in the history of mankind) was undiluted sensuality. Perhaps beauty carries the memory of this quality, which Nietzsche sought as a counterweight to the codification and elision of individuality inherent in logic.[lxxvii] Beauty is unique and singular, it cannot (according to Kant) be meaningfully included in a logical-communicative conceptuality because its foundation refers to taste and opinion, which "cannot be discussed".

But that is not true either. The perspectival codification of the depicted world turned out to be as "unnatural", as conventional as the symbolic forms of the theories.

The Convention "Art"

Following closely on the heels of the self-criticism of science, art also came to terms with its ideals. This showdown was carried out with the vehemence of one for whom nothing is at stake and therefore has nothing to lose. And it was far more profound than the one that philosophy spearheaded, since practically nothing of the old remained afterwards.

We can conveniently divide the artistic upheaval and the break with naturalism into three phases with successively radicalised claims on how the truth of art should be expressed: A. Questioning the naturalness of *perspective* (cubism) B. Questioning the naturalness of *pictorial elements* (Kandinsky), and C. Questioning the very *concept of art* (Duchamp).

Cubism and the Decentralised Point of View

Since pictorial naturalism began with a spontaneous centring of the imagined observer's perspective, it follows that its dissolution began with a decentralisation of the point of view. Following Nietzsche (but not necessarily influenced by him), the Cubists did away with the claim that only *one* dominant point of view in relation to a subject is correct. Already in Cézanne, we can see how the subject-object relationship changes, which Rainer Maria Rilke was one of the first to notice.

In letters to his wife, he writes of his impressions of Cézanne's landscapes and still lifes: '…as he turns to landscape, they start missing the interpretation, the judgement, the superiority.'[162] According to Rilke, this makes the landscape appear *in its own right*, without the intervention of an interpreting subject. In

---

[lxxvii] There was a late Nietzschean movement including Adorno and Marcuse who perceived it that way.

Cézanne's painting, the artist/subject's sentiment is not transferred to nature/object, but on the contrary, it is nature's own elements that assert themselves on man. The novelty of Cézanne is particularly evident when Rilke compares his work to the *Stimmungsmalerei* that was so popular at the time.

The atmospheric painters, Rilke writes, exhibit their love for nature; for a thing. 'They'd paint: I love this here; instead of painting: here it is,'[163] without the intervention of an active subject. It was as if the new kind of painting called for one to *feel for oneself* or in the case of Cubism to *see for oneself* as the overall naturalistic context of meaning had been lost. That, too, was a task for the *Übermensch*.

Nietzsche said that our knowledge is "perspectival". Perspectivism means that if we choose to (theoretically) view the world of phenomena in a certain light; if we let the spotlight of theories fall on existence from a given position, so to speak, this entails that other aspects fall into *shadow*, and are made theoretically invisible. The multi-perspective of Cubism, which still operates on the premise of central perspective insofar as it is still about perspective, attempts to circumvent this "shadowing" by positing a number of simultaneous possible viewpoints.

But Nietzsche's *Übermensch* surrenders the communicatively given connection as a shaper of reality and understands himself instead as a subject who is conscious of the perspectival codifications. Similarly, a superhuman approach is demanded of a viewer of postnaturalist representation, when the isomorphism between image and original subject that has been the ideal of both visual and theoretical communication has been broken. Or, in other words, when the communicative unity contained in the image and which can be conveyed to someone by saying, for example, "this depicts X" no longer applies.

The image no longer "pretends" to be, *or claims to represent*, anything, but is merely what it is: an image; a detached point of view; an unarticulated argument; a *perspective* in Nietzsche's sense. The ideology whose more or less disguised companion is the central perspective, takes the existence of an objective, general human viewpoint on existence for granted. The decomposition of the central perspective, Cubism, implicitly asserts that there is no such thing. It no longer posits an ideal counter-world of real-identical *beings* that it is possible to have a dominant overview on. Instead, it presents a set of divergent perspectives, which allows for many different, yet equivalent, points of view.

Kandinsky and the Secondary Qualities

There were two ways out from the theoretical framework of naturalism. One way was to link up with the currents of thought that criticised the classical foundations of naturalism. Duchamp chose this route, as his main inspiration was Poincarés critical epistemology. Kandinsky, however, chose a very different and a totally divergent set of theories. Kandinsky praised the method of gaining knowledge that anthroposophy, especially Rudolf Steiner, had devised as an *alternative* to Newtonian and Galilean physics.

'In science, these men are positivists, only recognising those things that can be weighed and measured. Anything beyond that they consider as rather discreditable nonsense, that same nonsense about which they held yesterday the theories that today are proven. In art, they are naturalists, which means that they recognise and value the personality, individuality and temperament of the artist up to a certain definite point. This point has been fixed by others, and in it, they believe unflinchingly,'[164] Kandinsky writes. But 'Painting has [only] two weapons at her disposal: 1. Colour. 2. Form.'[165]

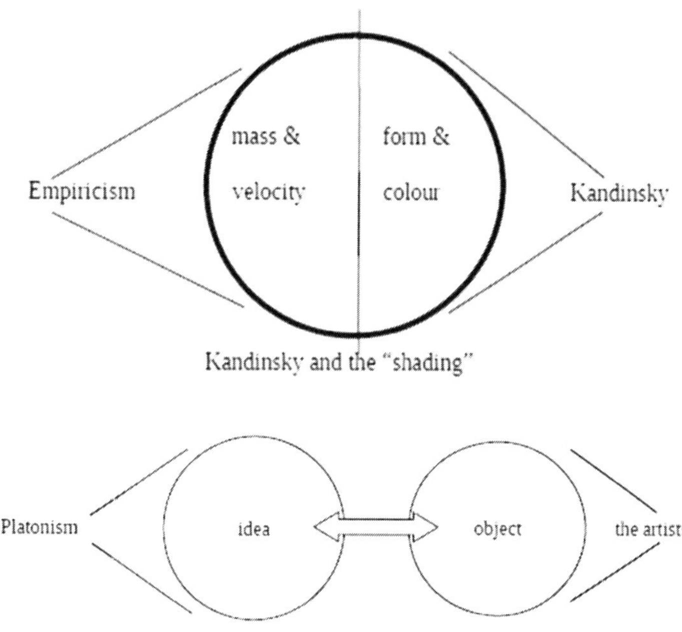

Plato and the "shading"

In Kandinsky, art presents a different set of cosmic laws than those of naturalism; subjectively experienced laws that have not been chosen due to their efficiency or utility. 'Abstract painting leaves behind the 'skin' of nature, but not its laws. Let me use the 'big words' cosmic laws. Art can only be great if it relates directly to cosmic laws and is subordinated to them. One senses these laws unconsciously if one approaches nature not outwardly, but—inwardly. One must be able not merely to see nature, but to experience it. As you see, this has nothing to do with using "objects". Absolutely nothing!'[166]

In the theoretical and abstract perspective from which empiricism viewed the world, sensory qualities were put in the shade. But Kandinsky turned the empiricist procedure on its head, and—preserving the abstraction—saw only what had previously been in the shadow; *colour* and *form*. Kandinsky pictorially produced pure colour and pure form, without any specific material connection. He thus does what the empiricist ideal presupposed—but in reverse.[lxxviii] Thus, the "shading" is an aspect of instrumentality; of the subject-object relation.

Kandinsky visualised the sensory qualities relegated to secondary phenomena in physics, the pure forms, the pure colours and nothing else. In Kandinsky, colours and forms lack, in his own words, "base and foundation", i.e., they lack physical materiality. Colour and form are not a secondary aspect of materiality, but, in contrast to the relationship of Hume and Locke, for Kandinsky colour and form become *primary qualities* in the pictorial representation of existence.

And in so far as the artists flirted with occultism (as also Duchamp is said to have done), epistemologically it meant linking back to insights and principles of inquiry that applied before Galilean physics simplified and unified the world, and before the *qualitative differences* that, according to the contemporary philosopher *à la mode* Henri Bergson, are the hallmarks of a genuine experience of the world, had been reduced and transformed into *quantitative* ones.[lxxix]

We can also look at Kandinsky's ambitions from a different angle, pairing them with the radical nominalism that Nietzsche—and Duchamp later on—

[lxxviii] But unlike empiricism, which gave existence its abstract quantitative character on objective grounds, when it comes to the abstraction of both form and colour Kandinsky refers to the "Principle of inner Necessity"; to the lonely human soul. Kandinsky 1959, p. 64-69

[lxxix] For example, the experience of time: in historical time, every interval is unique. Time in physics, on the other hand, that which is assumed when the *experiment* defines the truth, assumes that all passages of time are identical.

represented. When Kandinsky makes colour *pure* colour, and form *pure* form, he simultaneously abolishes the "natural" connection between the image and the original subject, between image and physical reality.

Just as the nominalists denied that there was a *naturally given* relationship between symbol and reality, only a conventional one, in practice Kandinsky denies that the pictorial relationship between a visual image and external reality is anything other than a convention and that it is valid only as long as this is maintained.

But it is not necessary for it to be maintained: even what colour and form represent are only conventions, for "actually"—and Kandinsky shows this—colour is only colour and not a representative for something or a metaphor; likewise form is only form and not a representation or a depiction of something else. There is no natural homology between things and their ritualistically produced pictorial forms. Only a conventional one: what reality is in reality, is completely indeterminate.

Marcel Duchamp

The life's work of Duchamp is undeniably the result of the strangest artistic work of our time. With uncommon consistency, he created one enigmatic work after another, seemingly forming an unbroken chain in which one work often refers to another, so that taken as a whole, they form a kind of trail. As if strange material forms have crystallised along the points where two slowly rotating galaxies of separate dimensions crossed each other.

As if a listless universe of comfort, on its way to the suttee of galaxies deep in the void, encountered a future-dimensional desire galaxy along an intersection in whose flashpoints events are materialising and unfold into our world as enigmatic things and carriers of dual but undecipherable knowledge. As if one could imagine that a galaxy of water on its path through space would be crossed by a galaxy of nothing but cold and that the memory of the encounter would be a stretch of strangely shaped ice crystals which would be neither water nor cold, but something third. Or a cryptic array of ideograms that do not know what they refer to.

Duchamp used the concept of *nominalisme pictural* to characterise the turnaround that took place in his art sometime between 1912 and 1913, when, by his own account, he ceased to *paint*. With that decision, art in the sense of "naturalism" or art as *depicting* or *representing* something else, definitely dies.

In 1913, Duchamp asked himself: 'Can one [as an artist?] make works which are not "works of art"?'[167]

This question has many layers; on one of them Duchamp's query could be transformed into: Does the name "art" come to an object from an (eternal) *idea* of art, is it linked to what the *artist* produces, or does it accrue to the object via an individual labelling?

As a historical phenomenon, nominalism (as we have seen) belongs to the late medieval stage when the metaphysics that underpinned the ancient instrumental patterns of rationality were eliminated and a new and more concrete foundation was laid.

If we allow ourselves a retrospective extension of the phenomenon of nominalism, we can add the Sophist criticism of Athenian academic philosophy to the extended family of nominalism—a negative nominalism, as it in the absence of contact with the currents that would later change the conditions of knowledge, lacked positive alternatives, but which nevertheless contained the same aspiration as genuine nominalism, namely to relativise the absolute in Platonism.

Duchamp's characterisation of his art as a *nominalisme pictural* is "nominalist" in this latter sense. So is Nietzsche's critique of Kantian metaphysics. That is, it is a critique that is directed against the very core of contemporary science, against its metaphysics, without having anything to replace it.

Nietzsche's critique of science can be summarised in the following posthumously published lines: 'We have measured the value of the world according to categories that refer to a purely fictitious world. Final conclusion: All the values by means of which we have tried so far to render the world estimable for ourselves and which then proved inapplicable and therefore devaluated the world—all these values are, psychologically considered, the results of certain perspectives of utility, designed to maintain and increase human constructs of domination—and they have been falsely projected into the essence of things.'

'What we find here is still the hyperbolic naivete of man: positing himself as the meaning and measure of the value of things.'[168]

Marcel Duchamp knew of, and had probably read Nietzsche. In his book on Duchamp, Ulf Linde says that it 'would be strange if he had not read him [Nietzsche]—carefully.' Further: 'If someone anticipates Duchamp, it is

Nietzsche. Duchamp committed two acts that alone would have been enough to earn him a place in art history: the introduction of chance in *3 stoppages étalon* and the act of signing a readymade. And both are foreshadowed in Nietzsche. [---] But Duchamp must have encountered Nietzsche elsewhere as well.'

'His interest in Poincaré's scientific essays is well documented, and in 1911, a book was published on those very essays, *Un romantisme utilitaire* by René Berthelot. Its subtitle was: *Le pragmatisme chez Nietzsche et chez Poincaré.* The book contains an excellent account of Nietzsche's theory of knowledge, reinforced by numerous essential quotations, all of which show surprising similarities with formulations by Poincaré.'[169]

So Duchamp's theoretical baggage also included Henri Poincaré—and Henri Bergson. That both Bergson and Poincaré were *à la mode* in the 1910s (for example, Poincaré's most famous work, *La science et L'hypothèse* had appeared in twenty editions by 1912) gives an idea of the knowledge-critical climate that prevailed at the time of Duchamp's debut as an artist.[170] The latest philosophical ideas were widely discussed, of course, in the theoretically very knowledgeable circle of friends around the Duchamp brothers.

In connection with the publication of Poincaré's books of popular science, there was a minor debate about nominalism in France. In 1901, M. le Roy had stated his physicalist position in the journal *Science et Philosphie, Revue de Métaphysique et de Morale,* as "nominalist". Already in the preface to *La science et L'hypothèse* Poincaré makes a rather vehement outburst against this position. These nominalists, Poincaré says, 'have asked if the savant is not the dupe of his own definitions, and if the world he thinks he has discovered is not simply the creation of his own caprice.'[171]

Poincaré's own position is that the so-called laws of nature are indeed conventions, but not arbitrary ones.[172] They could, therefore, be described as conventionalist. On the geometrical construction of space Poincaré, for example, says that 'The geometrical axioms are therefore neither synthetic *a priori* intuitions nor experimental facts.' They are, he says in the spirit of Nietzsche, *conventions.*

'Our choice among all possible conventions is guided by experimental facts; but it remains free, and is only limited by the necessity of avoiding every contradiction, and thus it is that postulates may remain rigorously true even when the experimental laws which have determined their adoption are only approximate. In other words, the axioms of geometry [---] are only definitions in disguise.'[173]

And as for the concepts that are central to our physicalist constructions of understanding, i.e., "mass" and "force", Poincaré says that we do not even know what they are. According to Lagrange, force is 'that which moves or tends to move a body,' while Kirchoff defined force as 'the product of the mass and the acceleration.' Poincaré comments: 'When we say that force is something that causes motion, we are speaking metaphysics, and this definition, if we are forced to be satisfied with it, would lead to absolutely nothing.'

And he concludes, 'The principles of dynamics appeared to us first as experimental truths, but we have been compelled to use them as definitions.'[174]

At the end of *The Value of Science*, Poincaré returns to le Roy and his nominalism. Poincaré reveals here that he passionately believes in the search for truth as a noble and (almost) useless virtue, and that this virtue constantly saves science from decaying into arbitrariness—such as creating a science of chess![lxxx]

Among the practical ironies is that Duchamp was not only an accomplished chess player, but also, together with the German chess master, Vitaly Halberstadt, wrote a book on the "theory" of chess; a book which in fact turns out to be the draft of a "science" of the singular and the unique.

'The theory of chess can never become a science,' Poincaré writes, 'for the different moves of the same piece are limited and do not resemble each other.'[175] This was the theory Duchamp had set out to write, even though he knew it would be utterly useless. Because the problems it addresses are of such nature that, according to Duchamp, they appear at most "once in one's lifetime".[lxxxi]

The first non-depictive work Duchamp made was aimed squarely at the core of the linearly unified Euclidean conception of space: he constructed the so-

---

[lxxx] Poincaré does not ask, however, what virtue is, but in the search for truth he sees an absolute value. But bravery and glory were virtues when they had a practical meaning, i.e. during warlike ages when prosperity was tied to the ability to to conquer or retain territories. As we saw in Archilochus, glory could be rejected as soon as one could buy oneself a position. So a virtue is nothing that exists outside of man and his practical expectations, and as we know, the search for truth was no noble virtue during a time in history but, on the contrary, a vice. In this way virtue is part of an interaction; it is a mediator between the individual and the general. That which the general intellect needs most, is produced within the individual as a virtue. The search for truth is thus noble only as long as it is useful. The ideal of beauty is subject to the same terms and conditions.
[lxxxi] Duchamp was thus engaged in a bit of the same thing that Alfred Jarry had done a little earlier in the Pataphysical College: with "the science that governs the exceptions". See Sandqvist 1990, p. 263

called *Trois stoppages étalon*; an alternative *metre* in three variants which not only relativised the unit of length, but also, because he cut out rulers after the randomly curved lines, gave the axiomatics of Euclid's geometry a completely different meaning. Duchamp kept his standard metres/rulers almost with the same care as the archival platinum metre, which is kept by *The International Bureau of Weights and Measures* in Sèvres.

In the geometry of Duchamp, "a straight line" was then the line produced by any of the rulers in *Trois stoppages étalon*—as close to an axiom as one can come. Regarding the standard units (*les étalons*), Poincare had written that 'What, then, are we to think of the question: Is Euclidean geometry true? It has no meaning. We might as well ask if the metric system is true, and if the old weights and measures are false; if Cartesian coordinates are true and polar coordinates false. One geometry cannot be more true than another; it can only be more convenient.'[176]

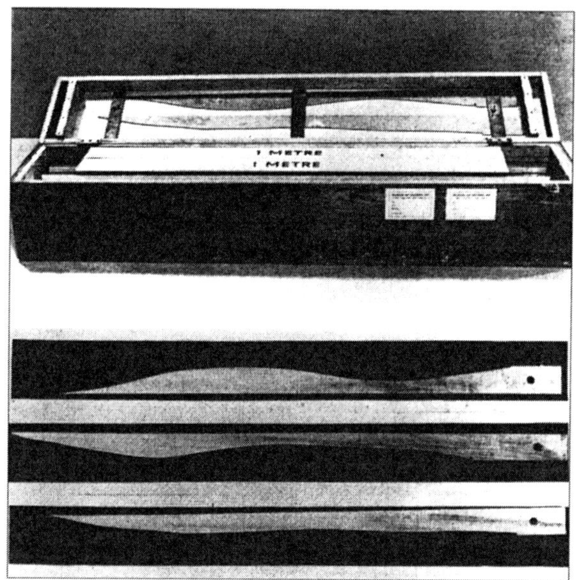

Marcel Duchamp: *Trois stoppages étalon*

In his personal interpretation of the unity of the *Trois stoppages étalon*, Duchamp, (admittedly playfully) does precisely what Nicolaus Cusanus had already resisted, namely asserting that 'scientific principles are pure arrangements to its logical conclusion [and—] that all standards are equally valid, however personal, arbitrary, or capricious they may be. This, the first of

Duchamp's non-paintings, is an image of relativism and subjectivism. It states that there is no necessity, no objective interrelation in nature or in society. According to this work, scientific thought is nothing more than a human presumption, at best self-deception.'[177]

In the *Trois stoppages étalon*, the influence of Poincaré is evident. But there are quite a few other works in which Poincaré's ideas appear to various degrees. Take, for example, *Nu descendant un escalier* from 1912; the painting that was refused, against all principles, by the *Salon des Indépendants* in Paris and which later caused a scandal in New York[lxxxii]. In *Science and Hypothesis,*[178] Poincaré makes an attempt to visualise the fourth dimension—child's play, says Poincaré—by showing how it could be represented on one plane.

'Well, in the same way that we draw the perspective of a three-dimensional figure on a plane, so we can draw that of a four-dimensional figure on a canvas of three (or two) dimensions. To a geometer, this is but child's play. We can even draw several perspectives of the same figure from several different points of view. We can easily represent to ourselves these perspectives, since they are of only three dimensions. Imagine that the different perspectives of one and the same object to occur in succession, and that the transition from one to the other is accompanied by muscular sensations.'

(This muscular sensation of an executed action is, for Poincare, the primary condition for the experience of space as a continuum.)

[lxxxii] Moreover, on the basis of the refusal, another hypothesis for Duchamp's first turn towards nominalism can be made. Duchamp was in fact told by the exhibition commissariat, to which his brothers belonged, that the painting could be accepted if he only changed its *name*! Thus, the *name* would have determined what was art and what was not. It seems to me that the decision of the commissariat was made for reasons of national prestige, as earlier that year, the Italian Futurists held a major exhibition in Paris, which caused a great stir but which the French artists would have preferred to ignore. A couple of days after the opening Apollinaire wrote that "the originality of the futurist school is derived from its endeavour to represent movement. This is a perfectly legitimate aspiration and discovery, but the French painters have solved the problem long ago, to the extent that it has a solution". One of the Futurists, Umberto Boccioni had, moreover, in his manifesto, spoken equally disparagingly of the Cubists – the only one who was good enough for him was Picasso, but he was a Spaniard with a *mother from Genoa*! – Well, the fact is that the *Nu* of Duchamp shows a striking resemblance to Luigi Russolo's *Plastic Synthesis of the Movements of a Woman*, which admittedly was not exhibited among Russolo's other works in Paris, but which Duchamp may have been aware of. The crux for the exhibition curators was that Duchamp represented *movement* in the same way as the Italians. But if he would have agreed to change its title to something *static*, something cubist.

This could be a program for *Nu descendant un escalier* and, if so, would not be Duchamp's only attempt to illustrate "the fourth dimension".

Marcel Duchamp: *Nu descendant un escalier*

Among other ideas that might have originated with Poincaré might be the one where he rotated space by 90 degrees by nailing a coat hanger to the floor. As, according to Poincaré, there was no up and no down, no right and no left. Or when he invented *"physique amusante"*—a variation on Nietzsche's *Gay Science*. Or the fanciful idea of *ironic causality,* and many others.

But the shocking thing about Duchamp is not just that he so ingeniously reworked and undermined the basic postulates of physical naturalism; no, the real startling thing is that, that with his playful irony and derisive criticism, he also made pictorial naturalism impossible.

The Bottle Rack as a Slave

If we understand the increasing relativisation of the elements of art so that Kandinsky, so to speak, denatured the "given" substantiality of colour and form, and the Cubists broke with the magisterial validity of the perspective or point of view, then Duchamp with *The Bottle Rack*, *The Fountain* and the other readymade objects took one further step—the definitive step—in that he questioned the very *concept* of art. This, too, is in line with the nominalistic critique: there is no *general concept* of Art; there is only *actual* Art—Artefacts.

There is no (absent) *beauty*; there is only beauty in that which exists. A kind of hope and a kind of faith are thus shattered; in the possible *constructability of everything* that had been inscribed in the great rotating mechanistic galaxy and whose synonym had been freedom. Now that the inner mass of that galaxy has been consumed it is heading for dissolution into nothingness.

Duchamp recapitulates the origins of *The Bottle Rack* in an interview: 'In 1914, I *did* the *Bottle Rack*. I just *bought* it, at the bazaar of the town hall. The idea of an inscription came as I was doing it. There was an inscription on the bottle rack which I forgot. When I moved from the rue Saint-Hippolyte to leave for the United States, my sister and sister-in-law took everything out, threw it in the garbage. [---] It was in 1915, especially, in the United States, that I did other objects with inscriptions, like the snow shovel, on which I wrote something in English. The word "readymade" thrust itself on me then.'

'It seemed perfect for these things that weren't works of art, that weren't sketches, and to which no art terms applied. [---] The choice of readymades is always based on visual indifference and, at the same time, on the total absence of good or bad taste.'[179]

The original Rack was thus never exhibited, but the copies, whether bought or made, gave the thing-world a different and "higher" life. A simple bottle rack became *The Bottle Rack*, a thing with a proper name, and not only that, for the thing became *art*. Thus, in Nietzsche's words, the bottle rack was "redeemed from the servitude of purpose" and transformed into *something for itself*, an object of admiration or contemplation.

And somewhere in the extension of Duchamp's gesture towards the contemporary, one can presage the contours of an understanding that the conditions of existence of Western Man have once again become fundamentally contradictory. It is an understanding that is in the process of articulating the knowledge, that it is the *machine* and no longer man that sets the boundary conditions for the realisation of human ideals.

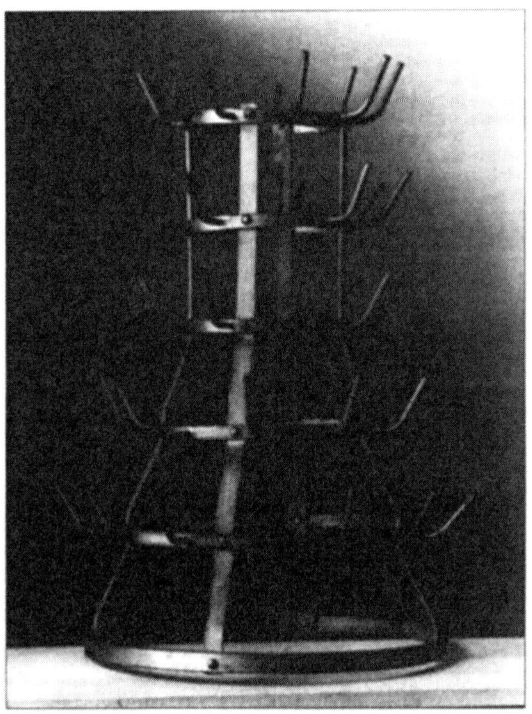

Marcel Duchamp: *The Bottle Rack*

I intend to draw two conclusions from *The Bottle Rack* as art:

First, that the actions and works Duchamp did were of a "nominalist" nature; not only in his own self-understanding but also in their historical *consequences*. This is shown by the fact that after Duchamp no *normative* demands can any longer be made on art. Art is what "one" (= the aesthetic community) agrees upon being art, and "one" is aware of this being the case.

After Duchamp, art is not a reflection of a nature, but of a "second nature", which includes both the first nature as well as the relative conditions of its interpretation. Of Descartes' strong *doubt-belief* model, only scepticism and doubt once again remain.

Second, the *historical* significance that a *tool* is placed in the academically hallowed place where people have become accustomed to encounter a finely tuned, subtle emblem of man's sovereign place in nature, is of the same kind as when sculptors in the Greek cultural area after the erosion of Athenian state rationalism exhibited the image of a living instrument as an object of admiration. But instead of visualised aspects of the dialectic between master and servant, now, from the recesses of cluelessness, there are omens that another and equally fundamental dialectic, the dialectic between man and nature, has reached the turning point where the subject's *counterpart* has begun to claim recognition, in a manner of its *own*. The emphasis on the one hand on the inhuman—the slave— and, on the other hand, the unnatural—the dryer—implies a negation of the subject's former blind idolatry.

The first sign of this is, therefore, that the *differentiating*, the tool, is exhibited *in itself*, in order to become the object of visual attention and reflective contemplation in its own right. The denial of naturalism has the same origins as the denial of idealism by Hellenism. They are born of the same spirit and they declare that the categories of reason are turning against reason itself, insofar as a certain rationality of production has lost its self-evident justification.

And just as the changes in the plastic image of man in antiquity contained an underlying message of freedom, so the new shape of art can also be projected onto the broad canvas of freedom. If, as Kant says, we produce freedom by the means of the *thing*, or as in Hegel and Marx by the means of *work*, and that the synthesis is that freedom for us is produced by working things, the analogy with the demise of ancient political rationality can be made clearer: *We* can see that antiquity produced freedom instrumentally because they could and had to deny the general concept of *human*.

We also produce freedom instrumentally but cannot—in the same manner as the Greeks—see the dilemma, because we have imagined that we are *above* nature with the absolute right to use nature for our own purposes. We have denied that we and nature would have anything essential in common. Or as Nietzsche says: 'We speak of nature and forget to include ourselves: we ourselves are nature, *quand même*. It follows that nature is something quite different from what we think of when we speak its name.'[180]

One is subject and the other object. The age of machinal existence has enslaved nature, but the question is whether it has not equally enslaved itself.

The Transition from Innocence into Insight

In his book on Marcel Duchamp and pictorial nominalism, Thierry de Duve bestows one of the last "real" paintings Duchamp made, the remarkable canvas *LE PASSAGE de la vierge à la mariée (THE PASSAGE from Virgin to Bride)* of 1912 a decisive importance.[lxxxiii]

According to de Duve, it is not only about a PASSAGE from innocence to knowledge (for the BRIDE does not become guilty by her marriage; but probably becomes aware of the matter, and possibly also disillusioned) but the passage concerns, in a broader sense, an epistemological rupture which, according to de Duve, metaphorically marks a 'passage from an ontology to an epistemology, from painting as Being to painting as Knowing.'[181]

Marcel Duchamp: *The PASSAGE Passage from Virgin to Bride*

I agree with de Duve, though on different grounds. For Leonardo, painting was also a *cosa mentale*, so the epistemological foundations as such are not new. It is a new kind of knowing that intervenes in the creative process, a knowledge that I in the same spirit as Hegel with regard to antiquity would call *unhappy*, in the sense of lacking all prospects.

In Hegel's interpretation of Greek scepticism, the sceptic's misfortune is that he is divided. What was previously existentially separated, is united in the sceptic

[lxxxiii] de Duve 1987, p. 115ff. & p. 173. I have written the title in upper and lower case in the same way as Duchamp did, to make it clear that it is above all a PASSAGE. The two adjoining paintings, *static* in name, are called VIERGE and MARIÉE respectively, and were made during the same, for Duchamp's development, crucial summer. The titles thus explicitly *belong* to the paintings, since they are written in the place where the artist usually only signs his name. The name is the painting; the painting is the name.

into a double in that he himself unites two opposite, and within the framework in which he operated, incompatible states of knowledge: the self-understanding of the master and the self-understanding of the slave.

'The doubling, which was previously distributed between two singular individuals, the master and the servant, is thereby brought back into one singular individual. Although, the doubling of self-consciousness within itself, which is essential in the concept of spirit, is thereby present, its unity is not yet present, and the unhappy consciousness is the consciousness of itself as a doubled, only contradictory creature.'[lxxxiv]

The same incompatibility and the same unhappiness in the sense of hopelessness is found in modern scepticism or nihilism which in its expression has internalised the modern subject-object split; which suffers from the conventional lies but at the same time sees that the affirmation of only a pure being lacks prospects, a being uncluttered by logical and grammatical categories

---

[lxxxiv] Georg Wilhelm Friedrich Hegel: *The Phenomenology of Spirit* 2018, p. 123. I know that there are those who think that Hegel's interpretation of scepticism is nonsense; who think that scepticism is a pure logical approach which has its origins in the problems that Aristotle's logic and categories gave rise to. I ask these sceptics to consider the following: one of the crucial contradictory determinations in Greek philosophy concerns *motion*. There were those who, referring to Zeno for example, said that motion does not exist. More realistic people said that it does exist. Or, to follow Diogenes Laertius: "Some claim that it exists and some that it does not; the Pyrrhonists (i.e. the sceptics) that it neither exists nor does not exist." In Aristotle the main aspect of movement is that movement is a traversal towards a *static* goal. The most essential expression for the category of *motion* is thus static and stationary. But the *telos* of Aristotle (and the still more static *idea* of Plato) is most certainly the expression of a philosophical master-position. For if one does not see it – and, by the way, teleology permeates all levels in Aristotle, including the practical ones in a pattern that explicitly states that things exist to be appropriated by those who have the power to do so --; if one does not see that Aristotle has essential ideological values to defend and that this rubs off on his ontology, his ontology becomes, as I see it, completely incomprehensible. One is almost forced to believe that he was a bit stupid. (This is not my judgement, but that of half a millennium) He wasn't stupid, but instead a brilliant interpreter of the theoretical potential of a successful constellation of power. When one then deprives the Aristotelian categories of power, which in practice happens when Alexander treats barbarians and Hellenes equally, then teleology disappears, and movement (later on) essentially becomes a *dynamic* aspect of work. But the sceptics, who were situated in the middle of the epoch, in the turning point the Greeks called *epoché*; the sceptics who affirmed both the head of the master and the corporeality of the slave, could not make up their minds; movement both existed and did not exist (as a dynamic phenomenon). For example: (borrowed from Pliny the Elder) If one is travelling in a sedan chair, then movement is rest and the knowledge of the goal or address is the essential aspect of movement; if one, on the other hand, has to carry the chair, then movement is an activity, work and a result of the use of force.

in a constantly new now. Which neither can identify itself with the activity of the (technologically superior) subject, nor utilise the pure naturalness of the object—nature.

The misfortune of nihilism is that it tries to overcome knowledge with knowledge; to overcome the subject with more subjectivity. And as in classical scepticism (and stoicism), both fall back to the only project that scepticism and nihilism can realise while maintaining their premises: the *ataractic* or *superhuman* self. The self that "philosophises with the hammer" (Nietzsche), or who has a habit of bursting into "incomparable explosions" when "left to itself" (Duchamp).

In an interview with Arturo Schwarz, Duchamp is reported to have said that 'when he was librarian at the Bibliotheque Sainte-Genevieve [when he had "stopped painting and started working" in 1913] and had the opportunity to go through the Greek philosophers once more, the one he appreciated most and which was closest to his own interest was Pyrrho.'[182] Pyrrho of Elis was the founder of the sceptical school and, according to Diogenes Laertios, made his living as a painter.

A combination that certainly could have piqued Duchamp's interest. It is possible that Herbert Molderings is right when he says that what Duchamp found in Pyrrho was 'a philosophy that asked how one should live; how one should behave in life.'[183] But if it were merely an initiation into ataraxia and the art of living, one might imagine that there would have been more articulate moralists among, say, the Stoics—Pyrrho we know very little about. It is rather a form of *ambivalence* that unites Duchamp with his ancient colleague; *ouden mallon*—being indecisive.

For Duchamp, who was going through his "nominalist crisis", this was a welcome stimulus. Pyrrho had taught that all values depended on human conventions, and that every proposition was as well-founded as its contradictory counterpart. To choose, in the sceptical context, thus implied choosing a set of *conventions*, in practice the system of norms of the master or the slave. And that, according to the sceptics, was impracticable.

Duchamp accepted the sceptics' challenge with delight, and in the ambivalent space between opposites, cultivated his particular art form, which certainly included "the art of living". The interplay between opposites most easily found in Duchamp are those between male and female; between art and non-art; technology and nature; trivial and subtle; beautiful and ugly; calculated and random; mass-produced and unique, etc.

In the background, however, there is a subject-object problem just as in Pyrrho, and a deeply felt dissatisfaction with the principles of naturalism and with the cultural values and scientific truths associated with them.[lxxxv]

But Duchamp, of course, worked primarily in the modernist tradition he himself had created, so when de Duve says that to 'paint after Duchamp means to paint in the hostile conditions set up by industrialisation,'[184] these are conditions that Duchamp himself shared. Where Leonardo da Vinci stands at the dawn of an industrial epoch as the supreme introducer in pictorial form of its productive strategies, Duchamp stands at its end and observes its results with an ironic smile.

(Incidentally, the Leonardian imprints in Duchamp are perhaps more numerous than one could imagine. These include not only the immodest bearded Mona Lisa, but also the androgynous characters, the fascination with machines, the reproduction of anatomy as a form of dynamic-pneumatic mechanics, and indeed even an element of form, *The Glider*, is present in both of them. The relationship between Duchamp and Leonardo in all of these cases is like the play of irony with seriousness.)[lxxxvi]

The "hostile conditions" de Duve speaks of could conceivably consist of the indeterminacy that arises when the premises that sustain the aesthetic system begin to contradict each other. If A and non-A simultaneously apply within a set of norms, *anything goes* within the system. In the later stages of Hellenism, both human and un-human could be set up as idols. This contradiction eroded *idealisation* as an aesthetic norm; after that "everything was permitted", i.e., Greek realism became possible. (The change of thought-categories was subject to the same conditions.)

After Duchamp, the concept of art could include representations of nature as well as un-nature, which in turn led to *naturalism* as an aesthetic norm losing its

---

[lxxxv] In a late interview Duchamp voiced his Pyrrhic scepticism in the following manner: "After all we have to accept those so-called laws of science because it makes life more convenient, but that doesn't mean anything sofar as validity is concerned. Maybe it's all just an illusion. We are so fond of ourselves, we think we are little gods of the earth – I have my doubts about it, that's all."

[lxxxvi] The Glider is on sheet LXXXII in Leonardo 1939. The original is included in Codex Adanticus, which after its Bonapartist tour of Paris, is now kept in Milan, but a copy of Richter's book which first appeared as early as 1883 should probably have been kept in the Bibliothèque Sainte-Geneviève.

unambiguous validity. *The Bottle Rack* and the *Fountain* as aesthetic manifestations had exposed the contradiction between the beautiful in Kant's sense (the work of art) and the originally beautiful (nature) because Duchamp, in the place of art, had inserted an object (that was yet) alien to art, which did not refer to nature and therefore could not lay claim to being beautiful.

The demand for isometry between nature and a work of art, that had already been woven into the grammar of naturalism's imagery by Bonaventure and Nicolaus Cusanus, and where *likeness* was seen as a synonym for beauty, no longer applied. The *work of art* itself became the centrepiece and the *likeness* became the likeness of the work to itself. Naturalism as an ideal and aesthetic norm was thus dissolved and everything became possible once again. In the words of de Duve: 'With the readymade, however, the shift from the classical to the modern aesthetic judgement is brought into the open, as the substitution of the sentence 'this is art' for the sentence "this is beautiful".'[185]

However, the two sentences are neither symmetrical nor syntactically equivalent. If I go into a museum or a gallery and I see an object arranged according to principles with which I am familiar, I *know* at once that this object is a work of art, and I know it in relation to classical as well as modern art[lxxxvii]. I do not have to explicitly state it to myself.

No, something else is going on. When I stand in the gallery looking at a foreign object that I know is art, I don't exclaim: "this is beautiful", but neither do I exclaim: "this is art". Possibly, about an object like the *Bottle Rack,* I could say: "how useful", but then I would be suspending its status as art. But I know that my reaction would be: "how interesting/uninteresting"—or synonymously: "how relevant/irrelevant"; "how convincing/pointless", etc.

And these are statements that are symmetrical with "this is beautiful/ugly", where "the interesting" in the same way as "the beautiful" in Kant refers to an "indeterminate concept", which we can identify after all.

So now we can reconnect to the remaining conceptuality in Kant's view on art, namely 'the supersensible substratum of phenomena.' What did Kant mean

---

[lxxxvii] This argument applies to the observer's perspective de Duve deals with in connection to Kant. From the artist's perspective it looks a little different. The artist makes a *proposition* with his work: this is beautiful (in classical aesthetics); or: this is art (in modern). Thus far de Duve's observation is valid. But above all it applies to the paradigmatic case extensively studied by de Duve (de Duve 1996, ch. 2), which concerns the reception of *Fountain* in New York in 1917

by this, and what role does this strange entity play when we form an opinion of a work of art and pronounce it beautiful or not beautiful/convincing or pointless?

Kant's conception of art is far more subtle than that which is found among the majority of art theorists today. He does not see art as an independent, autonomous phenomenon, but sees it as an integrated part of a larger whole, the endpoints of which can be described as, for example, Necessity and Freedom. In Kant, Art (or more generally: Culture) is the mediating instance between Necessity/Nature and Freedom.

The concept of Nature and the concept of Freedom stand in absolute opposition to each other,[186] (these are the words of a pupil of Francis Bacon, Newton and Hume), but Art as a mediator stands in relation to them both, (thus speaks the spiritual father of Hegel and Marx). The free relation to Nature is portrayed as *beauty*, but this is not enough for beauty to be beautiful. It must also have a natural relation to Freedom, and this *supersensible relation* presupposes that 'the beautiful is the symbol of the morally good.' (§ 59).

It is then this teleologically related *supersensible substratum* which we refer to when assessing the value of a work of art.[lxxxviii] Art is not, and never has been, ethically neutral in relation to the conditions in which it was created. It has always highlighted the underlying conditions that must be met for one to be able to realise a life in accordance with good morals.

As long as the dichotomy Freedom—Nature could be unquestionably maintained in the realm of thought as well as in productive practice, the naturalistic concept of beauty in art functioned as a reflection of man's sovereign freedom in relation to nature. But as soon as it was challenged, when in other words, it was no longer unquestionably "morally good" that freedom and convenience were created out of a mastery of nature, that which reported the other way—i.e., beauty—changed at the same moment. It became naive or impossible.

At the same time, the concepts became blurred and man became part nature, while nature partly was acknowledged with freedom. Art changed completely. It became, as it had been in antiquity, aware of the norms and instruments that maintained this contradiction. The sense of beauty, which in Kant's aesthetics was the intermediary between knowledge (freedom) and desire (nature), Duchamp ironically turned against them both. He made fun of both knowledge

---

[lxxxviii] Sometimes this substrate has appeared as a normative condition with the name of *academism, socialist realism, etc.* and sometimes not.

(science) and desire—by exhibiting them. He made knowledge irrelevant and free, while mechanising desire (*The Bachelor Machine* in all its variations).

The aesthetic actions of Duchamp and his successors—e.g., Joseph Beuys—thus implicitly contain an argument against Kant which says that Kant was only temporarily right when he claimed that 'between the realm of the natural concept, as the sensible, and the realm of the concept of freedom, as the supersensible, there is a great gulf fixed, so that it is not possible to pass from the former to the latter (by means of the theoretical employment of reason).'[187] Freedom is not free in absolute terms, and nature is not absolutely natural. They are both a creation of culture.

The interesting thing, then, is that when the philosophers and artists of the beginning of the last century did away with naturalistic metaphysics, the gap between the concept of nature and the concept of freedom disappeared, and it became possible, for example, to speak of "rights of nature". At the same time, the qualities that had manifested the sensible and supersensible substrates of nature and freedom disappeared, namely beauty and freedom as *end goals*. There was no point in demanding "more beauty" (of art) or "more freedom" (of society).

In a way that at least makes me recall the events that took place two thousand years ago, when an abstract freedom was given to the slaves and an abstract slavery was placed on the masters, it now seems that *nature* would be allowed to share the hitherto abstract idea of freedom, while man, on the other hand, will have to learn to observe the hard laws of necessity once more.

But let us return to LE PASSAGE:

The experience of the wedding night and the transition from virginity to experience is an irreversible process; there is no way back to innocence. The experience of the consciousness in the PASSAGE makes it enlightened about itself and its *opposite*, the other sex—i.e., about the totality which, due to matters of custom, it has hitherto not had the means of fully comprehending. The transition from virgin to bride is also a transition from innocent freedom to conscious unfreedom; freedom is an untenable ideal in the married state.

If Modernity is filled with innocent confidence and unabashed optimism for the future, her name becomes Postmodernity after the espousal with inevitable Fate: no old truths apply anymore, freedom has become meaningless, and even that which Postmodernity initially placed so much emphasis on, that everything would always be New, is ultimately not even fun. There is no *promise* in contemporary life anymore. The aspirations, hopes and expectancies that form the force field that rationality orients itself around, have ebbed away. Reason has entered a directionless zone with no poles; all directions are equally indeterminate and equally diffuse.

And when (the great) future is missing, (the great) history disappears as well. Everything becomes equally valid but also equally indifferent. In the end, perhaps our time will reach the same stage as a maturing marriage: the dream of freedom is replaced by the demand for morality. In this, we can also recognise something from the past, and in a manner, we are right back where we started: and in another infinitely far from it.

Bibliography

Abelard, P., d'Argenteuil, H. (2004) The Letters of Abelard and Héloïse, Transl. Betty Radice, London.

Alberti, L. B. (1969) Della Famiglia, Torino.

Alberti, L. B. (1956) On Painting, Transl. John R. Spencer, Yale UP.

Anderson, P. (1974) Passages from Antiquity to Feudalism, London.

Antal, F. (1947) Florentine Painting and Its Social Background, London.

Aristotle: Perseus Digital Library. keyword Aristotle.

St. Augustine (1997) Confessions, Transl. J. M. Lelen, Catholic Book Publ.

St. Augustine, De civitate Dei.

Austin, M. M., Vidal-Nacquet, P. (1977) Economic and Social History of Ancient Greece, Berkeley.

Averroes, (1986) Averroes' Middle Commentary on Aristotle's Politics, Transl.C. E. Butterworth, Princeton UP.

Bacon, F., Spedding, J. (ed. et al.) (1857–1869) The Works of Francis Bacon, New York.

Bacon, F., Johnston, A. (ed.) (1974) The Advancement of Learning, Oxford.

Bacon, R., Burke, R. B. (ed.) (1928) The Opus Majus, Philadelphia.

Barasch, M. (1987) Giotto and the Language of Gesture, Cambridge.

Battisti, E. (1960) Giotto, Lausanne.

Baumgarten, A. G. Aesthetica.

Baxandall, M. (1971) Giotto and the Orators: Humanist Observers of Painting in Italy and the Discovery of Pictorial Composition 1350–1450, Oxford.

Blumenberg, H. (1973) Der Prozess der theoretischen Neugierde, Frankfurt/M.

Boccaccio, G., The Decameron, Transl. John Payne, Standard eBooks.

Boeder, H. (1959) Der frühgriechische Wortgebrauch von Logos und Aletheia, Archiv für Begriffsgeschichte, No. 4.

Boëthius, The Consolation of Philosophy, Transl. W. C. Cooper.

Boyle, M. O. (1991) Petrarch's Genius: Pentimento and Prophecy, Berkeley.

Bramly, S. (1988) Leonardo da Vinci, Transl. Siân Reynolds, Penguin Book.

Burke, P. (1986) The Italian Renaissance, Princeton UP.

Cassirer, E. (2010) The Individual and the Cosmos in Renaissance Philosophy, Transl. Mario Domandi, Chicago.

Cassirer, E. (1911) Das Erkenntnisproblem, Berlin.

Cassirer, E. Substance And Function/Einstein's Theory of Relativity III. I, (online text), Transl. William Curtis and Marie Collins Swabey.

Cicero, De natura deorum, De officiis, De finibus, in The Loeb classical library, Transl. H. Rackham.

Crombie, A. C. (1953) Robert Grosseteste and the Origin of Experimental Science 1100–1700, Oxford.

Dante Alighieri. The Divine Comedy: Inferno.

Dante Alighieri. Dante to Cangrande, Transl. James Marchand, (online text), Georgetown UP.

Davis, C. T. (1957) Dante and the Idea of Rome, Oxford: Clarendon.

Descartes, R. (1899) Discourse on the Method of Rightly Conducting the Reason, and Seeking Truth in the Sciences I, Transl. John Veitch, La Salle, Ill.

Diels & Kranz (1952) Fragmente der Vorsokratiker, Berlin.

Diogenes Laërtius, (1853) The Lives and Opinions of Eminent Philosophers, Transl. C. D. Yonge, London.

Drews, A. (1964) Plotin und die Untergang der antiken Weltanchauung, Aalen.

de Duve, T. (1996) Kant after Duchamp, Cambridge: MIT Press.

de Duve, T. (1984) Pictorial Nominalism: On Marcel Duchamp's Passage from Painting to the Readymade, Transl. Dana Polan with the author, University of Minnesota Press.

de Duvc, T. (1991) The Definitively Unfinished Marcel Duchamp. Cambridge: MIT Press.

Eco, U. (1986) Art and Beauty in the Middle Ages, Transl. Hugh Bredin, Yale UP.

Elias, N. (1969) The Civilising Process, vol. I, Transl. Edmund Jephcott, Oxford.

Farrington, B. (1964) The Philosophy of Francis Bacon, Liverpool.

Finley, M. I. (1973) The Ancient Economy, Berkeley.

Foucault M. (1977) Discipline and Punishment, Transl. Alan Sheridan, London.

Foucault M. (1978 -) The History of Sexuality, Transl. Robert Hurley, New York.

Foucault M., Gordon, C. (ed. et al.) (1980) Power/Knowledge: Selected Interviews and Other Writings, Transl. C. Gordon.

Galileo Galilei. (1953) The Dialogue Concerning the Two Chief World Systems, Transl. Stillman Drake, Berkeley.

Gibbon, E. (2003) The History of the Decline and Fall of the Roman Empire, New York.

Gilson, É. (1955) History of Christian Philosophy in the Middle Ages, New York.

Gosebruch, M. (1962) Giotto und die Entwicklung des neuzeitlichen Kunstbewusstseins, Köln.

Gregory, T. (1992) Mundana sapiential: Forme di conoscenza nella cultura medieval, Roma.

Gurevich, A. J. (1985) Categories of Medieval Culture, Transl. G. L. Campbell, London.

Guthrie, W. K. C. (1962) A History of Greek Philosophy I, Cambridge.

Hannestaed, N. (1986) Roman Art and Imperial Policy, Århus.

Hegel, G. W. F. (1975) Aesthetics: Lectures on Fine Art, Transl. T. M. Knox, Oxford.

Hegel, G. W. F. (1979) Hegel's System of Ethical Life and First Philosophy of Spirit, Transl. H. S. Harris and T. M. Knox, New York.

Hegel, G. W. F. (1932) Jenenser Realphilosophie I. Ed. Georg Lasson (1911), Leipzig.

Hegel, G. W. F. (2018) The Phenomenology of Spirit, Transl. Terry Pinkard, Cambridge University Press.

Herodotus (2013) The Histories, Transl. J. Marincola, New York.

Huizinga, J. (1922) The Waning of the Middle Ages, eBook, London.

Hume, D. (1993) An Enquiry Concerning Human Understanding, Indianapolis.

Immler, H. (1985) Natur in der ökonomischen Theorie, Opladen.

Janson, H. W. (1962) History of Art, New York.

Jaspers, K. (1964) Nikolaus Cusanus, München.

Jünger, E. (1960–64) Der Arbeiter (1932): Werke, Bd. 6, Stuttgart.

Kandinsky, W. (1977) Concerning the Spiritual in Art, Transl. M. T. H. Sadler, New York.

Kant, I. (1952) The Critique of Judgement, Transl. J. C. Meredith, Oxford.

Keuls, E. C. (1978) Plato and Greek Painting, Leiden.

Ladurie, E. R. (1978) Montaillou, Transl. Barbara Bray, New York.

Leonardo da Vinci, Richter, J. (ed.) (1939) The Literary Works, London.

Lindberg, D. C. (1976) Theories of Vision from Al-Kindi to Kepler, Chicago.

Linde, U. (1986) Marcel Duchamp, Rabén & Sjögren, Stockholm.

Lucretius, C. T. (1977) The Nature of Things, Transl. Frank O. Copely, New York.

Meyboom, P. G. P. (1995) The Nile Mosaic of Palestrina: Early Evidence of Egyptian Religion in Italy, Leiden.

Monk, R. (1990) Ludwig Wittgenstein: The Duty of Genius, New York.

de Montaigne, M. (1958) The Complete Essays of Montaigne, Transl. Donald M. Fame, Stanford.

Murray, A. (1978) Reason and Society in the Middle Ages, Oxford U.P.

Mussato, A., Berrigan, J. R. (ed.) (1975) Ecerinis, München.

Müller, H. (1987) Früher Humanismus in Oberitalien, Albertino Mussato:

Ecerinis , Frankfurt/M.

Nicholas of Cusa (Cusanus, N.), De Ludo Globi, Transl. Jasper Hopkins.

Nicholas of Cusa. (1954) Of Learned Ignorance, Transl. Germain Heron, Yale UP.

Nicholas of Cusa. Metaphysical Speculations, Transl. Jasper Hopkins.

Nicholas of Cusa. (2001) Complete philosophical and theological treatises of Nicholas of Cusa, I-II, Transl. Jasper Hopkins, Minneapolis.

Nietzsche, F., Montinari, M., Colli, G. (ed.) (1992) Sämtliche Werke. Kritische Studienausgabe, Berlin & Nördlingen.

Nietzsche, F., Levy, O., Guppy, R. (eds.) The Complete Works of Friedrich Nietzsche, onlinebooks.library.upenn.edu.

Nietzsche, F. (1964) The Will to Power, Transl. Anthony M. Ludovici, Pennsylvania State University.

Nietzsche, F. (1998) Twilight of the Idols, Transl. Duncan Large, Oxford UP.

O'Daly, G. J. P. (1993) Plotinus' Philosophy of the Self, Shannon: Irish University Press.

Ovid (1986) Metamorphoses, Transl. A. D. Melville, Oxford UP.

Panofsky, E. (1968) Idea: A Concept in Art Theory, Transl. Joseph J. S. Peake, New York.

Panofsky, E. (1991) Perspective as Symbolic Form, Transl. Christopher S. Wood, New York.

Panofsky, E. (1940) The Codex Huygens and Leonardo da Vinci's Art Theory, London: Warburg Institute.

Pearson, C. (2011) Humanism and the Urban World: Leon Battista Alberti and the Renaissance City, Pennsylvania State UP.

Petrarch, F. (2015) Secretum, Transl. J. G. Nichols, London.

Petrarch, F., Rerum Memorandarum Libri.

Petrarch, F. (2000) The Canzoniere, Transl. J. G. Nichols, Manchester.

Petrarch, F. (2010) Sekretum, Transl. J. G. Nichols, Richmond Surrey.

Petrarch, F., Lokaj, R. (ed.) (2006) Petrarch's Ascent of Mount Ventoux, (the Familiaris IV, I), Rome.

Petrarch, F., Bernardo, A. (ed.) (1975–1985) Familiares o Familiarium rerum libri, Albany.

Plato: Perseus Digital Library. keyword Plato.

Plotinus, The Six Enneads: The Internet Classics Archive, Transl. Stephen MacKenna & B. S. Page.

Poincaré, H. (1905) Science and Hypothesis, Transl. V. J. Greenstreet, New York.

Poincaré, H., Gould, S. J. (ed.) (2001) The Value of Science, Random House.

Polanyi, K. (1957) Aristotle Discovers Economy: In Trade and Market in the Early Empires, Ed. Karl Polanyi, Glencoe.

Poulsen, V. (1965) Från grottorna till Rom, Transl. Kerstin Karling, Stockholm.

Riegl, A. (1927) Spätrömische Kunstindustrie, Wien.

Rilke, R. M. (1985) Letters on Cézanne, Transl. Joel Agee, North Point Press.

Ringbom, S. (1991) Det ytliga djupet, Essäer om den abstrakta konsten och dess förhistoria, Helsingfors.

Rossi, P. (1957) Francesco Bacone, Laterza, Bari.

Roy, J., Shipley, G., Salmon, J. (ed.) (1996) The Countryside in Classical Greek Drama: In Human Landscape in Classical Antiquity, London.

Sandqvist, T. (1990) Vid gränsen, Kristianstad.

Sappho, Transl. Julia Dubnoff, https://www.uh.edu/~cldue/texts/sappho.html.

Sartre, J. (1956) Being and Nothingness, Transl. Hazel E. Barnes, New York.

Schanz, H. (1990) Hvad er metafysik? Hvad er moderne?, Århus.

Schwarz, A. (1969) The Complete Works of Marcel Duchamp, New York.

Seneca (1969) Letters from a Stoic, Transl. Robin Campbell, Penguin Books.

Sløk, J. (1974) Cusanus' dialog om visdomen, Skjern.

Snell, B. (1953) The Discovery of the Mind, Transl. T. G. Rosenmeyer, Blackwell.

Spivey, N. J. (1996) Understanding Greek Sculpture, London.

Stierle, K. (1979) Petrarcas Landschaften: Zur Geschichte ästhetischer Lanschaftserfahrung, Krefeld.

Suger, (Sugerius) (1948) On the Abbey Church of St Denis and Its Art Treasures, Ed. and Transl. Erwin Panofsky, Princeton.

Summers, D. (1987) The Judgement of Sense: Renaissance Naturalism and the Rise of Aesthetics, Cambridge.

Taylor, C. (2005) Hegel, Cambridge: Cambridge University Press.

Thesleff, H. (1990) Platon, Lund.

Thode, H. (1904) Franz von Assisi und die Anfänge der Kunst des Renaissance in Italien, Berlin.

Thomas Aquinas, Summa Contra Gentiles, Transl. Anton C. Pegis, University of Notre Dame Press.

Thomas Aquinas, Summa Theologiae, Transl. by Fathers of the English Dominican Province, Online Edition.

Vogt, J. (1974) Ancient Slavery and the Ideal of Man, Oxford: Blackwell.

Warner, M. (1990) Alone of All Her Sex: The Myth and the Cult of the Virgin Mary, London.

Wiedemann, T. (1981) Greek and Roman Slavery, Baltimore: Johns Hopkins UP.

Xenophon (1179) On Revenues: Ways and Means, Transl. Henry Graham Dakyns, Project Gutenberg Release #1179.

Yavets, Z. (1988) Slave and Slavery in Ancient Rome, New Brunswick.

Zanker, P. (1988) The Power of Images in the Age of Augustus, Transl. Alan Shapiro, Ann Arbor.

Endnotes

[1] *Kuva ja ajatus,* 2017, transl. Jarkko S. Tuusvuori

[2] For how the Greeks unified knowledge and power see e.g., Ewen Bowie: *Greeks and Their Past in the Second Sophistic.* In *Studies in Ancient Society.* Ed. Moses Finley, 1974, p. 166–209; T. A. Sinclair: *A History of Greek Political Thought,* 2010, p. 47.

[3] Aristotle*: Metaphysics*, 982a. I will use the concept of metaphysics in a broad manner, allowing myself to speak of the "metaphysics of an epoch", as in the dominant modes of understanding that underlie that epoch's interpretations of existence.

[4] Leonardo da Vinci: *The Notebooks of Leonardo da Vinci*, fr. 1154. Transl. Jean Paul Richter

[5] Friedrich Nietzsche: *The Will to Power* 12 B, Transl. Anthony M Ludovici

[6] Aristotle: *Politics* 1253b; 1254a, transl. H. Rackham

[7] Aristotle: *Politics* 1282b

[8] Aristotle: *Politics* 1328a

[9] Aristotle: *Politics* 1333b-1334a

[10] Xenophon: *On Revenues. Ways and Means,* I.17, 23-24

[11] G.W.F. Hegel: *Hegel's System of Ethical Life and First Philosophy of Spirit* 1979 p. 230 , transl. by H.S. Harris and T.M. Knox. Ernst Jünger defined technology in 1932 in the following manner: "Die Technik ist die Art und Weise, in der die Gestalt des Arbeiters die Welt mobilisiert. [---] Technik in diesem Sinne ist die Beherrschung der Sprache, die im Arbeitsraume gültig ist. Diese Sprache ist nicht weniger bedeutend, nicht weniger tief als jede andere, da sie nicht nur Grammatik, sondern auch Metaphysik besitzt."(Ernst Jünger Bd. 6, Stuttgart 1960-64, p. 165)

[12] Ernst Cassirer: *Substance And Function / Einstein's Theory Of Relativity* 1953, p.68. Transl. William Curtis Swabey and Marie Collins Swabey.

[13] Ludwig Wittgenstein: *Tractatus*, 6.371 and 6.372. Transl. C.K. Ogden

[14] According to Karl Polanyi the concepts were used for the first time by Ferdinand Tönnies and Sir Henry Summer Maine; see *Aristotle discovers the economy*, in Polanyi 1957

[15] Aristotle: *Rhetorica ad Alexandrum,* ed. W. D. Ross, chapter 28. Transl. E. S. Forster

[16] Thomas R. Martin, Christopher W. Blackwell: *Alexander the Great. The Story of an Ancient Life*, 2012, p. 181

[17] Cicero: *In Verrem* II.V 57; cf. the *Book of Acts,* 22:25-28

[18] See e.g. Seneca: *On Benefits* or the famous passage in *Letters from a Stoic* (letter 47) in which he argues for the human rights of slaves.

[19] Aristotle: *Politics* 1253b. Transl. H. Rackham

[20] Erwin Panofsky: *Idea: A Concept in Art Theory* 1968, p. 38. Transl. Joseph J. S. Peake

[21] Aristotle: *Metaphysics* 982b

[22] St. Augustine: *Confessions*, V.3

[23] See Niels Hannestaed: *Roman Art and Imperial Policy,* 1986

[24] Vagn Poulsen: *Från grottorna till Rom*, 1965, p. 342 -

[25] Paul Zanker: *The Power of Images in the Age of Augustus*, 1988. p. 332 -

[26] Emperor Constantine VII Porphyrogenitus quoted in Robert Byron, David Talbot Rice: *The Birth of Western Painting* 2013, p. 45

[27] See e.g. *Galatians* 3:13. For an explicit formulation of the metaphor of manumission see 1 *Corinthians* 7:20-24 that is preceded (7:19) by the other strategic moves Paul made in enabling Christianity to become a Roman religion: The Jewish injunctions regarding circumcision and the dietary regulations peculiar to Greeks and Romans did not have to be observed. "You can eat anything sold in the meat market without raising questions of conscience", he wrote, and "circumcision is nothing and uncircumcision is nothing. Keeping God's commands is what counts". See also Joseph Vogt: *Ancient Slavery and the Ideal of Man*, 1974, p. 165 f.

[28] *Gal.* 3:28

[29] Joseph Jacobs and Emil G. Hirsch → *Salvation*, in www.jewishencyclopedia.com

[30] *Rom.* 10:13

[31] Theodoret of Cyrus: *Commentary on Romans*, ch. XIV: 7.

[32] Zvi Yavetz: *Slave and Slavery in Ancient Rome*, 1988, p. 154

[33] Jean-Paul Sartre: *Being and Nothingness*, 1956, p. 301 – Transl. Hazel E. Barnes

[34] Ibid, p. 358

[35] Michel Foucault: *Discipline and punish*, 1977 p. 202 – ,

[36] Jeremy Bentham: *Panopticon or the Inspection-House*, 1787, Letter V

[37] Michel Foucault: *Power/Knowledge. Selected Interviews and Other Writings*, 1980 Ed. C. Gordon, transl. C. Gordon et al, p. 155

[38] John Huizinga: *The Waning of the Middle Ages,* 1922, p.20

[39] Schulz, W. *Der Gott der neuzeitlichen Metaphysik.* In *Cusanus, Philosophisch-theologische Schriften* III. ed. Leo Gabriel Herder, Wien 1967, xii.

[40] Nicolaus Cusanus: *De visione Dei*, chapter iv. Transl. Jasper Hopkins.

[41] Ibid. chapter v

[42] Nicolaus Cusanus: *De beryllo* 6; *De coniecturis* II.19 See also Pauline Moffitt Watts: *Nicolaus Cusanus: A Fifteenth-Century Vision of Man*, 1982, p. 180

[43] Augustine: *De civitate Dei,* 7.13.

[44] Marjorie O'Rourke Boyle: *Petrarch's Genius. Pentimento and Prophecy,* 1991, p. 23

[45] Peter Burke: *The Italian Renaissance* 1986, p. 198

[46] Nicolaus Cusanus: *De venatione sapientiae*, p. 17.

[47] Adhemar; bishop of Le Puy 11th century. From Marina Warner: *Alone of All Her Sex*, 1990, p. 115.

[48] Ibid. p. 130 -

[49] Ibid. p. 211

[50] Frederick Antal: *Florentine Painting and Its Social Background,* 1947 p.23 -

[51] Boccaccio: *Decamerone* VI.5

[52] Leon Battista Alberti: *Della Pittura,* 1956, p.78

[53] See Martin Gosenbuch: *Giotto und die Entwicklung des neuzeitlichen Kunstbewusstseins,* 1962, p. 82 –

[54] Moshe Barasch:, *Giotto and the Language of Gesture*, 1987 p. 38

[55] Nicolaus Cusanus: *Idiota de mente,* ch 13

[56] M.I. Finley: *The Ancient Economy*, 1973 p.28

[57] Eugenio Battisti: Giotto, 1960 p. 99

[58] Freely translated from Albertino Mussato: *Ecerinis*, 1975, p. 48 -

[59] Till Davis: *Dante and the Idea of Rome,* 1957 p. 45. Also see Dante, *Convivio* IV. v.

[60] Petrarch: *Familiarum rerum libri* II.14

[61] Perry Anderson: *Passages From Antiquity to Feudalism*, 1974 p. 193

[62] Plato: *Cratylus* 390; Francis Bacon, *The Works of Francis Bacon* IV, 1857-1869 p. 441

[63] According to A.C. Crombie: *Robert Grosseteste and the Origin of Experimental Science 1100–1700*, 1953 p. 174 and p. 294

[64] Erwin Panofsky: *The Codex Huygens and Leonardo da Vinci's Art Theory*, 1940 p. 90-

[65] See Norbert Elias: *The Civilizing Process,* vol. I

[66] Sappho: frgm, 48 Transl. Henry De Vere Stacpoole

[67] Sappho: frgm. 47 Transl. Julia Dubnoff

[68] Bruno Snell: *The Discovery of the Mind, 1953* p. 48

[69] Ibid. p.69-

[70] Ernst Cassirer: *The Individual and the Cosmos in Renaissance Philosophy*, 2010 p. 52 Transl. Mario Domandi

[71] Umberto Eco: *Art and Beauty in the Middle Ages,* 1986 p.102

[72] Abbot Suger: *On the Abbey Church of St. Denis and Its Art Treasures.* Ed. Erwin Panofsky, 1948 p.36

[73] Ibid, p.1

[74] Ibid. p.94 and p. 36.

[75] Ibid. p 48 and 49.

[76] *Eph.* 2:19-22; Suger 1948, p. 104-

[77] Slicher van Bath: *The agrarian history of Western Europe,* here Anderson: *Passages* 1974, p. 195.

[78] See Umberto Eco: *Art and Beauty in the Middle Ages,* 1986 p.81

[79] Karlheinz Stierle: *Petrarcas Landschaften. Zur Geschichte ästhetischer Lanschaftserfahrung,* 1979 p. 51

[80] Joseph Vogt: *Ancient Slavery and the Ideal of Man,* 1974 p. 20

[81] Ibid. p. 21

[82] Zvi Yavets: *Slave and Slavery in Ancient Rome,* 1988 p.158

[83] Edward Gibbon: *The Decline and Fall of the Roman Empire*, 2003 p. 1234

[84] Eugenio Battisti: *Giotto: Biographical and Critical Study*, 1960 p. 117

[85] Petrarch: *Familiarium rerum libri* II.9

[86] Petrarch: *Il Canzoniere* 122

[87] Ibid. 212

[88] Edward Gibbon: *The Decline and Fall of the Roman Empire*, 2003 p. 1232.

[89] Marjorie O'Rourke Boyle: *Petrarch's Genius. Pentimento and Prophecy,* 1991 p.14

[90] Ibid. p. 55

[91] Petrarch: *Il Canzoniere* 292

[92] Karlheinz Stierle: *Petrarcas Landschaften. Zur Geschichte ästhetischer Lanschaftserfahrung,* 1979 p.34

[93] Petrarch: *Il Canzoniere* 192

[94] Karlheinz Stierle: *Petrarcas Landschaften. Zur Geschichte ästhetischer Lanschaftserfahrung,* 197, p.34

[95] See e.g. Petrarch: *Il Canzoniere,* 71-73

[96] Alexander Gottlieb Baumgarten, *Aestetica,* § 7

[97] Petrarch: *Il Canzoniere,* 235

[98] Petrarch: *Secretum,* p.63

[99] P.G.P. Meyboom: *The Nile Mosaic of Palestrina. Early Evidence of Egyptian Religion in Italy.* 2015 p. 76

[100] Friedrich Nietzsche: *Twilight of the Idols,* 1998 p. 20

[101] Francis Bacon: *The Advancement of Learning,* 1974 II.xiv.3

[102] Plato: *The Republic,* 598-99

[103] Plutarch: *Parallel lives; The Life of Pericles,* p. 2

[104] Erwin Panofsky: *Perspective as Symbolic Form,* 1991 p.123 n.47

[105] Petrarch: *Il Canzioniere* 237; see also 259 or 35.

[106] Galileo Galilei: *The Dialogue Concerning the Two Chief World Systems,* 1953 p.419

[107] Hegel: *Philosophie des Geistes,* 1973 p.116

[108] N. Spivey: *Understanding Greek Sculpture,* 1996 p. 95 and 168.

[109] Erwin Panofsky: *Perspective as Symbolic Form,* 1991 p.71

[110] Plotinus: *The Enneads* I.6.2

[111] See E. Gilson: *Christian Philsophy in the Middle Ages,* 1955 p.279

[112] Aristotle: *Politics,* 1256b

[113] Austin & Vidal-Naquet: *Economic and Social History of Ancient Greece,* 1977 p.162

[114] Ibid. p. 336

[115] See A. Murray: *Reason and Society in the Middle Ages,* 1978 p. 193

[116] Giordano Bruno praises Nicolaus as a new Pythagoras: "*Wo findet sich ein Mann vergleichbar jenem Cusaner, der je grösser ist, um so weniger zugänglich ist? Hätte nicht das Priesterkleid sein Genie da und dort verhullt, ich wurde*

zugestehen, dass er dem Pytagoras nicht gleich, sondern bei weitem grösser ist als dieser." (Here according to Karl Jaspers: *Nikolaus Cusanus*, 1964 p. 227)

[117] Nicolaus Cusanus: *Of Learned Ignorance,* 1954 I.1

[118] Ibid.

[119] Nicolaus Cusanus: *Idiota de sapientia* I.5

[120] Johannes Sløk: *Cusanus' dialog om visdommen,* 1974 p. 37

[121] Henri Poincaré: *The Value of Science,* quoted from de Duve's *The Definitely Unfinished Marcel Duchamp* 1991, p. 257

[122] Aristotle: *Metaphysics,* 985b

[123] Daniel de Morley; here in Gregory 1992, p. 107. Or Paracelsus: *. . also was auss der Natur wachst dem Menschen zu nutz, derselbige, der er dahin bringt, dahin es verordnet wirdt von der Natur, der ist ein Alchimist,* here according to Cassirer 1911, Bd.l, p. 221

[124] Lucretius: *The Nature of Things,* IV 426-433

[125] H. W Janson: 1962 p. 353

[126] Martin Gosebruch 1962, p. 90f. According to Gosebruch, Giotto would have been with Cimabue in Rome in 1293, where he would also have made the acquaintance with Cavallini's works – thus before he begun on the frescoes in the Upper Church of Assisi.

[127] In 1314 Giotto had 6 lawyers engaged in the collection of his claims; see Frederick Antal: *Florentine Painting and Its Social Background.* 1947, p. 161

[128] Petrarch: *Rerum Memorandum Libri* I.19.

[129] Leonardo da Vinci: *The Literary Works of Leonardo da Vinci*: from. 1154

[130] Serge Bramly: *Leonardo. The Artist and the Man*: 1988, p. 272

[131] Leonardo: *Codex Atlanticus,* here in Serge Bramly 1988, p. 284

[132] Leonardo 1939, from. 22 and 1148B. *"Sanza ragione"* can also be translated as "without reason", which would harmonise with the scholastic view on existence. As we can see, Leonardo's Tuscan mother tongue differs slightly from modern Italian.

[133] Leonardo: *The Literary Works of Leonardo da Vinci*: from. 606

[134] Ibid. from. 470-71

[135] Ibid. from. 1147

[136] Ibid. from. 1148 A

[137] Francis Bacon: *Novum Organum* II.4

[138] Leonardo: *The Literary Works of Leonardo da Vinci,* from. 660

[139] Nicolus Cusanus: *De beryllo,* chap. 32

[140] Leonardo: *The Literary Works of Leonardo da Vinci,* from. 1133

[141] See Leonardo: *The literary works,* from. 797 and 805.

[142] Roger Bacon: *The Opus Majus II*

[143] Leonardo: *Paragone I.1; in The Literary Works* 1939, p. 31 ff.

[144] See e.g. Paolo Rossi: *Francesco Bacone.* 1957, p. 87

[145] Wittgenstein: *The Blue book* 1958, p. 18

[146] Baumgarten *Aestetica, § 440*

[147] Aristotle: *Politics 1254 b*

[148] Poulsen, V: *Från grottorna till Rom*

[149] Virgil: *The Aeneid I.1*

[150] By Bernard Andreae, see Spivey 1996, p. 216

[151] Sandqvist 1990, p. 260 f. (Translated from Swedish by the translator)

[152] Charles Taylor: *Hegel* 1975, p. 153

[153] Taylor 1975 p. 157 f.

[154] Taylor 1975 p. 159

[155] The *Works of Francis Bacon,* ed. Ellis & Spedding, Vol IV, p. 24

[156] Farrington 1964, p. 119. n. 2

[157] Nietzsche, *Kritische Studienausgabe* 13, p.371

[158] Nietzsche: *The Will to Power,* 495 & 515

[159] Nietzsche: *The Will to Power,* 555

[160] Nietzsche: *The Will to Power,* 512 & 532

[161] Nietzsche, *The Will to Power, 480 & 555*

[162] Rainer Maria Rilke: *Letters on Cézanne* 1985, p. 59

[163] Rainer Maria Rilke: *Letters on Cézanne* 1985, p. 46

[164] Wassily Kandinsky: *Concerning the spiritual in art* 1977, p. 11

[165] Wassily Kandinsky: *Concerning the spiritual in art* 1977, p. 28

[166] Kandinsky, interviewed by Karl Nierendorf in 1937. Kandinsky *Complete Writings*, p. 807

[167] Herbert Molderings in Thierry de Duve (ed): *The Definitely Unfinished Marcel Duchamp* 1991, p. 245

[168] Nietzsche, *The Will to Power,* 12 B

[169] Linde 1986, p. 76

[170] Herbert Moldering in *The Definitely Unfinished Marcel Duchamp* 1991, p. 243. *La science et L'hypothèse was published in 1902.*

[171] Henri Poincaré: *Science and Hypothesis,* (S&H) 1905, p. xxiii

[172] Poincaré 1905, p. 110

[173] Poincaré 1905, p. 50

[174] Poincaré 1905, p. 97 ff.

[175] Poincaré 1905, p. 16

[176] Poincaré 1905, p. 50

[177] Herbert Molderings in Thierry de Duve (ed): *The Definitely Unfinished Marcel Duchamp* 1991, p. 248

[178] Poincaré 1952, p. 69

[179] Pierre Cabanne: *Dialogues with Marcel Duchamp* 1987, p. 47, italics by the author.

[180] Nietzsche: *Human, All Too Human* p. 327

[181] de Duve: *Pictorial Nominalism: On Marcel Duchamp's Passage from Painting to the Readymade.* 1984, p. 83

[182] *The Complete Works of Marcel Duchamp* 1969, p. 38, n.23.

[183] de Duve 1991, p.274

[184] de Duve 1991, p.167

[185] de Duve 1991, p.302

[186] Kant: *The Critique of Judgement,* Introduction IX

[187] Kant: *The Critique of Judgement,* Introduction II